"THE SPREE OF '83"

by Freddy & Catherine Powers
with Jake Brown

Featuring Exclusive Commentary from Merle Haggard and
Willie Nelson

Published by Waldorf Publishing

2140 Hall Johnson Road

#102-345

Grapevine, Texas 76051

www.WaldorfPublishing.com

The Spree of 83

ISBN: 978-1-945174-94-0

Library of Congress Control Number: 2016956993

Copyright © 2017

Photo Chapter design by Baris Celik

Co-Author Dedications

Freddy and Catherine Powers
We dedicate this book in the memory of Freddy Powers' and Merle Haggard's loving friendship!

Jake Brown Dedication
I dedicate this book to my lovely wife Carrie, and hope in 50-years' time we have the kind of marriage my co-authors do!

Author Thank You(s)

Freddy and Catherine Powers: Over the years I have many many people to thank and I wish I could list them all so many that it worked with me so many that had opened doors for me so many that taught me so many that gave of their time and support, but I must start with my parents who without them I would have probably never had a music career there's support was truly beyond what any child could have grown up with. My upbringing was that in a musical home with family of musical background . My brother Wallace who introduced me to the guitar my sister Mary Lou who introduced me to songwriting. To my brotherDon for being my best friend and one of my biggest fans and supporters. To my sister Norma who was there for me when I needed her the most and my brother and sister Jerry and Susie for their love and support. So much thanks to Paul Buskirk who recognized my talents and mentored me to become the musician I became. To Willie Nelson for the many years of friendship and support. To my best friend and brother in music the mighty Merle Haggard I love you dearly you I could never thank you enough all the time the energy the love and the support you've given me over all these years and all you taught me about songwriting I will forever be indebted to you. So many thanks to all the cast and characters that shared your time and stories for this book. And Final to my wife Catherine who was my rock and always there for me you are the love of my life and my best friend thank you for loving me so much your love was a Pillar of Strength for me. You held my hand and stuck by me through all the ups and downs and all the struggles without your love and your strength I would not have been able to continue my life through my Parkinson. I love you forever and thank God for the blessing of you.

Catherine Allen-Powers Thank You(s): My first Thank You is to my wonderful husband for choosing me to spend the rest of his life with blessing me with a wonderful romantic adventurous life full of many experiences fulfilling dreams that all girls only dream of. You are the love of my life and I will love you only for the rest of my life. And like Freddy, there are so many people that we would both like to thank that have stood beside us and supported us and been the best friends that we could have ever had. Unbelievably huge large thank you to Freddy's younger sister Norma Marlowe for helping us get the bus that Freddy's spent his final years in living the way he loved and most accustom to without her no telling what would have happened and how long he would have fought the Parkinson's so he could live and enjoy his life. Forever indebted to you and your beautiful heart that you shared with your brother Many abundant Thank Yous for all those that at times without Freddy's knowledge because felt there was no need for him to worry helped me keep him on the road and active. Without your help and support, I wouldn't have been able to keep his life QUALITY as well quantity. Willie Nelson, thank you for all your generosity and paying off our car and credit cards giving us a fresh start when I felt it was more important to put fuel in the bus and keep Freddy active and a part of the music life he loved, also putting his needed medical supplies first rather than to keeping up with our car payments and credit cards. I will forever be indebted to you and all your family for all the love and support you all have shown Freddy and I.

Deep sincere Thank Yours to Merle and Theresa Haggard, Marc and Greg Oswald, John Rich and Big Kenny Alphin, Gretchen Wilson, Tanya Tucker, Mary Sarah, Todd and Patty Gross, Joe Gilchrist, CW Colt, Susie Cochran - who more than once, twice, even three times when this bus broke down paid for the repairs and sent me numerous gas cards to keep fuel in the bus so Freddy could still come out and see you on your shows, and kept Freddy out touring and performing while he still could. Huge , huge thank you to my road warrior girls my sister Debbie Langham, Cass Hunter, our granddaughter Kasie Finkie, Tanya Tucker, Joi Davis and past (or ex I just like past or better yet just daughter) but always our daughter in law Carrie Powers and boy roadie our grandson Freddy Powers the 3rd who all took turns going out to assist me in taking care of Freddy so I could drive the bus and keep the wheels rolling. If they weren't already a nurse like Joi Davis, they pretty much learned to be one from doing simple things like setting on the side of the bed and feeding Freddy tiny bites of food for an hour so he had less chances of joking and mixing his water with thickeners to learning to give him his medication and feeding him through a feeding tube.

Thank you Joi Davis for all the days you spent at the hospitals with us leaving your job at your hospital in Muscle Shoals and your responsibilities to be with us and all the many hours you sitting with him at his bedside giving me a break for rest and food and for helping me understand the doctors when I didn't that several times made the difference in his life and death. And once again to John Rich for having flown Joi all over the country when or wherever needed. Thank you to Freddy's niece Vickie?(I'll have to call her about the last name) our daughter Karen Finkie for coming wherever we were and staying nights in the hospital, washing my clothes, feeding me, ect.all the large and small things you did. Thank you Debra Richardson for being my best friend 56 yrs of my life to date being my rock and shoulder every time I needed one and all the things you did helping with Freddy every time we were near you. Thank you to Terry Booth and all the Coondicks of Austin Texas for seeing to it that we had a hospital bed installed into this bus so Freddy could not only ride safely but in comfort not to mention making it easier on my back cuz it's at the front door not all the way to the back of the bus where his original bed was that I carried him to on my back.

A thousand billion thanks to Joe Gilchrist who saw the need for Freddy to have a good healthy place to spend his last days but also affording Freddy to stay within realm of the music scene he loved so much with a view we all wish for and blessed we had, being able to lay in his hospital bed and look out his front windshield watch the Dolphins swimming by see the boats and fisherman but also able to see the blue angels fly over on their practice days and always making sure I had what you call walking around money. Which I also have to include in that thank you for our beautiful location for living along with Joe Gilchrist other owners of the Flora-Bama John McInnis, Pat McClellan, Cameron Price and the Tamary family even at a time of going against county codes for us to love in the Flora-Bama parking lot with hook ups they especially had setup. I owe the world to the Flora-Bama family all the owners and their families to all the customer service that help me get Freddy in and out of the bus and helped get him to and from the Flora-Bama for Freddy to be able to listen to his favorite musicians and songwriters, always paying tribute to Freddy by singing one of songs to him and introducing him to the audience and boasting about his career to them, you could always see the twinkle in eyes beautiful blues eyes when they did.

I also Salute with many thanks to the United States Marines who many times showed up at shows and also here at the Flora-Bama to get Freddy from one location to another and for providing him with a beautiful Marine Military service with full honors and doing your homework not only knowing his status and rank in his military career but also his music career and fame. Huge gratitude of thanks to Diane Strict and Tine? (Will get her last name last) with Covenant Hospice Care for all that you did helping me take care of a Freddy and seeing that all his medical needs were met and he was comfortable and clean. Last but not least to all our friends and family each and every one of you so many to list that if I listed you all it would take all 356 pages leaving no room for this story, that came and set with Freddy so I could go to the store or run to the doctor or do whatever I needed to do and all you that just came to visit with him and spent time with him and let him know that he was loved and respected by you and many more thank you all sincerely you have all been a very special blessing in both of our lives and we want you to know we couldn't have done it without you and we love you deeply deeply deeply so much and sincerely thank God for you. Never to be forgotten so many wonderful thank yous to our sweet Lord who without him nothing would be possible and the blessing of my Church Worship On The Water at the Flora-Bama that has become the most important thing in my life. Without my congregation a friends from the church my survival would never been possible helping me with small bills keeping food on my table all those that kept food on my table and cook for me thank you thank you thank you so much I'd be even skinnier without you. To Donna and John Mason Smith for taking me under your wings and teaching me about God and the love he has for me. Thank you to Pastor Jeremy Mount I miss you so much. Thank you to Pastor Joe Brantley for being a wonderful Bible school teacher and a wonderful friend. To my loving and caring Pastor Dan Stone and Robin Harpster thank you for being with me during his final hours holding my hand and praying with us you both were such strong rocks for me. Robin your friendship means the world to me thank you for sharing your love and your family with me. A million thank yous to all the people that contributed with helping me with some of Freddy's medical bills and raising the money to put me in the Playa Del Rio RV Park and covering one whole years rent in advance that took so much worry off my shoulders I will forever be indebted to each and everyone of you. And finally to Jake Brown who saw that this book needed to be published and needed to be read by all Freddy Powers fans, with you this book went from a dream to reality, and Waldorf books for accepting to publishing it and bringing the dream to life. Please know if

I have left anyone out please know in my heart I thank you and I treasure you all.

Jake Brown Thank You(s): Its fitting I'm handing this beautiful story of Freddy Powers' life in on his birthday, October 13th, 2016**,** <u>Happy Birthday Freddy!</u> I began working on this book four years ago after meeting Catherine for the first time in the I.C.U. of the Nashville V.A. Hospital when Freddy was on life-support, and I was immediately humbled at the thought that I might not get to write this book WITH Freddy, which thankfully, is precisely what I got the chance to do over the next year, meeting with both of my co-authors each week on Music Row on their bus where I had the privilege to spend the last talking times of Freddy's life with him. Though it was clear Parkinson's had control of much of his body, his mind and wit were as sharp as ever, and at times when he'd be up to speaking, he'd be talking and break out into song in mid-story. That to me best sums up Freddy, and it has truly been the most humbling and rewarding memoir to co-write over 44 books and 15 years doing so, so THANK YOU Freddy and Catherine for trusting me with your story. Thank you as well to my wife Carrie Brock-Brown and my parents, James and Christina Brown, brother Joshua T Brown, best Dog Buddy Hannie and in-laws, Bill and Susan Brock, for your love and support throughout the workaholic nature of this profession. I'd also briefly like to thank the amazing collection of Country Music treasures who took the time to give us beautiful interviews for this book, beginning with the late, great Merle Haggard; the legendary Willie Nelson – who took time out of his Christmas Day to speak to me for the project; our wonderful publisher Waldorf Books, and specifically Barbara Terry, for taking this brave chance on us!; our editor Carol McCrow; John Rich of Lonestar/Big & Rich for the wonderful descriptions of/about Freddy; Tanya Tucker for the lovely conversation; fellow Texas Hall of Famer Sonny Throckmorton; Norma Powers-Marlow, Freddy's only living sibling, for the wonderful memories of childhood on the plains of West Texas; Edith Royal, widow of Coach Darrell Royal; Linda Mitchell for the memories of life on the lake; Marc Oswald for the fantastic memories of traveling with Freddy on the road, and of your times out on Lake Shasta; Biff Adams, thank you for taking the time to share your memories of playing and partying with Freddy in the Strangers; the lovely Ann Reynolds for recounting so eloquently the memory of your late husband, Deaniebird Reynolds; Todd & Gross and their lovely daughter, Mary Sarah (2016 The Voice Finalist), Molly McKnight and Pauline Reese for discussing Freddy's mentoring so openly and eloquently; Tom Roland at Billboard Country for the great plug on the book's release; Stephen Betts and Rolling Stone Country for the BEAUTIFUL back-of-book-jacket review quote and your support of celebrating Freddy's legacy in all; and finally, the Flora-Bama crew: Joe Gilchrist and John McGinnis, co-owners, for all you do, and Catherine's crew:

Robin R. Harpster, Joi Vinson Davis, Cass Hunter, Chris Newbury, Auggie Savage, and everyone else who helped support and celebrate this beautiful couple of souls.

Table of Contents

Meet the Cast of Characters in Our Crazy Life Story

Freddy and **Catherine Powers:** Co-authors

Norma Powers-Marlow: Freddy's sister

Merle Haggard: Freddy's best friend and songwriting sidekick, bandmate, and pickin' partner

Willie Nelson: Freddy's longtime friend, Prankster and fellow picker

Paul Buskirk: Represented in Spirit, Texas music legend / Mentor to Freddy and Willie

Coach Darrell Royal: Represented in Spirit, Legendary Texas Longhorns Football Coach / Longtime friend of Freddy and Willie's, Supporter of Songwriters

Edith Royal: Widow of the late Coach Darrell Royal

Ann Reynolds: Widow of the late DeanieBird Reynolds, Freddy's longtime bass player

Bill McDavid: Freddy's late co-host of the Cable Ace-Nominated *Rogers and Hammerhead* Songwriters Television Show

Marc Oswald: Longtime Merle Haggard Manager/Freddy Friend

John Rich: One half of hit country act Big & Rich and longtime Freddy fan/friend

Tanya Tucker: Multi-platinum Country Music legend and close friend

Biff Adams: Longtime Drummer for Merle Haggard's The Strangers

Mary Sarah: 2016 The Voice Finalist / Freddy Powers Protégé

Pauline Reese: Freddy Protégé and Texas Country Music Star

Linda Mitchell: Manager, Silverthorne Resort, Merle Haggard's Former Assistant

Sonny Throckmorton: Legendary Texas Country Music Songwriter, Friend of Freddy's

Joe Gilchrist: Founder of Frank Brown Songwriter Festival, Co-owner of the Flora-Bama

John McGinnis: Co-Owner of the World Famous Flora-Bama

Joi Vinson Davis: Freddy's Personal Nurse & Daughter by Another Mother and Father

Cass Hunter: Catherine's Road Warrior/Close Family Friend

Foreword by Tanya Tucker

I remember one of the first times I ever met Freddy, he sang the whole chorus of "*Delta Dawn*" to me! That was incredible, I was so freaked out over that, because he wasn't talking really at all at that point. So when he sang that whole chorus to me, I was just elated and Catherine was sitting back with her mouth open, she couldn't believe it and I was like "*O.M.G!*" I felt so honored that he would sing that for me, like I was the only one he would do that for. Freddy is a great singer; I love to hear him sing. I love his voice, and I could listen to a whole album of Freddy singing because his voice is so easy and so calming to the ears.

I loved to watch him play guitar too. I remember I used to watch him on Austin City Limits, and do different things with Merle, and he's not just a great songwriter, but he has great melodies, which I think comes from being a great guitar player. He really has that Jazz kind of sound in his songs, and his music is so palpable to the ear. Its so easy on the ear, and just floats, and is a beautiful experience to listen to some of his melodies. Of course his words are great, but he just creates these melodies that are unforgettable.

He's just as great a writer too, and I think he's one of the least-recognized of the great country songwriters, and doesn't really get his credit due. He's not just a writer of country music either, I love songs of his like "*Little Hotel Room*," and a lot of the older stuff he's written years ago I have in my head to record later on. He's got so many songs that I think would be good records to this day, just certain songs that stand the tests of time. His music will be great in any era, no matter what year it is, you'll still want to hear a Freddy Powers song.

"Freddy is a Troubadour…" – Catherine Powers

Introduction: Sir Frederick

Catherine Powers: Freddy was born in Duncan, Oklahoma, the middle child of seven. His father was a cotton farmer and worked on oil rigs, and when he was seven years old, the family moved to a farm outside Seminole, Texas.

Norma Powers-Marlowe (Freddy's Younger Sister): When we moved down to Seminole, Texas from Oklahoma, we came through Andrews, Texas into Seminole, and oh my God, the sand storms! They used to have horrible sand storms out there – I remember the sand was blowing and the tumbleweeds were crossing the highway, and we got to the city limit, and Daddy says "We're home," and my mother started crying! She's got seven kids in the car like sardines, and she says "How could you move your family to this God forsaken place?" (laughs)

Back in Oklahoma, there were trees and creeks and all kinds of stuff to do, you know. My little sister Suzie was just a baby and my brother Jerry was really small too, and I wasn't much older but I remember it well: there wasn't nobody saying a word in that car, and that's how we started out in Seminole. Later on, we ended up buying the Mayor's house, and it was a nice house, and behind it, we had a cow lot back there.

When we moved out in the country, we had more company than we did when we lived right there in town, because when they would come out there, it was like anything goes because we had all this space so you could be outside with no neighbors telling you to be quiet or anything like that. We lived a life that was a lot more interesting than the Waltons, or any of those other families you'd see on T.V., because we did things together. They liked to hunt, and were really good at catching rabbits, and would kill birds with their slingshots and whittle and all kinds of stuff. We used to go a lot in the pasture, and we would find a hole out there and pour water down it and drown out these little ground squirrels, and they would run on that little wheel and everything, it was real cute.

Catherine Powers: At night, the whole family gathered in the living room and made music together. His whole family was musical, and in fact, his mother had grown up on stage performing in Vaudeville shows with her sisters, traveling around, and his father was a fiddle player. As kids, on the weekends, Freddy's parents would throw parties where all their family and friends would come out to the house and they would move the furniture out, so the house could become a stage and a dance floor.

Freddy and his older sister Mary Lou were singers, and they both entered and won school talent contests, and after Freddy's older brother Wallace came home from the Service, he had learned to play a little guitar, and Freddy picked that up from him and first started learning how to play guitar while he sang. Freddy's sister was a writer, and she'd had a couple songs she'd written and had been recorded already by a Texas country music star Hank Thompson, and that intrigued Freddy: that his sister was writing songs and getting paid for it. So his sister helped him get into songwriting after that, but they had a family band. They all sang and they all played.

Norma Powers-Marlowe (Freddy's Younger Sister): My mother could sing and grew up in a very musical family as well. My grandmother would play the drums and my grandfather – we called them "Big Mama" and "Big Daddy" – and Big Daddy would play the trombone, and some other instruments. They lived in Ft. Worth, Texas when she was growing up, and they had a garage that they made into a little theater, and my Aunt Thelma played the piano very well as a matter of fact and all the other girls – there were five sisters – I'm telling you, they could put the McGuire Sisters to shame! They sang until they started dying off, and had beautiful voices, so it was kind of in our family through my mother's side that the music came from I'm sure.

At night, just about the time everybody was supposed to go to bed, everybody got wound up and nobody wanted to go to sleep and Freddy would start making up songs and every night all the kids would put on these little music shows! We did all kinds of stuff. Wallace and Freddy would play guitar and Don and Freddy and Wallace – all of 'em – would sing, and Freddy always stood out because he was the most vocal and it was just in him to be a performer, it was in his blood.

My father participated in our antics and stuff like that. He would do a jig and would move his head funny, and Daddy would just have a big time, a fine time, and Mama would usually sing right along with the kids! She could really sing those Rhythm and Blues numbers like "*A Good Man is Hard to Find*," and we all participated in all of that. It was like a family band, and we sang sometimes all night long! We would be playing music and doing all kinds of funny stuff!

Back then when we were living out in the country, Hank Williams was really big, and Don used to sing that "*Love Sick Blues*," and he could really sing. Our older sister Mary Lou played "*Boogie Woogie*" and other popular songs of the day on the piano, and in our household growing up, we had a lot of the Rhythm and Blues, Country Western, and Bud Killen came to see us one time and raved over my mother's biscuits! (laughs)

Freddy also would do some slapstick and tell jokes, and sing. Freddy had a high voice when we were growing up, I always used to joke that we had our very own Alfalfa! (laughs) He had a high voice, and he loved to dance, Freddy was really good, he would tap dance and then when he would enter talent shows, he'd do acrobatics on the stage and the whole family would always come watch him perform. We used to joke that Freddy was our little crooner, and there was always some little girl involved he was singing too…. (laughs)

Ft. Worth Star Telegram: "Seminole, Texas (was)… where 12-year-old Freddy Powers taught himself to play the guitar so he could join his two brothers in country dance bands playing the area."

Texas Music Magazine: "With the guiding apron strings and euphonious vocals of their mother Mary, who had already dabbled with her own success as a singer, they formed a family band to tour VFW halls and honky-tonks from West Texas to Hobbs, NM."

Freddy Powers: "I started in it when I was real young, just a kid in family bands, you know, with my brothers. Everybody in my family either played something or tried to. Out in West Texas, in Seminole, if you didn't play guitar or do something, you'd go out of your mind. There wasn't anything else to do and as my dad used to say, 'Everything that crawls, bites, everything that flies, stings and every bush that grows out there, has a thorn on it'. That's just about telling the whole story… My musical indoctrination occurred – at the ol' country dance. Each week, it would be at one ranch or the other, all of them good people, church people, but on Saturday they would loosen up. That was my

training ground and the training ground for all great
country musicians." 1

Catherine Powers: Freddy grew up poor, but he
didn't know it, in fact, when they were young boys, their
mother made Freddy and his brothers' shirts out of potato
sacks, and at Christmas, to get a whistle or a little toy gun
was huge for them. The way kids celebrate Christmas today
did not compare to anything like they got, they got
homemade gifts and maybe one bought gift. It was an
extremely humble existence materially but the house was
always full of life and love because Freddy came from such
a big family. Freddy and his older brother Don were the
two middle children and they were very close in age, just
like the two oldest children, Mary Lou and Wallace, were
close in age, and then there was Norma and Jerry and Suzie,
so Freddy and Don were extremely mischievous.

Norma Powers-Marlowe: Freddy growing up was
never, *ever* without friends. Freddy was always upbeat and
looking back, of course, he was bound to be in show
business of some kind, because every time they would have
something at school, Freddy would be in anything. If they
had any kind of play or talent show, and around the house,
he was like our little "Song and Dance" man. He liked to
sing, and Don did too, he had a really nice voice as well.
You'd never see Don without Freddy, they were close as
any twins or just like best friends, I've never known them
to fight or disagree or fuss, they went along together just

like they were joined at the hip. Freddy and Don liked to crack jokes, and they would work together, they kept us laughing all the time.

They were good boys. I can truthfully say that Freddy was always a gentleman, he never was disrespectful or anything to any of us kids, and they didn't get into too much mischief. I remember one time there was this filling station, and I mean it was a little bitty thing, and they crawled in the bathroom window one time and took a couple of packages of cigarettes and climbed back out the window. Well, Daddy found out about it and took them downtown where the jail is and scared the daylights out of them, they thought they were going to have to go to prison! (laughs) Another time, we had a haystack, and they would bundle it and stack it where if it rains, it won't leak and back then, we didn't have a garbage service, so you had to have a garbage barrel and burnt your garbage and they'd pick it up. Well, they had gone to get the last load of that and there was an old tire they'd been burning, and Freddy or Don was poking at it with a stick to put it out and a piece of flaming tire flew back up onto that haystack, and boy, you talk about a fire!! Oh my God, this looked like the end of the world, and the fire department was there at our house and everything. So they were like normal boys, they got into mischief but never did anything to harm anybody.

Catherine Powers: One of the funniest family stories came when Freddy and Don became known as "The

Chicken Thieves", because around the age of ten, they were stealing their daddy's chickens and sell them over in another part of town for a quarter, and that quarter would pay both their ways into the movies, and buy them each a popcorn, a candy bar and a drink way back then. So one day, their dad was at the Post Office when this woman came up and said, "Ah, Mr. Powers, you need to send your boys around with another chicken. They're the best fryers, you need to tell Don and Freddy to bring me around another one of those chickens!" So when their dad got home, instead of running in the house immediately and jumping on the boys for stealing the chickens, he waited till dinner that night when the whole family was sitting around the table and said, "Boys, after dinner, we need to have a man to man talk."

So after dinner, their daddy Roy said, "Boys, we've got us a chicken thief, and I figure the best way we're gonna catch this chicken thief is we're gonna take turns spending the night in the chicken coop till we catch him." So they set up cots in the chicken coop for Freddy and Don, and in those little chicken coops, you have snakes and rats and spiders and all those creepy little things that as a kid would be scary, and that first night, they both stayed in the chicken coop. Neither one of them slept because they were scared to death, so the next night comes along, and their daddy said, "Boys, I'm gonna let you boys take watch again tonight, I've worked hard today and I need to get some rest." Well, when they got in there, all of a sudden,

Don couldn't handle it and started crying, "Daddy, we don't have to sleep out here, we know who the chicken thieves are!" That was their daddy's way of punishing them, and making them come in and own up to it.

Norma Powers-Marlowe: He and Don didn't like me to mess with their pet snakes. It was a big old blue Texas Indigo snake, and I'd sit on the porch and wait till they got out of sight till I could really get out there and get that snake, and scare everybody in the neighborhood! I'd terrorize the neighborhood, then I'd put it back like nothing happened. It's hard to zero in on just Freddy because we were a family, and were together a lot, so it was like all kinds of mischief! (laughs)

One day, a bunch of us kids were out there in that pasture way off from our house and everything, and we came up on an old cellar where there'd been a house there long before, and found a bootlegger's stash down there! Well, we went back across the highway and got our little old wagon that had sides on it, and loaded that wagon up – I never will forget – it was these little, tall bottles of beer, and all kinds of stuff. We made I don't know how many trips, back and forth, back and forth, and the neighbor eventually came home and saw us with all that stuff and said, "Where in the world did you get all this stuff?", and we told him, "Oh, we found it," and then he asked more pointedly, "*Where* did you find it?" So we told him, "Over there in the pasture," and his response was funny because then he asked, "Is there any more of it?" (laughs) We told him "No, we got it all," and he told us not to go over there anymore. The funny part is: all of us kids over there, we were barefooted and had tracked sand all down in the bottom of that cellar and everything, so you could see these little old bitty feet prints everywhere! It was fun growing up, we did have a good childhood.

Catherine Powers: His whole family, everybody in his family and every one of them coming up today, it totally amazes me, it's the wittiest family I've ever seen in my life. Every one of them is funny, they all could have been comedians – his son, his grandson – so it's like it was born in Freddy and instilled in him to be comical. So Freddy used that in his music, combining comedy into his performing persona, and that's when he got into the banjo and that's where he started developing his unique style of guitar playing as well, which is rooted through his banjo.

Norma Powers-Marlowe: I have to tell you another really funny, true story: Freddy was home, and we all went on Saturday to the theater to see what was usually a Country and Western show, and by this time, we didn't live in town at the Mayor's house anymore. We lived out in the country on the other side of the city limit, and when we walked out of this show, we heard Freddy playing that steel guitar out in the yard and he was playing that thing wide open! We heard him from outside the theater all the way out there at our house playing steel guitar out there in the yard! He wasn't always Country and Western either, not at all, the times when I really enjoyed Freddy's music the most actually was when he got into Dixieland Jazz. Freddy could really play the banjo, oh my God, he was *really* good at playing that banjo!

Catherine Powers: But as a teenager, Freddy was always a comedian. One time when their daddy was out somewhere, Freddy and Don decided to take their father's car for a little joyride, so they're driving around the fields and all of a sudden pull up on the sand embankment, were bogged down and got their daddy's car stuck! Well, they were trying to dig it out, and before too long, ran the battery down, so now they're really starting to panic, and all of a sudden, over the horizon, they could see their daddy riding up on his horse, looking like a Texas Ranger or something, boots, cowboy hat and all. Now they both know they're about to be in real trouble, and their daddy asks, "What's going on here boys?" Well, they had to own up to joyriding, and this was one of those old cars that had the crank, so their dad gets the tool out to crank it up, starts to wind it up, and as he did, the crank came off and hit him in the head and knocked him back onto the ground. Well, now Freddy and Don are staring down at him, and their daddy looks up at the two boys and says, "Well, don't just stand there like a monument of shit, help me up!"

Back in those days, growing up in that little town in Seminole, Texas, when the police would be working, driving around at night checking on the neighborhood and stuff, they would pull up to a donut shop and leave the car running so they could hear the dispatch radio. Well, while they were inside that shop getting a donut one night with the patrol car sitting outside and running, Freddy and Don and two other guys decided to up their game and thought it would be funny to jump in the police car and drive it out to the city dump, and they left it out there.

Needless to say, it was huge news in that town on the front page of the newspaper, and for a week, they were searching, looking for this police car and they would see it sitting out at the city dump, but every time, they'd just assume it was a cop out there watching, so they never went and checked it out. Well, after a week of seeing that car, they finally went, checked it out, realized it was the stolen car, and Freddy never got caught! It wasn't until he was older and out of the service that he and Don owned up to his daddy that they were the ones who had stolen that police car, and his dad said, "It was a good thing I didn't know back then because I'd have tanned your hide!"

Another time, Freddy, Don and some buddies of theirs found this swimming hole, which was in a tank, because being out there on the plains of West Texas, there weren't any lakes or ponds around where they were. So the kids would go swim in these tanks that they used for the cattle to drink out of. Well, this one old man didn't like them swimming in his tank, so he decided he was going to put an end to it, and put some barbed-wire down in that tank. Well, when they showed up to go swimming the next day, they discovered that barbed-wire and went home and told their daddy. So he jumped on a horse, went over, and was gonna jump on this guy, and the guy looked up at him, and said "Roy, for little or nothing, I'd yank you off that horse, and kick your ass!" And Roy looked down at him and said, "Now, what the hell do you think I'm gonna be doing while you're doing all this ass kicking?"

Norma Powers-Marlowe: My father was a hard-working man, but he was fun. Let me tell you something, we had good parents. That's not to say that my daddy would put up with any crap because he wouldn't! It didn't make a difference if you were the girl in the family or who you were, if you got into trouble, you got punished. I remember Don would never cry, he'd lean over and just take it, but once my daddy got ahold of Freddy, oh my God, he would carry on like it was the end of the world, screaming, he'd go crazy… but it was all an act! (laughs)

Catherine Powers: Because his older brother Wallace had been in the service, and this was after WWII when all those John Wayne movies made war seem that it was glamorous, so Freddy looked at the joining the military as being something glamorous, and at age 15, it was the first time he ran away from home and joined the Air Force.

Once he got in there and they realized he was under age, they called his father, who came and got him and took him back home. Well, a year later, at 16, Freddy ran off again, and this time joined the Marines.

He'd gone down to the enlistment office, and when he walked in, the recruiter looked him over and said, "You don't look 18 to me son," and Freddy said "Okay, see you later!", and the guy goes, "Oh, no, no, no, now *wait a minute*, and sat Freddy back down, and he ended up BS-ing his way through the interview and was able once again to join the military. Well, as soon as he got into boot camp, it didn't take long for these experienced drill instructors to realize Freddy wasn't 18, and once again, his father picks up a ringing phone back home telling him déjà vu, your son's done it again. Well, this time, when his father drove down to the base where Freddy was stationed at, they all sat down and talked it out and saw that he was determined to be in the military, and decided to let him stay in under a special set of conditions: 1.) he would finish high school in the service, and 2.) he was restricted to the base until he came of age.

Norma Powers-Marlowe: We were very, very patriotic at our house and we had every reason to be. I remember when the boys were in the service, back at home, we turned our kitchen into like a candy factory or something; we made fudge, and meat loaf, and all kinds of stuff like that and sent packages to the boys. They'd divide everything up, and we did this with my oldest brother Wallace when he was in World War II, and Wallace saw a lot of awful things over there. A lot of people didn't come back, but fortunately, all of my brothers came back alive. Jerry, my youngest brother, was in the Navy, Freddy was in the Marines, Don was in the Army and Wallace was in the Navy too. They were all during different wars, and they all proudly served. When Wallace went into the service he was 18 years old, and Freddy was 16 when he ran off to join the Marines. In fact, Freddy was in a car wreck that kind of hurt his back, and he missed going over there in that first division of the (Korean?) War, and they wiped them out. So that wreck really was kind of a blessing or he probably wouldn't even be here.

Catherine Powers: Freddy was so gung-ho that when the Drill Sergeant would come and get right up on his nose and scream at him, Freddy was one of those that would stand at attention and yell right back, "Yes sir! Yes sir!" He wanted to be in that military so bad that he ended up being a six-year Vet in the Marines, he became C.I.D. during the Korean War, and during that war, not everybody who went to Korea came back. Every night he would lay in his bed and hear guys in the barracks who knew they were being shipped off the next day to Korea crying, just scared to death to go.

So Freddy wanted to be in the military, but he didn't want to go kill anybody and didn't want to be killed, and at the base, was running the cleaners, and it was a safe gig, and he was even able to make money on the side because on his off days, he would still go and work the cleaners and wash his buddies' clothes and they'd pay him a couple of bucks. So every time Freddy's number would come up, they couldn't let him go until he trained somebody else to run the cleaners, and naturally, every time they'd send somebody over, after a bit when somebody asked him, "Well, how are they doing?", Freddy would say, "Ehhh, I don't think they're gonna get it," and so they never could afford to get rid of him. Through that luck, he was able to stay on American soil while still staying in the Marines through running the cleaners.

One time in the service, Freddy was standing post at the guard gate, because everyone in his (platoon) had to take turns on guard gate duty, and so Freddy was leaning up against the building falling asleep standing up. So the sergeant came through and of course, yelled "POWERS!", and Freddy jumped and he said, "You know I could put you in the brig for sleeping on the job," and he replied, "Oh no Sir, I wasn't asleep, I was resting my eyes," and the Sergeant said, "It looked to me like the rest of your body joined in too!" Another time, Freddy, was in the guard house standing post, and this was down in Ocean Side, and he was playing around with his gun and it went off and he shot a hole through the guard shack, which is a big, big no-no. That hole is there to this day, and he took me back years later to see it.

After he'd been in the service a while, Freddy came home for a visit driving his very first car, and he was so proud of this car, so that night, a few of his buddies got in the car for a ride around the country, and the way he tells the story, they came upon this watermelon field, and pulled Freddy's car up into this patch and loaded his trunk with watermelons! Well, they saw lights come on at the farmhouse, all jumped in the car and were getting ready to get the heck out of there, but when Freddy tried to crank up his car, it was so weighted down with watermelons that it was bogged and he couldn't get out. So now all his friends leap out of the car and take off running just as the farmer who owned the watermelon patch comes running up on Freddy with his shotgun in hand, yelling and cussing! Initially, Freddy had followed the rest of his buddies running off into the darkness until he remembered, "Hey, wait a minute, that's my car!" Sure enough, when Freddy got back to the car, that farmer took a closer look, lowered the shotgun, and said "You're one of the Powers boys!" (laughs) Freddy and Don were known so well around town for being the mischief-makers while they were growing up that the farmer recognized him right away, and then made Freddy feel bad, "There's no reason for you boys to come over here and steal my watermelons. All you had to do was come and ask me, and I'd have told you to take all the watermelons you want!"

Norma Powers-Marlowe: One time when Freddy had just come home from the Marines, he bought a little Coupe that was solid black and then he went off somewhere, and I thought I'd surprise him and clean up that little car, and I got out there and used Old English Furniture Polish on it, which is an *oil*. So I got out there and polished that little old Coupe up and then here comes a horrible sand storm, what a mess! He never growled at me or snapped at me, but he just got out there with soap and water and worked like a Trojan horse trying to get that grease off of there! (laughs)

Chapter 1: Over the Rainbow

Freddy Powers: It was the 8th of August, 1987 and the temperature in Redding, California had been in the 100s and up for a few weeks, and the thoughts of winter were beginning to come into my mind. Not only was I winding down the summer, I was also winding down a life that I had lived for the past six years, and as I was driving in my pickup loaded down with guitars and amps and all the things that I would be needing for my change of life, I started thinking about how it all came about. Here I was on my way to Nevada to start my new life back where it all started.

My mind wandered back to a day in 1980 in Reno, Nevada when I was visiting with Willie Nelson at Bill Harrah's house. By the time the 1980s came along, I had already spent 20 years of my life on the music circuit playing throughout the United States, mostly in Nevada lounges. At the time, I had a Dixie band where I also performed comedy and it was a great bunch of road musicians. After years on the road in the mid-1970s, we'd finally landed a dream-sit down gig at the Eldorado Hotel/Casino in Reno. The family who owned the hotel, the Corona family, was a wonderful Italian family with three boys, one girl and father Don Corona running the family business. They were always good to me and all my memories of the family and casino are among my favorites.

In reality, my Eldorado days had me all oiled up and ready for the Spree of 83 and that rock and roll style of living. Leading up to the point when I met Merle Haggard, from the mid-70s on, I'd been named the Entertainment Director and had a show there with my band. I was known as 'Ambassador of Good Will,' and had the *power of the pen*. This meant I could buy anything for anybody I wanted to. I kept half of Reno drunk for those four years! I lived on top of the hotel in the penthouse suite, and the party always ended up in my suite just about every night. Why not, everything was free. The hotel wasn't dumb about giving me the power of the pen and putting me up in that suite either because these guests of mine would wind up staying half the night with me, getting so drunk they were almost out of their minds, and this was all on the house to turn them loose in the Casino. Need I say more?

The Austin Chronicle: "Hired to lead the house band at the Stardust, the flagship enterprise of Allen Glick's Chicago Mafia-backed Argent Corp. In the plush red booths at the back of the lounge… Powers spent his evenings drinking with notorious gangsters like Lefty Rosenthal and Tony Spilotro, who were running operations at the Stardust behind titled fronts like 'Entertainment Director'. Rosenthal and Spilotro would later become the inspiration for Robert De Niro and Joe Pesci's characters in the film *Casino*."

Freddy Powers: Reno was a top-notched party town back then, especially when you're the most popular entertainers in town and the star of a nightly show living on the top of one of the hottest hotel and casinos in a penthouse suite. I had my pick of a WHOLE lotta ladies to choose from every night, and I say Ladies because some of them became good friends I even wrote a song about it:

There are some ladies
that know I did wrong
Because I was weak
When I should have been strong

There are some that I loved
And some that I used
Some that were willing
And some that refused

We took of the things
That would cloud up our minds
And loosen resistance
For a sexual time

The touch of a woman
The world's greatest high
I'm addicted to women
Till the day that I die

Many big-time entertainers came by to see my band back in those days, and a lot would sit in with the band, including Willie Nelson. I remember Willie was playing Harrah's when I was across the street at Harvey's Hotel/Casino once when he came over to sit in with me and my band. They wound up having to shut down the gambling tables around the lounge because it filled up with so many people that were crowding in to see us. It got so crazy so quickly that the dealers couldn't tell who was playing on the tables and who wasn't.

I'd actually first met Willie way back in the late 50s shortly after I'd gotten out of the Marines. I'd come straight back to Texas with my heart set on breaking into the music business. I'd grown up in a musical family that played Dixieland Jazz for local town dances in our hometown of Seminole, and when I'd returned back home in my early 20s, I went to Barber school in Dallas to make ends meet while I was getting things going- Johnny Gimble was actually a classmate of mine. While I was playing in Dallas, I began taking guitar lessons from Paul Buskirk – my hero and mentor, and a major influence – who in turn introduced me to Willie when he was just another young country singer-songwriter. In fact, I actually wound up being one of the first country artists to ever record one of Willie's tunes, '*Heartaches of a Fool*,' back in 1955!

Willie Nelson: The first time I remember seeing Freddy, he was playing in a Banjo band in Arlington, Texas

and it was like a noon-time show at some club; that was
many years ago. Then we ran into each other up in Houston
when he was down there with Paul Buskirk, and he and
Paul and I played a lot of music together and had a lot of
fun.

Catherine Powers: He was living in Arlington, Texas
in an apartment complex back then where one of his fellow
neighbors turned out to be Paul Buskirk. Before he'd ever
first introduced himself to Paul, every day, he would see
this guy dressed in a nice suit walking around with his
instrument, and Freddy was like, "Wow, this guy looks like
somebody I need to meet," and so whenever he would see
that Paul was pulling into the parking lot, Freddy would
open up his door and start singing and playing his guitar as
loud as he could to get his attention, and that's how he first
caught the attention of Paul Buskirk.

Freddy Powers: "Paul was a wonderful friend of mine!
My first paying job was with him. He was such a father
figure to me. We played Europe and Vegas together, my
gosh, son. I knew him so well. He was even the one who
introduced me to marijuana, hahaha! Paul was hardnosed
when it came to music. He was a serious player, and a
serious musician!" 2

"We met in Dallas in the 1950s. I had just gotten out of
the service and was there to become a barber. Paul drove a
big ol' white Buick. I would sing extra loud by the window

and Paul heard me one day, and came to talk to me. He hired me and things moved fast from there. We started doing a noon day Jones show in 1955. It was a news/weather show. Neil Jones was the emcee and Paul was the sidekick." 3

"Later we started doing *the Pat Boone Show* around 1955/56. We played service clubs and officers clubs in Europe. We had a show with three banjos, three vocalists, and a tuba. Paul had a gypsy wagon built on wheels with a stage and lights in the 1960s. We would pull up on a Saturday afternoon to places like furniture store parking lots and Paul would sweet talk the owners into letting us play. We made good money! Paul was never a honky-tonk player. He was so far advanced and beyond us, he was like a professor of music, and he got better with age!" 4

"Here's a funny story for ya'. One time a young guy came up to him at the National DJ Convention Festival in Nashville in the 1950s and said, 'Paul Buskirk, the greatest mandolinist in the world.' Paul remarked, 'The only one in the world!' That was Elvis. Elvis had a WSM corncob pipe and was surrounded by girls, by the way. Willie was a standup DJ when they met. With all absolutely due respect, Paul could eat Bill Monroe alive. Buskirk was from a different mold. If I hadn't met him, there's no telling which direction I'd have gone." 5

Willie Nelson: The first time I heard Paul, he was playing with Johnny and Jack out of Memphis, TN, and then I heard him again when I ran into him down in Houston. I taught guitar with him down there, he had a music studio, and so besides making some records together down there, I would teach guitar in his studio.

Freddy Powers: We all had some great times together traveling around the country. I'm sure Willie misses Paul as much as I do, God rest his soul…

Catherine Powers: Once he got out of the Marines, Freddy got married immediately because he'd been brought up to focus on having a family while young, but his goal and dream was still to be a professional musician. His oldest daughter was born in 1954, and because he still had to be the breadwinner, he worked in the oil industry with his father and opened up his own bar knowing it guaranteed him a place to play, and another thing he did to put food on the table was he went to barber school. Back then, a lot of musicians went to barber school, because 1.) he could control his schedule, and 2.) make money during the day and still go play music at night. So that's how Freddy kept food on the table and his career going at the same time in the early years.

Freddy Powers: "My first professional gig was in 1953 in Dallas at a place called Diamond Jim's, way down on Elm Street, and on my opening night, I got hit in the middle of the face with a salt shaker that they threw at me so hard it damn near knocked me crazy. That was my introduction to Dallas nightclubs… and show business." 6

"I got my start playing over in Hobbs, New Mexico. They had those old Honky-Tonks that hired bands. Lots of people would come through there, like Bob Wills. That's when I got interested in songwriting. All of those old acts would come through and I'd get to see 'um live – closest thing to 'show biz.' That was in the (late 40s)." 7

Catherine Powers: His parents were both always very supportive of Freddy's musical development growing up, and it's kind of sweet, because though I'm not going to say in any way that his parents loved any one child more than they loved the other, Freddy was "Sir Frederick" to his Mama and Daddy. So much so, that on the last day of his mama's life, she still addressed him as "Sir Frederick," and that nickname stuck around the house when Freddy was a kid because one of Freddy's first bands was Sir Frederick and his Little Men. Because his parents came from musical backgrounds themselves, not only were they extremely supportive when he was still living at home, but after he'd gotten out of the service and was getting his start in the music business touring around Texas, his parents would follow Freddy to watch him play. The family moved to Arlington when Freddy did, and when Freddy moved to Houston, the family moved, so even though he was the middle child, wherever Freddy lived, they followed him.

As a matter of fact, with his baby brother Jerry, Freddy was more than a big brother to him, he was his hero. He was his idol, and when you would say Freddy's name to Jerry, he'd get this smile as big as Texas on his face because he was so proud and looked up so much to his older brother. Whenever Freddy would pull back into town when he'd been out on the road, his whole family – mother, father, brothers, sister – would all get the instruments out and they would play music together. His sister would play piano, his daddy would play fiddle, his brothers would play bass and lead guitar, and Freddy would play rhythm on his banjo, so they were a very close family.

Norma Powers-Marlowe: Daddy would have given us anything, any kind of lesson pertaining to anything musical or any other kind of education that we had the ambition and get-up-and-go to go do it. So my father and mother were absolutely supportive of Freddy, or any of us if we'd wanted to do that.

Elston Brooks, Ft. Worth Star Telegram: "The real break came when NBC-TV's TODAY show came to Texas. Producer Don Silverman, a ragtime nut, heard about the boys and asked for a special audition. It was at the un-musician-like hour of 9 a.m. in Powers' empty Arlington nightspot… They made the show. Later Silverman invited them to New York for more appearances on the 'Today' show. A spot on the TONIGHT SHOW followed. TODAY

31

and TONIGHT were just logical culminations of day and nice practice for Tuba man Bobby Hollingsworth. Freddy Powers: 'Bobby had only played the tuba for a short while in the Waco High School Band. I thought it would be an interesting sound to go with the banjos, but the first night it was awful. It was 117 years before he could take that vacant building in Arlington and make it into his Crestview Club. I just named it after the Arlington telephone exchange. If I had known the banjoes were going to go so good, I've had called it the River Boat.'"

Catherine Powers: Back then in the early 50s, Freddy had this nightclub, and one day, he got wind of the fact that Tonight Show was coming through town, and at the time, his band consisted of three banjos and a tuba, The Powerhouse 4. So he picked up the phone, called Today Show host Dave Garroway and told him he had this really unusual band that would be a great fit for the show, and at first, they'd told him they were really busy and didn't know if they'd be able to get over to see him play, and Freddy cleverly said, "You all gotta take a lunch break, right? You come over to my bar and we'll feed you lunch and do our show for you." Well, they were so bowled over by his show that he was invited not only to appear on Today Show, but also its companion Tonight Show, which back then was hosted by Steve Allen.

By this time in 1953, Freddy had already had a little bit of stardom, and Willie Nelson was still trying to break into the business and saw this and gave Freddy "Heartache of a Fool" to record, which made Freddy actually the first artist to record a Willie Nelson song, and to get radio play for a song written by Willie. Willie would play as a feature act at Freddy's club back then too, so through that their friendship grew, and they started touring around Texas together doing shows together. The funny thing about that was, back then, though both Willie and Freddy smoked pot, neither Willie nor Freddy knew yet that the other smoked. So when they'd all be out on the road together – Freddy, Paul, Willie and his wife at the time Shirley – and they would stop, because Freddy and Paul didn't know Willie was a pot smoker, they would take off and go their way and hide from Willie to get stoned while Willie and Shirley were going the opposite direction to do the *same thing*! The laws were so strict back then – especially in the Lone Star state – that getting caught with one joint could land you a stiff prison sentence. So after that, when they were on the road, to make sure they didn't get caught, they would sneak out into the middle of the desert where they could see cars coming for miles, and get high.

Freddy Powers: "My sister wrote a song for Hank Thompson, she wasn't a performer or anything, but she played the piano and wrote great songs. I think that's where

33

the idea came from, when she cut that tune, I started thinking, "Hey… maybe I could to that?" 8

Catherine Powers: Freddy's songwriting career got its start in the 1950s too when he was a writer on "There She Goes" by Carl Smith, and Freddy's father had been so impressed with his talent for writing that he'd paid for Carl to go in the studio and demo the song and record it. Freddy had run home and excitedly told his wife at the time, "We've broken into the business, we have a song coming out on the radio," the whole nine yards, but when it came out, Freddy's name was nowhere to be found on the songwriting credits. He'd been cut out, and all the money his father had invested had been lost, and in those days, if you didn't have a name as a writer to go and try and fight somebody that was already reputable in the business, you didn't have a chance. Then Freddy had a song recorded by The Wilburn Brothers where his name was on the record as a writer, *"Nothing at All,"* but that's exactly what he received in the way of songwriting royalties. It was another one of those rip-offs, and that discouraged Freddy and he gave up on writing for a while to focus on being a performer and just writing songs for his band.

Freddy Powers: "The Wilburn Brothers had some kind of hits out there on the Grand Old Opry, and I wrote a song with them. I soon found out that I was signed up with a publisher that was really unscrupulous. I never saw any money from that. I don't know what happened back in the days. I didn't have an idea on how to collect any money, and I sort of got disenchanted on selling songs." 9

Nothing At All

If you only care for things money can buy
You're a man who's found fortune and fame
Just remember before life has wilted away
Without true love you don't have a thing

Nothing at all nothing at all
Without love you've got nothing at all
Nothing at all nothing at all
Without love you've got nothing at all

When you find a love that will never grow old
Then you'll know dreams are free and not bought
You'll have your cup full without treasures of gold
And be richer than you ever thought

Freddy Powers: The Austin Chronicle would note an interesting fact not many fans know about Willie and my musical relationship in a cover story a few years back: "Nelson even joined Powers' band on bass for a short time, working the infamous honky-tonks along the Jacksboro Highway. They had to cover the tuba with a mesh screen to keep the crowds from flinging their beer bottles into the bell."

So years later, while Willie was in Reno, I remember we'd gotten together with another friend of mine Nate Green for a golf game. Willie and I got to talking about the old musicians we knew and soon got around to Django Reinhart. The next thing I knew we were making plans to get some of these old guys together and make an album. Will, at the time, was as hot as the Texas Rodeo, and out of the blue at a golf game one day, he asked me to help produce, sing and play on his next studio album, which became '*Somewhere Over the Rainbow*.'

Willie Nelson: *Over the Rainbow*, which Freddy produced, is one of my favorite albums. We've been in the studio many times together and I enjoyed all of them. He's a lot of fun to play with, and when Freddy was at his best, there was nobody better at what he did. I think '*Rainbow*' is one of the best albums I ever did because Freddy and Buskirk and Dean Reynolds were playing on it.

Freddy Powers: "I sang a little bit, on five or six of the tunes on the album, including '*I'm Gonna Sit Right Down and Write Myself a Letter*.' A lot of people didn't know it, because the disc jockeys that played it wouldn't say it, and a matter of fact, a lot of them didn't know that it was me singing on it. It was really strange, because every now and then somebody, they'd find out that it was me and they'd be real surprised because they'd heard it a lot of times and you know, somebody close to me sometimes, and all of a sudden, they'd find out two or three years later." 10

Willie Nelson: Freddy's strongest suit, I always thought, was his rhythm guitar playing. He was a great rhythm guitar player. I liked Django Reinhardt, and Django's brother was a great rhythm guitar player, and Freddy and Paul Buskirk both were the two best rhythm guitar players – other than Django's brother – that I've ever known.

Freddy Powers: "The biggest influence in my life is Django Reinhardt. In the 50s, I was introduced to Django. I was drawn to that fiery acoustic rhythm with Stephane Grappelli on the fiddle. What people don't realize is Western swing was framed right out of that style of music. I'm not saying that Django is the king of Western Swing, but he's up there with Emit Miller. He had a band back in the Milton Brown days. Johnny Gimble gave me some Emit Miller stuff and believe it or not, that's where a lot of the Bob Wills came from. I also heard a song on an Emmett Miller tape 'Got a Feeling That Blue, Oh Lord' just like Hank sang. Years before Hank did it!" 11

Rolling Stone Magazine 4-Star Album Review, June 11, 1981: "*Somewhere over the Rainbow* further establishes Willie Nelson as country music's preeminent conservator of America's pop tradition… *Somewhere over the Rainbow* is a lively acoustic record of simpler material, made in Texas, with no frills. Utilizing only a fiddle, a stand-up bass, a mandolin and guitars, the arrangements suggest a spontaneous musicale whose inspirations range from Django Reinhardt to Bob Wills to Les Paul. This all-purpose period sound perfectly complements Willie Nelson's Lone Star gypsy persona. Alternating with him on lead vocals is Freddie Powers, a Reno bandleader whose more casual swing style makes a nice contrast to Nelson's intensity...*Somewhere over the Rainbow* may be the most audacious album thus far in the revivalist phase of Nelson's career."

Freddy Powers: *"Somewhere Over the Rainbow"* went platinum, and Willie had credited me as the album's primary producer, so once it went to #1 on the Billboard Top Country Albums chart, overnight it was certainly a boost to my career. My first big sign of that came one day at Bill Harrah's house where I remember Willie and I were talking and playing the guitar. There were a lot of people in the house at the time, and we were sitting around smoking a joint that afternoon when none other than Merle Haggard walked in! Of all the country singers I had ever met, Merle made the greatest impact on me when I met him. That day, he was with his then-wife Leona Williams, and I'll have to admit Leona was the first one I saw, and I was thinking that she was a very beautiful lady. Then as Merle strolled in with his semi-cocky walk and all eyes in the room would follow Merle around, there was no doubt that he had a special "star charisma" about him.

I laid my guitar down and walked over a little nervous, introduced myself, and to my surprise, Merle replied, "Freddy Powers, I love the work you did on Willie's new album '*Somewhere Over the Rainbow*.'" He said that it was his favorite album, and I must say I was so flattered that I didn't really know what to say. Little did I know that this meeting with Merle Haggard would be the start of a new career, and that Merle would bring out of me new artistic gifts that I never knew I had (like the ability to write hit songs). From that day on until now, Merle and I were never too far away from each other.

Chapter 2: Meeting Merle

Freddy Powers: In truth, the first time I'd ever met Merle was years before, way back in 1961. He was an unknown side man playing bass for Wynn Stewart. They were working at the Nashville Nevada Club in Las Vegas, and I was working down the street at the Showboat Hotel/Casino. I had a Dixieland band on the bill with Spike Jones and his band The City Slickers. I remember one evening Merle came over either on his break or after their show, and told me he liked our show and our style of music. He told me he was working down the street and so the next night, I made sure to go over and catch his show. That soon became a nightly ritual for us where he'd usually come over and watch my show, then after I'd finished my set, I'd go over to the club he was playing and do the same. I always set up on the left side of the stage, that's the side Merle was on. We liked each other and had respect for each other's style of music so we became fast friends and hung out together during our engagement there, but lost touch as the 60s and our respective careers went on.

Catherine Powers: Freddy didn't go out to Nevada until 1960, so prior to then, in the late 50s, he was still touring around Texas and playing locally at the bar he owned in Arlington as well as frequenting the Dallas area clubs with his band. Through playing that circuit, he got to know another bar owner by the name of Jack Ruby, who became a good friend of Freddy's, and as a matter of fact, Jack even gave Freddy a puppy. Jack Ruby would of course go on to live forever in infamy after he shot and killed Lee Harvey Oswald following Oswald's assassination of President John F. Kennedy, who was Jack's hero. Jack was friends with all the police because of all the protection money that club owners paid to the cops back in those days, and Freddy in fact was still in touch with Jack in the early 60s when he shot Oswald. Freddy always thought they really took it too far, the whole conspiracy angle, because Jack Ruby, like Freddy, was just an extremely patriotic American.

Don Powers Jr: Freddy was supposed to play for President Kennedy and Lyndon Johnson and Governor John Connolly the next day after JFK was killed! The reason Freddy had that honor is because he'd campaigned for Governor Connolly during his re-election campaign, but sadly, the Governor also got shot sitting in the front seat in the same car with Kennedy. Don and Freddy both knew Jack Ruby, who had a bar in Dallas and Ruby would come over to Arlington, Texas to the Crestview Club, which Freddy and Dad used to own together, and they would swap entertainment so they'd have different bands, a variety of groups, and so my dad and Freddy both knew Jack Ruby.

Austin City Limits: "During the early '60s, he appeared on the 'Hootenanny' television show, and the next thing he knew he had jumped from the honky-tonk to the coffee house circuit."

Freddy Powers: "West Texas couldn't hold me, nothing ever could. I've known that for as long as I can remember. I've always followed my heart and my songs wherever they take me." 12

Elston Brooks, Ft. Worth Star Telegram: "Joe (Fingers) Carr calls it 'music with lumps in it'. Hugh Downs calls the musical mixture 'the greatest combination since Jimmy Valentine sandpapered his fingers and opened his last safe'. Freddy Powers, the local lad who is the subject of the professional adulation, calls it 'a different ragtime sound'. Powers leaves the more colorful quotes to those better equipped to describe the unlikely sound of three banjos and the tuba. Eight years ago, the 30-year-old Powers was just a barber dreaming of the time when he could be a 30-year-old success in show business. No more does Powers take just a little off the sides, his cut now is strictly off the top. What kind of a Barber was he? 'One of the best', he says without hesitation. Now, that's what others around the nation are saying about his 'Powerhouse IV', the little ragtime group that found its way from Arlington to Manhattan in less than a year."

Freddy Powers: "I was doin' stand-up comedy and Dixieland. We had these costumes of old-time knickers with argyle socks and little snap caps. By the 60s, I was doin' The Today and Tonight Shows with a little banjo band I had for a while. I did two albums as 'Freddy Powers and the Powerhouse IV' for Warner Bros. Records. That wasn't in the country vein. It was three banjos and a tuba. It was 'hell raisin' Dixieland like Bill Bailey and stuff like that. I kinda got lost from country music there during that folk period." 13

Don Powers Jr.: They did a 40s/50s show and dressed of that era in Zoot suits, and when they'd head for the stage, they'd come out of the elevator and would play walking all the way through the floor of the Casino – around the Blackjack tables, around the slot machines and all of that – and then head to the showroom to do their show, and people loved that! They would parade in with Freddy up front playing the banjo, then a guy behind him with the clarinet and so forth, and they did Dixieland Jazz and Comedy.

Freddy Powers: "When I hear an audience exploding with real belly laughs, I get cold chills up and down my spine. I love this business now more than ever, and I intend to stay in it until they carry me on and off – and then I'll play dead! I never felt I was truly successful until I got into comedy. My show is in real demand now." 13a

Elston Brooks, Ft. Worth Star Telegram: "State Rep. Don Kennard, who wanted to be State Senator Don Kennard, asked us to suggest a musical group for his campaigning. We mentioned the little group at Arlington's Crestview Club that had been setting the customers on fire, and Kennard engaged their services. The fact that Kennard now signs his letters State Senator, and Doyle Willis is running for the Fort Worth City Council, may… be traced to the musical attraction of the Powerhouse IV. In any event, it allowed them to play the Governor's inauguration party on the same bill with Joey Bishop, Vic Damone and the Ames Brothers."

Nevada Appeal: "Powers has been entertaining since he was 15 and he began appearing in Las Vegas early in the 1960s…" (Nevada Appeal, Star Talk, Thursday, Sept 21, 1989, by Pamela Bissell Crowell)

Freddy Powers: "(One slow night at Harvey's Casino playing opposite the DeCastro Sisters) the place was completely empty. I stripped down to my shorts, pulled on the long zoot suit jacket and slunk out into the chairs in front of the stage. Peggy DeCastro about melted into the stage." [14]

Catherine Powers: Once he was playing the Casino circuit, Freddy was always trying to pull publicity stunts, so one night – and this was after the whole Roswell thing –

Freddy decided that he was going to make people think Martians had landed. When they would see cars coming, they would run across the highway, thinking all these cars would stop, hoping that it was gonna make the front page that Martians had landed outside of Reno, then say "Hahaha, it was us!" It was little stunts like that Freddy would do, trying to get publicity.

Freddy Powers: "We went out on the highway… and one of the guys in the band and I wrapped ourselves in tin foil, put plastic bags over our heads, stuck antennas on the bags. We had a huge amplifier in the car, and played that warbling whistle you always hear in flying saucer films. Cars pulled over, trucks pulled over, people were shouting. Not one paper printed a word about it!" 15

Anne Reynolds, Deanie-Bird's Widow: That's one that still stands out! It's crazy, but Dean would always laugh recounting for me the time he and Freddy and the boys in the Powerhouse IV were acting silly and wound aluminum foil around themselves to look like Martins, and would stand in the bend of the road where the big truckers would be swinging their big rigs around the corner, and when their headlights would shine on Freddy and Dean all wrapped up in this tin foil, they looked like they were outer-space men. That's the kind of stupid stuff they used to pull, and even years later, they'd laugh themselves silly recalling it.

Don Powers Jr: Freddy used to play when he had the Dixieland band all over the state of Nevada: Elko, Wendover, Winnemucca, Las Vegas, Reno, pretty much everywhere. He was voted best Showroom Group two years in a row by Guy Richardson, who even bought a Cadillac for Freddy. My dad worked dealing blackjack at the El Dorado and I worked across the street. Freddy played mostly at the El Dorado Casino in Reno, Nevada, and they had Freddy redesign the showroom and he put red velvet all over the walls and hung banjos all over to decorate it, and he was the house band there and really started to pull that Casino out of the red after that.

Reno bandmate Augie Savage: "The best music I ever played was with Freddy. Every real musician wanted to play with Freddy, because he lets them play." (Source: The Lovelock Review-Miner by Debra Reid, July, 2012)

Freddy Powers: I was always meeting new musicians and new people at every engagement. I like most people can't remember ever person's name I meet. Most of them when you're traveling you never see again, but it seemed like Merle and I were meant to – and indeed we would – although that destiny would take 20 years to come full circle. So that night after Merle and I had started talking about '*Somewhere Over the Rainbow*,' he asked me, "When did you work there?", like I'd said something to jar his memory, and in the instant that followed we both realized at the same time that we had met back then all those many years ago!!!

Merle Haggard: Freddy and I go way back to the early 1960s. The first time I met Freddy, he was doing stand-up comedy playing a banjo. I remember seeing Fred was in Las Vegas, and I think he was playing at the Showboat at the time and I was playing at the Nashville Nevada club. I was playing bass for Wynn Stewart.

Freddy Powers: "In the sixties and seventies I was traveling – I had a territorial band out of Minnesota. Minnesota was a good training ground, because they had casinos of Elks Clubs. They had illegal gambling and they let them get away with it. It wasn't legal, but everyone in town did it, and we often got paid under the table." 16

Merle Haggard: Over the years, I'd hear about different things, and as the years went by, things got good for me and good for Fred, and I don't think we ran into each other again for about 20 years. By then, around 1980, Fred had been working in Reno across the street from Harrah's at the El Dorado, and he'd been doing mainly Dixieland up until that time, and was interested in trying to get deeper into country music, and I was wanting to play guitar.

We got together there, I think the first time we actually played together, we played for 18 hours up there at

Harrah's in Reno. We really enjoyed playing together because he knew a thousand songs and I wanted to learn them all, and he wanted to write some country songs and he did. Then we looked at a clock and it was time for both of us to go back to work, and so we did- I did two full shows at Harrah's and Freddy did I think four shows. Then when we got off, we did the same thing and played together for another 18 hours, me and Deaniebird and Freddy. After that, we played non-stop for about five years.

Freddy Powers: After I got acquainted with him again after so many years, we got our guitars out and began to pick. I had my bass player and best friend Dean Reynolds with me, we called him Deanie Bird. The two of us were the rhythm section with Merle and Willie taking turns on lead guitar. Merle really liked our style of swing and Dixieland jazz. Willie had to leave after a little bit to go and play his show, but the three of us – Deanie Bird, Merle and I- continued to play almost all night long, which turned into days and days of picking. Merle just couldn't get enough. I didn't realize it at the time but Merle was learning jazz from us. Not far out jazz but country jazz.

Anne Reynolds, Deanie-Bird's Widow: Dean got his nickname way back when he had first been in the Grand Ole Opry when he was 16 and Uncle Dave Macon and Minnie Pearl were in the show. Well, after that, he went on the road with Uncle Dave Macon, and one day in between shows, they were bathing together in a horse troft, and Uncle Dave looked at Dean's legs and said, "My God kid, your legs are just skinny as a bird, I'm gonna call you Deanie Bird." Then Minnie Pearl took him under her wing and kept all his money for him, and they would sneak into churches at night – they were always unlocked – when they were empty, and she taught him to play the piano. She taught him math, and kept him on the straight and narrow while they were out on the road, because he was in the Grand Ole Opry on the road at 16 without his folks.

Freddy Powers: The three of us became close and enjoyed playing so much together that if Merle wasn't in Reno, we were on our way to Redding, California to Merle's home to play. Dean and I were spending a lot of time in Lake Shasta where Merle was living on a houseboat and owned a marina with a great showroom and night club. Deaniebird and I started getting together with Merle anywhere we could and the three of us would pick for as much as 18 hours a day. Merle wanted to learn every song I knew, and I was in turn trying to learn every song Merle knew. This went on for months. Merle would come on my jobs and play guitar with me, and I would come on his jobs and play guitar with him.

One day, we were at Harrah's Hotel and Casino in Tahoe in Merle's room before a gig of his when I grabbed his guitar and sang '*I Always Get Lucky With You*' for him. When I finished the song, he just stared at me for a moment

49

saying nothing as if he didn't know how to tell me it was a shitty song! But instead, he jumped up out of his chair and said something about how the title of the song alone was a hit. When Merle said that, it was like a lightning bolt of confidence that hit me and that moment, unbeknownst to me, was the launching point of my songwriting career. One night not long after the phone rang and it was Merle's office manager Tex Whitson. He said Merle had rewritten my song and played it over the phone to me on a little tape recorder. I couldn't hear it too good over the phone, but it sounded awful good from what I could hear. Merle recorded the song on an album called '*Big City*,' which was one of Merle's biggest selling albums. Later George Jones had a # 1 on it, and it was nominated for song of the year.

I Always Get Lucky With You

I 've had good luck and bad luck
And no luck, it's true
But I always get lucky with you

I've been turned on and turned down
When the bars close at two
But I always get lucky with you

I've had two strikes against me
Most all of the time

And when it's down to just a phone call
I'm minus a dime

There's been good days and bad days
But when the day is through
I always get lucky with you
Oh, I always get lucky with you

I've had two strikes against me
Most all of the time
And when it's down to just a phone call
I'm minus a dime

There's been good days and bad days
But when the day is through
I always get lucky with you
Oh, I always get lucky with you

I always get lucky with you

It was somewhere around this time that Merle came down to Reno to see me (I was working at The El Dorado Hotel with my half-Country/half-Dixie band). After the last show that night, Merle asked me, "Would you like to give up a year of what you're doing and come live with me in

Redding and write songs with me?" Here I am at the top of the Nevada lounge circuit and I'm about to throw caution into the wind entirely and relocate to a lake to live out the next decade with Merle Haggard. Two members of my band I felt that I couldn't let go because they had been with me through thick and thin, so Merle agreed to hire Gary Church for his band, and Dean Reynolds was still working with me occasionally. At the time, the lounges of Nevada were getting to me, and already I had been writing a few new songs, so my decision was an easy one to come by. Merle was enjoying learning Dixieland jazz style that Deanie Bird and I were playing, and I was learning a hell of a lot about writing country songs, so I split up my band and relocated to the lake with Merle.

Chapter 3: Lake Shasta

Freddy Powers: It was 1980. I had just divorced my second wife and was free to go crazy- A 50-year-old playboy. Merle Haggard was working on a divorce and was primed for a party. At the time, Merle owned a resort called 'Silverthorne' on Lake Shasta: they rented house boats, ski boats, and had a 400-seat club with live bands, a restaurant, etc., it was an unbelievable paradise. Even though Merle had a beautiful ranch just 10 miles away, he spent most of his time on his private houseboat. Shortly after I arrived, Merle approached me with the idea that I should have my own houseboat as well, but I told him I didn't have that kind of money to buy one, to which he replied, "Don't worry, that's the only thing I have plenty of..."

Well, in a few days, we located a 57-foot boat with everything (including the kitchen sink), Merle wrote a check out for $85,000 and bought the boat. He had it put in my name, even though I was worried about paying for the boat. Merle joked matter of factly that "Your only worry is taxes," and he said I'd be making a lot of money soon and advised me to hire a tax attorney, and from that day the now-infamous 'Spree of 83' was on.

Merle Haggard: Of all the people I've met in my entire life in this business, Freddy is one of my closest friends. Some people thought we were homosexuals, we weren't, we both like women, and I can testify (laughs) that

53

that's the truth. It was a gas. The Spree of 83, we called it that, had actually started out in 1979, and went on that way for five or six years I guess. The Great Escape is what it was really. We had some adventures; I don't think fear was in our vocabulary very much. We both probably wanted to bite the dust some other way than the way we're going to.

We'd become really close friends. We were both getting a divorce, and we were both happy about it, and Lake Shasta seemed like the likely place to go. So for about the next seven years, we had the greatest times. Sometimes we'd eat, sometimes we'd have a drink, but mostly, we played all the time. Living out on the lake there, we had the boats hooked up to the shoreline where we had phones down there so we could call up and get whatever supplies we needed while we worked. We really enjoyed it, we were in shape, our chops were up, and I don't think I've played that good since then.

Linda Mitchell, Silverthorne Resort Manager: The guys would get into these long jam sessions out on the houseboats, they called it *Pickin'*, and sometimes during the day, they'd have a concert right out there on the dock! Freddy's best friend Deanie Bird Reynolds used to come up to the lake a lot, and if you wanted Catfish, he was the best in the world, but Deaniebird and Freddy and Merle and others would pick for hours. They'd play and play and play and play, and they spent a lot of time doing that. We'd get a phone call sometimes from Merle's houseboat after they'd been playing for hours, and he'd say "We're hungry," and I'd reply, "Do you realize it's two o'clock in the morning?" And he'd persist, "We're hungry, we want some biscuits and gravy," and everything. Well, because Merle was my boss, we'd get dressed, and go up to the kitchen in the resort and sometimes they would remember that they had called us to fix them something to eat, and sometimes they'd just keep playing and forget about all the food we'd cooked!

Freddy Powers: Here we were, two single, middle-aged men, living in a near-paradise lifestyle. Merle was hot as a pistol and his career was at its peak. I was being treated like a king and I was thinking what in the world am I gonna do to justify this treatment? For the first three years or so, Merle was extremely protective of me. I traveled with that circus to every state in the country. From the beginning, Merle and I were almost inseparable. Where one went, we both went. We would do an occasional tour where I would play guitar and sing a few songs in the show. Somehow, I knew that it was more than just a friendship with Merle, it was a mutual respect for each other's talents.

Haggard Manager Marc Oswald: Merle's life in the early 80s was insane, and it was such a crazy tornado around him all the time because of the fame and fortune and all the hit records, that Freddy was almost like 'Eye of the Hurricane' for him, where everything was still for a minute. Merle trusted Freddy no doubt with his life, and they were basically inseparable.

Merle and Freddy were what I call running buddies, and the thing about Freddy is he's like the ultimate wingman! So for a guy like Merle, who's a fighter pilot and is going into dangerous territory 24/7 as a star of the stature he was and still is, Freddy served as sort of comic relief, Yoda – in that he always had a philosophical angle if you needed one. So he was kind of a filter, so when everything got so big for Merle, so many people were trying to insert themselves into Merle's life that I think Freddy was a little reality check for Merle. They would discuss what was going on, who they were meeting, what they were doing, and it gave Merle something to bounce stuff off that didn't have an agenda. Freddy always had Merle's best interest at heart.

Freddy Powers: When we'd come home after a tour we would head straight for the houseboats, load up with as many as six or seven girls and head up the Pit River, a great place on Lake Shasta to hide out. The houseboats were located about 50 yards from the marina and club. At the resort, Merle built us a private dock with a security gate, electricity, phones, and everything he could think of to make things better.

Merle Haggard: The lake itself was just a different life than anything I'd ever experienced, and I think for

Freddy too. Its one of the most beautiful places in the world when the lake is up. Then when it went down, it changed, so every time it dropped a foot or so, it was a different lake. There was a period while we were living there where for 500 something days it wouldn't rain, and every day it was exactly perfect. It went two years without raining a drop, and the lake dropped 237 vertical feet when we lived out there. They thought the damn thing was going to dry up, then one day it started raining and rained for four months straight and filled that lake up in four months when they'd predicted it would take three or four years. I remember one night the lake raised 13 inches overnight; that's a lot of water. We docked in places that are all underwater now, so you can't even go back out there to the same place and find them because they're not there.

Longtime Haggard Drummer Biff Adams: When he moved up to Lake Shasta, Freddy's houseboat was right across the dock from mine. We lived on our own private dock behind a gate. At the end of the dock was Merle's big two-story boat, and right across the dock from Merle's was Freddy's houseboat. My houseboat was on the other side and we had our own little circle there, and it was a real nice deal, it really was.

Manager Marc Oswald: Silverthorne was a beautiful place, and it was Merle's field of dreams I think, and when you drove in there, you drove in this windy road into Lake

Shasta, and when you first got in there, there was a restaurant and this beautiful nightclub there. They had stars play that place all the time; I remember I saw Lynn Stewart play there with Freddy and Merle, so when you came in they had this big parking area, and then they had the docks so you would walk down this one main dock that then connected to all the docks where the houseboats were. I think there were 100 houseboats there, and it was in this little cove called Silverthorne Resort, and they had a private dock that was Merle's dock that had this gate on it.

It was mesh metal and you could see through it, but it was really pretty; it had carpet on it and I potted trees on it, and on that dock was The Hotel Troubadour, and then Freddy's boat, and one other that was a guest boat. So as fans would come down to try and look through that gate to get a look at Merle, he was super friendly with everybody, and people came by it all the time and would just stand out at the gate and look at the three or four houseboats they had on Merle's dock. So, your kind of like living in a fishbowl, and I also think that's why he was out at night so much, so he could have a little bit of privacy.

Linda Mitchell, Silverthorne Resort Manager: No one, unless they were invited onto that private dock, got on it, period. That was the rule. That was their serenity, I guess is the way to say it. It was their downtime; it was their time to take deep breaths from the tours and crowds and hub-bub of having to travel and have people swarm all over them, so

Silverthorne was their playtime, and they had fun. That was the neatest thing about them, they had fun.

We were out there in the snow, we were out there in the rain, we were out there when it was hotter than bloody hell, to put it very bluntly, and Freddy always wore pocket pants, as long as he wasn't swimming, he was always in long pants and that were always tan, and he always had a smile for anyone and everyone. Just the country gentleman that he always was, he was always so soft in his speaking, and the minute I met him, I fell in love with him. They were my boys, and I was like their *Mom*. He always had these twinkling eyes and this big smile and always a hug for you. He just had a Good Ole' Texas/Okie boy charming sense of humor, and he enjoyed everything he did, he just lit up: he enjoyed life on the lake, and songwriting, and performing and pickin' with other stars, he was enjoying his life.

Once we were all living out on the lake together, Merle started putting on his Merle Haggard Bass Tournaments, which brought in avid fishermen, professional fishermen, NFL football players, you name it, everybody who was anybody came out, and Merle and Freddy and the boys would jam up on top of Merle's boat out on the second deck. They just had a ball when we went out. In fact, Merle had a tour bus that was moored up there, and it had an actual recording studio built on board, and not only would they do the lighting and everything from there, but would record what he and Freddy and the boys were performing too.

Anne Reynolds, Deanie-Bird's Widow: Merle never got up until four or five in the afternoon, because they stayed up all night playing, and they'd take the houseboats out on the lake at night and kind of put them in a circle and they would jam on the front porches of the houseboats. Everyone would gather round, all the other houseboats would come up and listen. They never interfered with us, but they were getting a free show.

Freddy Powers: Merle had the biggest houseboat on the lake. Downstairs, he had a large living room, a kitchen in the front, and a large bathroom and bedroom in the back. Upstairs was another large bedroom with a hot tub and big screen TV. Its looked like an old-style whore house, but an elegant one. On the front of the boat it had a big neon sign that read "Hotel Troubadour." Merle took great pride in his boat. That boat stood high above all the other boats out there. So when we went up the famous Pit River, everybody knew it was us. We used two-way marine radios to stay in touch with each other. Naturally, that meant everybody on the lake could listen in, and did. You could make phone calls from the boat, but that meant the marine operator had to hook you up, so everyone could still hear any and all our conversations.

Manager Marc Oswald: On Merle's boat, of course, they had every contraption known to man, it was kind of like a MacGyver place, they were always fooling around with contraptions. So on Merle's houseboat, his coffee table was electric, and you hit like this clicker that looked like a garage door opener, and it moved out of the way and turned into a fishing hole. So they'd sit in the living room of his boat on the couch and fish through the floor while they were watching TV!

They also had this thing called a hovercraft that was round and was like a donut that came up on a little cushion of air, and had like a two-stroke engine in it and had handlebars, and it was maybe six feet across, and you'd it up and it would hover four or five inches off the ground. It had a fin right, and then it had another fin and you could ride it across the ground and also across the water, it was bizarre looking!

Linda Mitchell, Silverthorne Manager: Sometimes Freddy, Merle and the boys would go up the lake to go fishing, and you just never knew where they were. In fact, one year, they all went out on the fourth of July back when they used to do the fireworks display out on Shasta Dam, and Merle would take the Troubadour out and would have the band up on top and would serenade all the people that were watching the fireworks, but the Forest Service eventually shut that down.

Merle was always fighting with the Forest Service, let's just say they weren't houseboat friendly, and not wanting pollution and not wanting this and not wanting that out on the lake. We all had to have a permit, and give them their money too (laughs). I think the biggest honor I ever had was when Freddy and Merle asked me to put on a Willie Nelson Farm Aid event out at the lake. It was a big price he paid to the Forest Service, but they let us do it.

Freddy Powers: Its true, Hag was always fighting with the Forestry service. They were in control of the lake and what was allowed and what was not. That included the houseboats, their width, length, what you could have on them and what you couldn't. They made Merle take his side rails off because it exceeded the width rules. So as an act of defiance Merle started building upwards. When you thought he had gone as high as he could, he went and built a crow's nest. That made it about eight feet taller. My boat was moored next to Merle's about eight to ten feet away. They were about the same size, but I didn't have a second level. Merle's looked like a high rise houseboat going down the river. There was no doubt what was happening on our houseboats. You could hear the music and laughter, and the wild and wacky partying all over the lake.

Anne Reynolds, Deanie-Bird's Widow: Merle is such a character, he was always up to stuff and you never knew what he was gonna do, and the same with Freddy and Dean, you never knew who was going to pull the next prank – I mean, the sky was the limit! Anything was game. Freddy was usually the joker, and Dean played right into it, but Freddy was usually the leader. Freddy had a great sense of humor, like one night, I remember he untied our houseboat while we were asleep and we woke up clear across the lake!

You never knew what was going to happen next. One day it was raining, and Merle and Freddy and Dean and I put on a play, made costumes and everything, and they recorded it as we did a play on the houseboat. It was all just moving all the time, something was always going on. It really was like a family, I can't tell you how close we all were, and we just had such a good time. We were all like a bunch of crazy kids up there, like we didn't have good sense. We spent a lot of time just goofing around and laughing and doing silly things, we just had fun.

Chapter 4: The Spree of '83 Begins

Freddy Powers: By 1983, Merle and I were living on the boats full-time, writing and partying. We called it *'The Spree of 83'*. Now, I've always been a pot smoker and beer drinker and that was about the size of my vices up to that point, but 1983, 84, and 85, were the (fiend) drug years! It was as if we were deliberately trying to kill ourselves. We bought cocaine and speed by the bags and sometimes we would go for two or three days and never sleep. Merle was up one time I know for four, five days without sleep. It got to where he was almost afraid to go to sleep.

It seemed like we were living every day as if it were our last, which meant living for the moment. Sometimes we all got naked and stayed that way for days. It was just plain fun, and for the girls it was exciting as they always came back to do it again. We had these free spirits flying through us, and we chased the dragon on every adventure we could. The women were the fuel for our fires, and it seemed like they kept getting hotter and hotter, wilder and wilder till my life started to feel as surreal as a movie at times. I was definitely living the dream.

Biff Adams: Some of the parties out there at the lake were pretty wild. You didn't know quite what to expect when you went out there, but they were always having a good time. It was a riot, it was a lot of fun, and the women always went gaga for Merle. There were some days where

Freddy and Merle would be out on the lake just stark-ass naked passing some of these other houseboats waving at the girls.

Merle Haggard: The Rat Pack in Vegas, they were jealous of us, we had more going on over there than they did, and they knew about it and called us every once in a while. Frank Sinatra called me while that was going on, and invited me to play on the White House lawn for the President, but I got out of it because me and Freddy were busy partying and writing songs.

Freddy Powers: It's true! Merle and I were having one of our wild parties when Frank Sinatra called and asked Merle to go and perform on the White House front lawn with him, an invitation Merle politely declined because we were having too much fun! During The Spree of '83, there was a party going on 24/7. We were flying girls in from all over, and if we wanted to play music and jam, we flew the musicians in. The word was out where we were living and people did amazing things to get to Merle. We had women take off their clothes and swim out to the boat. People in boats would flash us, it was really a kick. Our parties were at the height of their time. Almost everybody was doing cocaine regularly.

Merle Haggard: We drank lemon water out there when a lot of guys were doing cocaine. Everybody had a little vile, and I remember before I quit in '85, it got pretty heavy. One time I was making a health drink, and it had all kinds of good things in it – fruits of different kinds, strawberries, blueberries, peaches and oranges- and I put it in the blender, got it all mixed up, and took that little vile and sprinkled a little bit of cocaine on it.

Freddy Powers: I, myself, had a love-hate relationship with cocaine. I didn't like the nervousness and uneasy feeling, but all the women loved it so Merle and I always had it around. If you had cocaine, the girls would come a running and be ready for anything. So I would catch myself doing another line even though I didn't like the feeling it gave me, I somehow thought it would get better. Either way, back then, it was the popular party drug and Merle and I for a while there both went through mountains of it – along with the girls of course, who always seemed to love it - during parties out on the lake.

Merle Haggard: I'm not going to go into any of the prostitutes or hookers, it's not necessary, because you all know Freddy, and at that time in our lives, we were in between women, and he would be up in his plane spotting fish and say 'Hey, there's a big school of bass located over here,' and we'd go over and catch the bass. Or he'd say, 'Hey, there's a bunch of naked women, and they're over just on the other side…'

Freddy Powers: Merle always referred to them as hookers and prostitutes but they were coke whores. Hell, there were girls around for free, we didn't have to pay for pussy as long as there was cocaine around. We named my boat the USSF boat, and you could watch everyone run to their boats when they heard either 'USSF houseboat calling the Hotel Troubadour' or vice versa. So we used codes like 'Your Aunt Patty was on her way with cookies.' Cookies? Yeah right, you know the old saying if you believe that... The Hotel Troubadour was host to a lot of strange parties and lots of very famous guests, some of whom can't be named here. One was this famous Hollywood Starlet we met at Universal Amphitheatre. She came up to the houseboat and was so quiet, she didn't really say much all day. She just sat back and watched whatever we were doing. Later on after everybody left, I went back to my houseboat. Merle later told me the minute the door closed she started stripping, throwing her clothes in the air hollering "Let's get after it." He said the only problem was she let loose and started talking, and they couldn't get much sex in because she wouldn't stop talking. Merle said she was still talking all the way to the airport the next day, and I'm sure if she reads this she'll get a big kick out of it.

Another notorious groupie I still remember to this day was 'Little Rock Connie.' Merle and I being constant partiers thought we were pretty wild, had the attitude everything goes and never thought there could be a woman who could be too much for us. That was, until we met

Connie, who back then was known as a famous groupie, and as we'd soon find out, for good reason too. She was a real good-looking gal, and actually a lot of fun, but she was WILD. Not realizing yet how wild she was, I got her phone number and called her up to invite her out to the houseboat for the weekend. I picked her up at the airport in a Limo with a sun roof- that should have been my first hint this woman was wild. The first thing she did was open the sun roof, take her top off, and stood up in the Limo flashing all of Redding, turning in all directions to make sure everybody saw her.

When the weekend was over and I was ready for her to leave, I talked the limo driver into taking her back to the airport without me. When he got back, he said "Boy that woman is wild! She was flashing everybody all the way to the airport, she nearly caused a pile up on I-5." Needless to say, it didn't help our reputation in the community. Later on, we saw her on a talk show. I was holding my breath, hoping she wouldn't mention my name and her weekend on the houseboats with Merle and I. She didn't, thank God.

We saw her again sometime later on at a concert in Little Rock. The famous 'Brown Sisters,' Maxine and Bonnie, were on the bus visiting Merle. Little Rock Connie showed up and just about the first thing she did was lift up her skirt and flash the Brown Sisters. Then she proceeded to tell Merle she liked him and he was a nice guy, but he, referring to me, 'is an asshole.' Merle liked that kind of stuff, but we preferred to be instigators at our own discretion. There were also people that did come to the party houseboat to see us that was not of the party type. And believe it or not, Merle and I and others around the marina were pretty good about cleaning up our act when need be. But when it came to partying, writing songs, or just playing music we went after it all the way with everything we had in us.

Linda Mitchell, Silverthorne Manager: There were girls, but I was *Mom*, so if any of the guys came up and said "You need to get rid of this person," whoever it was, I said "okay," went down and said "Young lady, you're going for a ride," and I'd already called her a cab, and gave her a bus ticket, and said "Don't come back." That was my job, I was *mom* like I said, I was kind of the mean one of the group I guess, but there were even times when we had what Merle and Freddy called the Red Line Express, where these parents would drop their daughters off and I'd get a phone call from the houseboats, "This is jail bait, we need to get rid of them," and again, I'd either have a cab take them to the bus station or have the houseboat drop them off.

Freddy Powers: Early on in our life out on the lake, Merle got the idea to have a weekly wet T-shirt contest on our private dock, with the First Prize being $200; Second Prize was $50.00 and a free trip on Merle's private houseboat with Merle (you can guess what went on during those outings), and I mean, we had some BIG turnouts. We must have had 50 women enter each week, it was really something. Now, I'm not going to say the contest was fixed, but you could lay your $ down on this: the Second place winner would be a good-looking girl. One time we had a wet dress contest, but I can't tell about that one in the book.

Merle Haggard: The Wet T-Shirt Contests were a Thursday night thing. We were both single, going through divorces, so we had lots of time on our hands. We had a resort there, and 32 houseboats, several cabins, and we'd rent them out starting on a Wednesday night, then on Thursday, have that wet T-shirt contest to see if there were any new women. A guy named Lewis Tally was the hoser, we had to have a hoser and old Willie would hose 'em down (laughs). The second prize was fixed, so we would give that one the first prize whatever it was, $100 or something, and the second prize was a trip up the Pit River with us. We were going to build this flush unit, where if they said the wrong thing or acted the wrong way, we'd just drop the floor and flush 'em right out.

Anne Reynolds, Deanie-Bird's Widow: Freddy and Merle used to call Dean "*José*" whenever they had wet T-Shirt contests, because Dean hosed them down.

Marc Oswald: They would bring in CARLOADS of girls from the Bay Area, and all conceivable intoxicants, and everyone was just on fire the whole time! But when

Merle was awake in the day time, he and Freddy would leave in their boats a lot and go up and fish the Pitt River, and they'd go up there, drop their anchors and stay up there for two, three, four days.

Freddy Powers: I know it sounds like all we did was party, and we did a lot, but there was also a lot of business going on too. Lake Shasta, the houseboats, and having a club made it the perfect set-up for entertaining and having other entertainers come to play. We had a houseboat set up right next to mine for guests and other entertainers that would come in to play the club. We had many, many big stars up there and a gate to try and keep everybody out so we could try and get some rest. But that was hard because the women would just take off their clothes and swim around the gate and come on over to the houseboats. Sometimes I felt like we were the Beatles or Elvis, it was girls, girls, girls.

Linda Mitchell, Silverthorne Manager: Jack, the original owner of Silverthorne, was the pilot for President John F. Kennedy on Air Force One, and when he got sick with cancer, he sold the resort to Merle and Jim Jabalsie, and eventually, Merle bought out his partner and it became strictly the Merle Haggard Silverthorne Resort. Whenever Freddy and Merle and the original Strangers performed there at the resort, it was always old-time Country music. I was kind of in charge of the bar and the restaurant and booking the entertainment, and we had all sorts of Country & Western singers come up, and Freddy and Merle would jam with all of them, Little Jimmy Dickens even came up one time, and I'd grown up listening to him. You name them, we had them: Tammy Wynette, Dwight Yoakam, and Rick Nelson came up shortly before he died in that horrible plane crash.

Freddy Powers: I'd taken two members of my band with me of course- Deanie Bird, my bass player, and Gary Church, who played trumpet and trombone – when I'd moved out to Lake Shasta. Merle hired Gary into his band the Strangers and Deanie Bird and I with a great guitar player Clint Strong that my son had introduced me to. For the next two years, we toured with Merle as his opening act, and we'd also play shows at Merle's nightclub out there on the lake.

Biff Adams: In the evening, we'd all go to the upstairs bar at the Resort that Merle owned there on the lake, Silverthorne, and it was a pretty nice nightclub that held 200 people, and we'd play at night and would have a lot of guest stars come and sit in with us. I did a lot of that booking of guest stars, and we had a lot of the players who worked the Northern Coast between San Francisco and L.A. that would come through in between tour dates and Merle would give them a free houseboat to stay at if they played at the resort. It worked out to be a pretty good deal for everyone all-around.

Linda Mitchell, Silverthorne Manager: The second floor of Silverthorne is where they performed, and when Merle and Freddy would put on a performance, I would always have to come backstage and tell them, "I can't put any more people in here," because the place was absolutely packed. You had people come from all over, they were on vacation and would hear that there was gonna be a concert; I remember one time The Strangers were performing and I had five cash registers up top working when we had a performance. 150 to 200 people was the capacity for the club, and we were always overcrowded up there because up to 300 people sometimes would pack into both floors, and you'd start to fear the roof was going to fall in! On stage, Freddy never wanted to upstage Merle. He never wanted to upstage anybody, that was Freddy Powers. Freddy didn't care if he opened or played background or if he was in a sense ever acknowledged, he just wanted to play his music. He didn't have to be # 1 and that's what made him # 1.

Freddy Powers: When we played there it seemed like everyone we knew came out- especially the 'girls' – so we'd end up afterwards with a party that lasted generally all night long. Most of the time, we'd party all night and sleep all day. By then, Merle wouldn't ever go near the Ranch. He said it was as if someone had died there, and he couldn't stand seeing memories of something that could never be. I truly felt for him because I had just gotten a divorce from my wife, who I dearly loved. What a setting for a bunch of hurting songs....

Merle Haggard: We were living on the houseboats when a lot of those things got written, and it was healthier out there. When you ride across country, a lot of people don't understand what I go through. I live out there, and every time I'd go to work, I've got to drive 2400 miles, and it can take three days to get over a trip like that, but when we were living out there on the lake, it would only take 24 hours. I got over it in one day. It's so much healthier because the air and the oxygen is plentiful out there.

Manager Marc Oswald: I think it was a combination of things that made Merle and Freddy such a great songwriting team, I would say the primary elements were: Freddy is a great listener, he's just such a great listener, and he and Merle wrote a lot late at night, and they both lived next to each other on the houseboats. Freddy had the Aircraft Carrier, which is what we called his boat, and Merle had the Hotel Troubadour, and because they were next door to each other and Merle's kind of a night owl, they were right there in the same physical space, and Freddy was a night owl too. I would just venture to say that for Merle, the only time it was ever quiet was at two, three, four in the morning, when the spotlights had been turned off, and all the fans that used to come to Silverthorne just to try and watch them through the gate to the dock late at night when it used to be quiet.

Freddy Powers: For all the good times, many of the songs we wrote during that time were about lost loves or love experiences. Merle wrote a lot of songs about his love and feelings for Leona. When I'd first hooked up with Merle, he was married to Leona Williams. We all traveled on Merle's bus together. Their relationship seemed great at first. But before long, I began to see problems slowly starting to take place, and their marriage falling apart, eventually ending in divorce. I always thought Leona was a beautiful woman. She's also a very talented, singer and star in her own right. But she was always walking in Merle's shadow, and I believe that's what caused a lot of the unease between them. Merle was the successful star getting all the attention, and she may have felt unnoticed for her work as a singer and writer too.

I think given more time they could have been a great songwriting team. But as a couple they just had too many problems and their marriage just fell apart. He wrote a lot of sad songs during that time. At the same time, I was writing songs about my past life, which gave us both a lot to write about. We wrote a few number ones and some that should have been number ones that just got overlooked in albums. Songs we wrote during that time were like an *audio*biography of our lives. And of course, for me, writing songs with such a great writer was a terrific ego boost. With my confidence at this level, I was putting my heart into every song.

Merle was always looking for ideas for new songs. I remember I went up to the ranch one day to talk to him about a song I'd written for him, and he was walking all through this big house as naked as a Jaybird playing Bob Willis stuff on his fiddle (and Leona laughing like a hyena). I'll always love Merle's sense of humor…. After he put his clothes on, he and I and Leona were sitting around in the kitchen talking and he said, "Let me hear the song." I played him one I'd written recently called '*The Silver Eagle.*'

Silver Eagle

Well, he rides into town,
On the back of a big Silver Eagle.
Strapped to his shoulders are
The burden of stayin' on top.
And the lines in his face
Tell the story of an uphill flight.
You can tell how he feels day by day,
By the songs that he writes.
He's loved by millions,
Somehow, he's their prisoner, as well.

As he rides down the road,

In his 10-wheel aluminum cell.
Now he lives for the day
That the Eagle will carry him home
'Cause the glamour is over,
Nearly all of his seeds have been sewn
Let him go, Silver Eagle.
There must be a better way of life.

For this great, American poet,
Who's singing his songs about,
The every-day, working man's life
One night on the road,
Just south of the I-dee-ho line,
We were smokin' some contracts,
And attempting to alter our minds
And just before daylight,
Hag pushed back his hat and he said,
"Are we puttin' too much emphasis on bein' a star?
Can't we do a little bit of livin' instead?"

Let him go, Silver Eagle
There must be a better way of life
For this great, American poet,
Who's singing his songs about,
The every-day, working man's life
Let him go, Silver Eagle
There must be a better way of life
This great, American poet, Who's singing...

After the song was over, Merle walked over to the big day window and stared out the window for a few moments. From where he was standing, I could see he had tears in his eyes and that he was truly moved by the song (again, he had given me more and more confidence). I started trying to think like Merle and find out where his mind was, so as to write things that he would relate to. The more I would find out about him, the more I believed that we were very much alike, in both background and our likes and dislikes.

Merle Haggard: Me and Willie were both in a position to influence him and to guide him a little bit. He didn't need much, he just wanted somebody to assure him he was on the right track I think. Fred wrote his own songs, I didn't help him write '*Natural High*,' he wrote that one himself.

Freddy Powers: Merle first took notice of my songwriting when I played him the first song we ever wrote together, '*I Always Get Lucky with You*.' At first, it was real hard for me to just open up and let loose my words for fear he would have something much better. He is such a great and profound writer, and with that in your mind at all times, it was overpowering. And just think how I felt when Merle Haggard looked at me and said, "I like your writing." After that my confidence grew and I felt very comfortable telling him any song idea I had, and I'm proud to say we used a lot of them.

In spite of the good times, every now and then, Merle would drop into a deep depression for several days, and sometimes he was mad at me. I think it was a combination of loss of sleep and the drugs. Merle was never a heavy drinker. I've only seen him drink a couple of times. When Merle was in these moods, I tried to stay over on my own boat or go out for a cruise on the lake. I would always know when he was over it because all of a sudden you would hear him singing some really silly song at the top of his voice, as if to let everyone know he was over whatever had come over him.

Merle and I didn't always just sit down and write a song together. A lot of times I would have an idea and I'd tell Merle about it, or I would start it and then give it to him and he'd take and finish it, or expound upon it or vice versa. Sometimes we'd pass a song back and forth to each other and make changes until we had a finished song. Together, we collaborated on some 40 songs he had recorded on albums as well as some that I wrote by myself. We had five # 1 hits, 'Song of the Year' and received the 'Triple Play Award' for writing three number one songs in a twelve-month period, and have since become what is called 'Members of the Million Air Play Club' for over one million plays on the radio. One of my favorite songs from this spree of hits was one I actually wrote by myself,

"*Natural High*," that has remained one of the fan favorites throughout my career. It went to # 1 in 1985 and Merle included it on both his "Kern River" and "All in the Game" albums, cementing it as one of his biggest hits of the decade.

Natural High

You stayed with me thru thick and thin
You watched me lose, you watched me win
You picked me up off of the ground
You never one time let me down
And you put me on a natural high
And I can fly, I can fly

I was drowning in a sea of make-believe
As helpless as a falling leave
You gave your hand to me that day
And you did it, 'cause you're made that way
And you put me on a natural high
And I can fly, I can fly

You always seem to let your feelings show
You love me and you let me know
Darling just remember these three words
I love you, I love you, I love you
And you put me on a natural high
And I can fly, I can fly

And you put me on a natural high
And I can fly, I can fly

Freddy Powers: "Merle did a marvelous job of that. I'm so proud of that song because, to me, you know Merle Haggard is the ultimate singer, the ultimate country singer." 17

Janine Fricke: "Merle was at Shoney's Inn, on his bus, and he had just recorded these songs. He said, 'Come on up here, I want you to listen to some tapes.' We liked the songs, and he said 'Well, how about you coming in and doing some things on 'em?' So we went right on in and did it."

Freddy Powers: Against the backdrop of all this newfound success and Lake Shasta itself, I felt myself coming alive as a songwriter again. To begin with, Merle to me is one of the greatest songwriters in the world. So to be asked by someone like him to co-write a song is the biggest honor a songwriter could ever ask for, especially because it was an untapped well of talent I never really knew I had before I met Merle. My confidence came from him in a big way, just as it did from Willie when he trusted me to pick the song list for '*Over the Rainbow*'. That was the first time anyone of that stature as a songwriter had ever trusted me to make that major a decision for him, and with Merle, co-writing songs together only made my awareness of that part of myself grow.

Linda Mitchell, Silverthorne Manager: Freddy and Merle were almost like twins, they knew what each other were thinking, is about the only way I can describe it, like they were one person. They were just in synch, they'd sit down and start doing something and all of a sudden, one would look at the other, and they would have a song, and it was just remarkable to watch how they worked together. They wrote from their experiences, and many a song that Freddy and Merle wrote, the inspiration came from out on Lake Shasta. It was something they lived. Music was just in their blood.

Freddy Powers: Until Merle, I had never had anything to really go anywhere and I had had a couple of real disappointments with songwriting that soured my attitude towards writing. One was a song I'd written that was recorded by the Wilburn Brothers back in 1953 called '*Nothing at All*' on Decca Records. I never saw a dime from that song. Another song that really hurt me and turned me off to writing was a song I collaborated on called '*There She Goes*', recorded by Carl Smith. Eddie Miller – who wrote '*Release Me*' – came to Dallas and I met him at Jim Beck's studio on Forrest Lane, and Eddie and I became good friends (at least I thought). He stayed with my wife and I in our apartment for a while. He had an idea for a song and had it partly written. I helped him finish the song.

Eddie didn't have any money and neither did I to go in and cut a demo, so I borrowed the money from my dad to go into the studio and cut it. I sang it and we thought we had a hit. Thinking this was my chance to become a recording artist, I borrowed more money to send Eddie to Nashville to see if he couldn't get me a record deal. That turned out to be the last I ever saw of Eddie. The next thing I knew Carl Smith was in the same studio I first recorded the song in, and when I walked in and heard the song being recorded by someone else and while I was disappointed, I thought at least I would get credit for my part in writing it. But I was once again wrong, didn't see a dime from that song, much less did I even get credit as a writer on it. So with those kinds of disappointments and betrayals I didn't focus on writing anymore as much as I did playing and singing.

I believe Merle has written more songs with Tommy Collins and me than any other songwriters he's ever written with. We had several other songs that I think should have been number one hits but they just got lost in albums. One Merle and I both agree on is a song off the 501 Blues album, *'Somewhere Down the Line'*. We had a couple that became famous and used in big albums or movies but we were never awarded. 'Texas' was used in the James A. Michener movie 'Texas,' and it's also on the film's soundtrack for the album 'Texas'. '*Friend in California*' was used as part of the 'Marlboro' Album.

A Friend in California

L.A. traffic is bad this time of year
But there's a friend of yours in California
Sure wishes you were here
And as you lay your head on your pillow tonight just remember
There's a friend of yours in California sure misses you

You've got a friend in California that misses you
You've got a friend in California that sure misses you

Fort Worth can get cold this time of year
But this southern California sun is warm
You should be here
And as you lay your head on your pillow tonight just remember
There's a friend of yours in California sure misses you

You've got a friend in California that misses you
You've got a friend in California that sure misses you

You've got a friend in California that misses you
You've got a friend in California that sure misses you

(Written by: Freddy Powers, 1986, Copyright Sony/ATV Music Publishing Ltd)

Merle Haggard: I like to write in the morning, my head is usually clear and so did Fred, so we wrote songs all the time. We didn't always have no reason beforehand, we just wrote songs and a lot of the sons of bitches we never heard again. Everything we wrote didn't go to # 1, a lot of them we threw in the God damn lake, because all of it was not good. We were always trying to write. We kind of helped each other sometimes when we'd have songs pretty well finished, then we'd give them to each other, and use each other's experience to see if we were on the right track; we did that a lot.

Biff Adams: Usually, the daily routine during those years when Freddy and Merle were writing neighbors was that one of them would get up in the morning, and Freddy and I were usually up a little bit earlier than Merle, and if it was Fred, he'd usually say something to me like 'Boy, I had an idea for a song last night,' and he'd go over to Merle's boat and tell him about it, and Merle would then typically tell me 'Hey, keep everybody away from the boat today, we're writing a song and don't want to be bothered.' So I'd say 'Okay,' and keep everybody off the dock while they went in Merle's boat and isolated themselves and sometimes they'd come out of there an hour and a half later with a hit song, and sometimes it wouldn't happen till maybe the next day or so and they'd keep working on it. I don't know numbers-wise how many songs they wrote over the years they lived together out there, but they wrote a lot of them.

Merle Haggard: My child Janessa was born while we still lived out on that boat, I think that was the year I wrote '*Twinkle, Twinkle Lucky Star*'. Freddy had no idea that I was going to write a good song that day. One morning I ran over and beat on his door and said 'I've got the complete construction for a # 1 song,' and he said, 'I don't feel good,' and gave that little look that he gets (laughs). I said 'Sick?' surprised, and he had the curtain pulled back, and said he'd been drinking the night before and he was serious because he didn't feel good that morning. I tried to get him out of bed, I said, 'I'm serious Fred, I got a really good format for the song.' See, there'd been a lot of songs written about fiddle tunes, but '*Twinkle Twinkle Little Star*,' there hasn't been a song written about that, it's just a fiddle tune. I said 'I'm telling you man, it's a hit song, the idea, I got the whole premise for it.' Well, he said 'Go ahead and write a little bit of it and I'll write some on it later around 12:30,' but never did get over there. So I went back over to my boat and wrote '*Twinkle Twinkle Lucky Star*,' then went back over and sang it for him, and I thought I'd tell that story on him (laughs). It became a # 1 song. So he missed that one.

Freddy Powers: I'd come down with a sciatic nerve condition. That had me in a lot of pain. All I wanted to do was stay in bed. Merle came over and said he had the title for a song, *'Twinkle Twinkle Lucky Star.'* The title didn't grab me as I said I was in pain, so I told Merle to come back later and maybe I would feel better. Needless to say, he wound up writing it without me and it became a big hit and won all kinds of awards and became a number one song.

Alongside all the partying, Merle and I also had some quiet nights fishing off the back of the Troubadour, telling stories about our past and making plans for the future. I can't remember a single day on the lake with the Hotel Troubadour and the USSF Boat that was not a magnificent one. And if there were any bad days, they have somehow been erased for my memory. Or maybe it's like a line in one of Merle's hit songs, 'These were the memories I choose to recall.'

"In Freddy's shows, he did a little bit of everything, all kinds of shows." – Merle Haggard

Chapter 5: The Bread & Butter Band
& Life on the Road with The Strangers

Freddy Powers: Merle came to me one day on a whim and said, "Let's start another band. We'll call it 'Bread and Butter Band.'" He suggested we get together the jammers from our bands and tour playing more of my and Deanie's swing-style of music.

Merle Haggard: Fred was doing the singing and playing rhythm guitar, and had a guy named Gary Church who was playing the clarinet and trombone, and a good friend named Dean Reynolds that we called Deaniebird. So that became a little four-piece band that we called the Bread and Butter Band.

Freddy Powers: Merle felt this would free him up to play more of what he wanted to and not pinning him down to just playing his hits. It wasn't the Merle Haggard and the Strangers show, and the public knew it when they came to see us. We had Deaniebird on bass, Gary Church on trumpet, Jimmy Belkins on Fiddle, Tiny Moore on mandolin, Norm Hamlet on Steel, Biff Adams on drums, Merle on lead and rhythm guitar, and me as well on rhythm guitar. Merle said we would tour California and split it

50/50. I felt that was unfair and insisted that Merle take a bigger cut- after all, he was the star. It ended up 70/30, and even that was a good deal for me.

The Oswald brothers, Marc and Greg had a booking agency called Luckenbach Productions and they had been booking Merle's shows. So we had them set us up a tour, as the 'Bread and Brother Band'. We toured mostly Southern California as far as I can remember because we were doing so much drugs and drinking during that time that it's all a haze to me. I could kick myself because this great experience even today is only a cloudy memory. I remember one time we were in Fresno and we went out and only did a 20-minute show. That happened a lot back then, whether it was drugs or something pissing Merle off, or he was just tired and wanted off that stage. And when Merle wanted to close a show he did.

Manager Marc Oswald: In 83, we did a tour called 'The Bread and Butter Tour', which began as seven shows across California, starting in San Diego, then Bakersfield, Fresno, Visalia, Santa Barbara, and a couple more. It was supposed to be Freddy's band – this is right after the *Country Jazz Singer* LP came out – and Merle was going to be a band member in it, so we weren't going to use his name in the promotion of the tour. It was going to be called 'The Bread and Butter Band', that's what they liked to call themselves as pickers, well originally it was just supposed to be Freddy, Merle, Deanie Bird Reynolds, and Clint

Strong, the four of them, doing an acoustic show where they'd all be equal on stage. Because it seemed like Merle liked being in the band, more than he liked being the star, it seemed like, he liked being in the band because he was such a musician. So, of course by the time everybody in the organization got wind of it, it went from being the Bread and Butter Tour with the four of those guys playing small Theaters to Merle Haggard and The Strangers & The Bread & Butter Band, so suddenly we were playing large venues and running three or four Semis and God knows how many buses.

In the Bread and Butter Band, Freddy was the lead guy, and it was really cool because as a live performer, when he was on stage, it was hard to not watch him. You know how certain people just kind of draw your attention? He was one of those players, because whatever he was doing, it was always interesting on stage. He was always understated, but always really confident too, he really had a sense of confidence on stage. Even when he was onstage with Merle – and Merle was such a presence on stage – Freddy was just fun to watch. It was like a ragtag band going down the road, and Freddy and Merle were like Butch Cassidy and the Sundance Kid, and whether we were on the Lake or the road, Freddy was always the funniest guy on the planet. He surrounded himself with funny people like Deaniebird Reynolds, and Merle, who's so funny and one of the best joke tellers I've ever heard. So Freddy and Merle were always up for a Shenanigan!

Freddy Powers: "My favorite food on the road. Well, I'll tell you, I don't eat beef, I only eat bacon, like in the morning, I'll eat some crisp bacon sometimes. Otherwise, I eat chicken and fish. So on the road, yes, I have chicken sandwiches. It's usually what I wind up ordering in a restaurant. When I'm on the road, I'm always lookin' for a seafood restaurant too." 18

Biff Adams: Whenever those of us who were also members of The Strangers would go out and play with Freddy during one of his solo shows, it was a change for us, and that was welcome, because being in Merle's band for quite a while by that point, you can get burned out a little playing that catalog of hits exactly the way it sounded on record. With Freddy, we had the freedom to play different styles of music and it was a different show so we dressed different.

Anne Reynolds, Deanie-Bird's Widow: Deanie and Freddy's relationship was awesome, and whenever they were together, the first thing they would do was to play. They would come out to the farm sometimes when it was just Dean and Freddy, and with Freddy singing and his rhythm and guitar and Dean picking bass, it was great, and all my friends would gather around on the patio, and we'd have jam sessions on our farm. Dean and I would have barbecues with 50 people and live music with Freddy and Dean jamming, and everybody could bring their guitar because of course, in Texas, everybody picks. Or they'd sit around and just watch Dean and Freddy, because even just the two of them was like a full-on concert all by itself, in fact, Dean was voted Best Bluegrass Bass Player for seven years in a row.

When they played together, it was just right, it was a love between those two. Dean would say, "Its just right Mama when I play with Freddy, its just right." And Freddy always looked back over his left shoulder at Dean when they were playing, Dean was always off behind him a little bit on the left, and he'd always be looking over at Dean. It was magic between them when they played. Freddy and Deanie Bird opened for Merle for one whole season, and were very well-received: they were the best damn trio you ever heard. They were really tight.

Freddy's a great entertainer, he's just so in command of the show, he's just so sharp, his music is so good and his fans just love it, they'd always yell and scream and carry on and he's a great emcee. Dean didn't talk during the show, except for "*Sweet Georgia Brown*," which was his show-off number, and he would do it in single time, double time and triple time and keep the flat bass going as well, so people would go crazy over that. And of course Clint Strong was just so awesome on the guitar, I don't know any guitar picker better than Clint, he's just an Ace and drove the audiences wild. So there was a lot of entertainment from three people, it was a great trio.

Freddy Powers: When we were on tour with The Strangers - Merle's band when he was headlining – we traveled in three buses and a big truck that carried the equipment. Merle's bus had two drivers, Dean Holloway and Biff Adams, the drummer for his band. The band had their own bus with several of the members who could also drive. Deanie Bird and I rode in the third bus with Lewis Talley and a guy who we called Steve Stone. His real name was Steve Van Stralen; he was the video man on the tours taping all our shows and whatever else we wanted videoed.

Merle Haggard: When Freddy joined The Strangers, he fit in perfectly because - as a rhythm guitar player - he played what the band was playing, so he was able to play whatever he needed to. He played rhythm guitar real well, he had the ability to play a banjo lick with his right hand from his years playing banjo, and it worked real good. He kind of needed a banjo-type rhythm because it was a swing band, and banjo was always kind of like the drums because it played to the snare drum. Freddy didn't play banjo anymore when he joined my band, but he played with a banjo rhythm on the guitar. I've worked for Freddy as a guitar player in his band and he's worked for me as a guitar player in my band, and I agree with the things that have been said about his guitar playing, I think he's one of the greatest.

Biff Adams: I think Freddy's style of guitar playing made The Strangers a better band. One thing I noted about Freddy as a guitarist right off was he was a damn good, solid rhythm player, he played real good stock rhythm. As a drummer, I always appreciated that, because the drums bass and a good stock rhythm guitar player makes a great rhythm section. At that time, though Merle was a good rhythm player, he was starting to play a lot more lead and getting off of the rhythm, so Freddy just fit right in there and I think it took a load off of Merle and in turn, he became a pretty good lead player.

Manager Marc Oswald: When Merle was on stage, you never knew who was going to play a lead. One of the things Merle liked to do during concerts, and I've seen it a zillion times, and he would either do what he would or point at somebody with the neck of his guitar, or with a fiddle bow. But he liked to do these songs onstage with the whole band where he would improvise all the time, whether he was saying 'I want to have a guitar lead or piano lead or horn or fiddle', whatever it was, and would just toss the leads off to people when they didn't expect it. He liked to do that, and so the show was never the same twice, which is really unusual. So Merle would be playing a fiddle and all of sudden, would take his fiddle bow and just almost pop it over his head behind him, and if he pointed at the piano, that piano player better be paying attention, because he was just throwing it all over the stage all the time. And Freddy of course could keep up with all that too, so they had fun doing that.

Willie Nelson: Freddy's strongest suit, I always thought, was his rhythm guitar playing. He was a great rhythm guitar player. I liked Django Reinhardt, and Django's brother was a great rhythm guitar player, and Freddy and Paul Buskirk both were the two best rhythm guitar players – other than Django's brother – that I've ever known. Freddy's one of the best guitar players, whether he's playing jazz or blues or country, all of it.

Freddy Powers: The road can be a tough place to be, but it can be a great place too. It all depends on what's happening while you're out there. Most of the time, we enjoyed ourselves and had lots of fun. Just think here you are traveling all over the country in high style with a bunch of people – about 20 or so - that you enjoy being with. Playing music that you love, to large crowds of people, who are yelling and screaming all through the show because they like you, and love the music. They came out of the woodwork to see Merle. The audience was good to me and they liked me okay, but make no mistake, they were there to see Merle Haggard.

Merle has had some big hits in his catalog by then, like '*Mama Tried*', '*Okie From Muskogee*', '*Fighting Side of Me*', and many more. But some nights, he would go out on stage and do Bob Wills' songs instead, or some new song that the public hadn't heard and his fans weren't familiar with and the audience would sometimes leave disappointed. They wanted to hear his hits and that's what they came for. Sometimes that would upset Merle, and he would then make the tour more work than it was supposed to be. Promoters back then I guess they half-expected it. Not just Merle but a lot of entertainers got by with more than they do today. Life seemed to be more of a party for everybody then. Now it's more business than party and promoters and venues are more likely to sue. One of my favorites on Merle: He had got into an argument with a promoter. He let him say what they had to, and then Merle said what he wanted to, and proceeded to walk out the door. The only problem is it wasn't the door to leave. Merle had accidentally walked into the broom closet. He walked back out like he meant to do that and waved his finger in the air, and said, "That's all I have to say," and walked out the door. The right door this time.

Manager Marc Oswald: One of the funniest road stories I remember from my years touring with Merle and Freddy was the time we pulled in for a date in Worcester, MA about 2 hours outside of Boston, and this was being billed as 'Merle Haggard & The Strangers w/Special Guest Freddy Powers', and we were playing the Theater in Worcester. Not surprisingly, because Merle was a huge superstar at the time, the show was sold out, and we were actually playing it as a make-up date because it had been cancelled the year prior. Well, what was cool is not one of Merle's fans had asked for a refund in that year, so we stopped in Boston, MA with the procession of buses – and there two Semis and four buses - and the reason we'd stopped was during that year in between the concert being cancelled and our make-up date, the theater had gone bankrupt because apparently the theater manager had run off with all the money.

So this really nice elderly lady that owned the Theater lived in Boston, and had arranged for me to meet her at the bank so she could pay us for the show, which was like $40,000 or something large, so Merle wanted it done in person. Well, when we stopped in Boston, we parked all the buses and trucks around The Common, which is the central city park where they have the big fountains and all the street performers playing music and doing mime acts, organ grinders with the monkeys; all those little sideshows. So we stopped there right in the middle of a Saturday or something with a bunch of people hanging out in the park and all this activity going on, and I jog on over the two or three blocks to the bank to meet the Theater owner, and I was going as fast as I did because we were running late for the show.

Well, by the time I got back, maybe an hour later and hopped on our bus to go, it was like a ghost town, I mean there was *NOBODY* on the buses, they were all gone, every last soul from the road crew, Merle's band, everyone. I couldn't find them, and it was really busy at that time of day, so I start looking around this park, and before too long, sure enough I come across this HUGE crowd assembled around the fountain, and I'm talking 300 people. I couldn't quite tell what was going on yet, but I knew I was onto something, and by the time I got over there and inched my way through all these people, there sat Freddy, Merle, Clint Strong, Deanie Bird Reynolds, and Tom Collins, all sitting there in their bus clothes – old t-shirts and sweats- picking. And the funny thing about this was, for as large a crowd as they'd attracted, because they all looked pretty beat up in their bus clothes, nobody knew who they were! Our buses didn't have the artist's name on them, so nobody had put two and two together, and again they looked damn near homeless the way they were dressed, but they had gotten out, set up shop and just started playing while I was gone. Well, they sounded so good that I threw my cowboy hat down right in front of Freddy just to see what would happen and threw a couple dollars in it, and before you knew it, the whole crowd started throwing money in the cowboy hat!

So as these guys played about three or four more songs – and they weren't playing hits, just jazz songs - another funny thing happened when I turned around to see the guy who was the Mime, along with all his fellow street performers who worked that park every day, ALL watching these guys playing. And you could almost feel they were pissed off because here's this new act stealing away all the attention – and TIPS – that would have been going to them otherwise, (laughs). So as all this money was piling up in the cowboy hat, I snuck in and whispered to Freddy, 'Dude, we have GOT to leave', because by that point, we were running REALLY late for the show we were supposed to be playing…. So we get everyone back on the buses without too much hustle and bustle because no one had put together that Merle Haggard was sitting there, and as we get on the bus, the final act of the comedy came when we're all finally sitting on the bus on our way up to Worcester, and it was Freddy, Deanie Bird, Clint, Merle and Me. Well, I had that Cowboy Hat full of tip money, and I set it on the kitchen table, and it makes me bust out laughing when I think back about it, because the next thing I know, I'm watching five grown men straightening out these $1 bills- I don't think we got a single $5 – digging into this hat, counting up all the tips. We wound up with $143 dollars between singles and all the change. So I remember I took my booking commission, which was 10%, for laying the hat down, and then the band took the other 90% and sat there and divvied it up between them for this 'Gig' they had just played, and everybody made their $25 bucks, and everybody was proud of that $25!

Merle got his cut too, because he was right in the middle of it, and what was funny to me was for all the fussing over this tip money they split up, the original reason we were in town was to pick up the fee for Merle's theater show, which was A LOT of money by comparison, and Merle NEVER asked me about it! So from the time we took off from the park to head to the show, it seemed to me that all he and the other guys in the band cared about was how they were going to cut up that $143 dollars. So when I turned that $40,000 over to Fuzzy, Merle's manager, he found the whole thing pretty amusing too, because there was just something funny about that cowboy hat full of tips that everybody wanted to get a piece of, and it served for me as kind of a metaphor for the whole operation out there. Because leaving the bus and going and playing that park and then worrying about how to split up $140 was a bigger deal than going to play a sold-out show for thousands of screaming fans, they'd rather be in the park in their sweats and wife-beaters playing Jazz.

To top the whole day off, after all that - and being late and barely making the show - when we finally got up there, they got everybody loaded into the theater, and we're getting ready to start the show, and security comes over and says 'There's been a bomb scare'! So they cleared everybody out of the theater – band and audience – and didn't find anything, then loaded everybody back in, and we finally did that show that everybody had first wanted to hear a year before. It was quite a day…

Freddy Powers: We both had - and probably still do have- a love/hate relationship with the road. Not the performing as much because when we're not on the stage, we're still playing. With Merle, I think it bothered him more. We'd be gone for four or five days and he'd be ready to go home. He really longed for the houseboat, not to say I didn't too. But we'd get home and after a few days he'd be on the phone with the agents to book us a short tour, which generally ended up being lesser paying jobs because of such short notice and what venues were available. But Merle has also turned higher paying jobs down to come and be my guitar player on a gig that I had booked somewhere. Naturally I seemed to draw bigger crowds (laughs).

Biff Adams: A lot of times, Freddy would be the one to take Merle off stage at the end of shows, so he'd take the mic and thank everyone for coming, and Merle and I would make a beeline for the backstage exit door to get out of there before it got too crazy with fan frenzy. Freddy would tell a lot of jokes and stuff. Freddy's timing was great for jokes, he always had a joke for everything. I watched a couple of his live shows from the audience and a lot of times, he'd tell jokes I'd already heard a couple years earlier, but the way he delivered it on stage just like I was hearing it for the first time. I'd laugh my ass off, so he was a natural born joke teller on top of being a gifted songwriter and guitar player.

That was versus Merle, who hardly ever talked on stage during shows. He used to say 'They're not here to hear me talk, they're here to hear me sing', and I'd say 'That's exactly right', so a lot of times, Freddy would do cover routine things during Merle's shows like introducing the band sometimes, that's one example how much Merle

trusted Freddy. He would always throw some humor in
there too, for instance, I'm a pretty big guy, I weigh around
290, so when it came time to introduce me to the crowd,
Freddy would joke and say 'And we've got little, bitty Biff
Adams back there on drums…', and the crowd of course
laughed because they could see me sitting back there.

Manager Marc Oswald: Sometimes Freddy was just
a musician up there, and other times, it almost seemed like
he was a bandleader to a degree, especially on the songs he
wrote with Merle. And sometimes he was a buddy up there,
so it was like he played a lot of different roles up there on
stage with Merle. He didn't just have one role, and it
depended on what song was being played, but I think as a
player, he gave sort of that Jazz 'Cred' and elevated the
game on the stage. But of course, Merle's band was so
freakin' good, that they were all Jazz players really.

Freddy Powers: Being a star can work for you as well
as work against you. We were at a concert setting on the
bus looking out and watching the crowd once when
someone called it a circus. I told Merle when I was a young
boy back in Seminole, Texas I had visions of running away
with a circus. I said if the circus had come to town on a
train, I would have hopped in a boxcar and went with them.
Merle asked me, "Have you ever heard of anyone running
away from a circus?" Of course, I had to reply no. Merle
said, "That's what I feel like doing, running away from this

circus right now." It was me, Dean Holloway and Deanie Bird. We all started agreeing, actually kidding saying, "Yeah, let's get the hell out of here and go fishing." The next thing I knew, Merle had convinced us to sneak off and get out of there. We were sneaking out the back and going up the ramp when I said, "Wait a minute, what are we doing, what are we running away from- our friends and our fans that love us and can't wait for you to perform your music for them?" Merle agreed and we all turned around and went on stage instead and probably played one of our best shows.

Biff Adams: On the road, Merle had his own bus, and Freddy would spend a lot of time over on Merle's bus and they'd sit over there and play a lot. I drove that bus a lot of times so I saw a lot of that, and it always kept them busy picking and writing songs. Freddy was a fun guy to be around, he always kept everybody in a good mood, and a lot of times Merle would come back after a show and might be complaining because something technical hadn't gone off quite right, and Freddy used to always be the one to cheer him up. He fit that part real good, and he did that both for Merle and for us in the band. If we were down or something, you could always count on Freddy coming by and saying 'Hey, what's the matter today Biff?', and he was a good guy to cheer you up or get your mind off something. He had a way with being able to get you off of thinking about it, and was always a good guy to be around, he really was. He always had a joke and a smile, or a good story to tell you because he'd had such a long, interesting life.

Catherine Powers: Freddy was always Merle's motivator, for instance, on tour, Freddy was generally the only one who could go on Merle's bus and wake him up to go out and play when Merle would be tired, and would say "Oh, I don't want to go do the show tonight." It was funny because Freddy would put his humor into it, and use Merle's old Prisoner number from when he was an inmate at San Quentin, and say, "Up and at 'em, on your feet!", acting like a prison guard, and Merle would do it! Merle used to laugh and joke with Freddy all the time about his time in prison, especially since all of Merle's crimes that sent him there were petty crimes. I think he broke into a restaurant that was open, so Merle would make jokes about it, and talk about how Johnny Cash had told him once, "Hey, you've been there, you've lived it, you let the world know it." There wasn't much Merle didn't talk about to Freddy, especially out there on that bus on the road. They spent a lot of hours just talking, and had a lot of really close, emotional, private moments together.

Linda Mitchell, Silverthorne Manager: Freddy would shake anybody's hand. Merle had an aversion to shaking hands because that was his livelihood, his fingers, and so Freddy was his surrogate out on the lake and road a lot of times.

Anne Reynolds, Deanie-Bird's Widow: You have no idea how bad that was for Merle. People were so… women tried to force their way onto the bus, they rocked the bus trying to turn it over, and were so rude and loud and demanding. I've seen lots of this, and once Merle finally came out and said "Folks, this is my home, would you please leave my home alone?", because they just went wild.

Freddy Powers: One time on the road, I remember Dean Roe, Deanie Bird and I were standing outside the bus talking when I turned around and saw Merle watching us through the port hole of his bus. Merle just couldn't get off his bus and roam around the venues or in public like we could. He generally can't walk five feet before someone has stopped him for an autograph, and if he stops for one, it draws a crowd. The burdens of staying on top made him a prisoner in that bus, and that's how the '*Silver Eagle*' came about.

Merle Haggard: We used to talk about things like that, we used to talk about 'Let's just set up and play here at 7:30 rather than going to the gig.'

Freddy Powers: For whatever the headaches of the road, Merle's name was always magic on tour. If you wanted a hotel room when the hotel was full, all you had to do was mention Merle and they would move someone if they had to. If a restaurant was closed, they would sometimes open up for him. One of Merle's pet peeves was when a restaurant would stop serving Breakfast at 11 AM. Hell, the only time Merle got up at 11 was when he never went to bed. Whatever time he got up, he wanted breakfast (and nothing else would do), and I have been with him when he would really raise hell, but it always seemed to get him breakfast.

Traveling around the world as stars – especially Merle – gave us the opportunity to meet and keep girls around all the time and boy did we like that! Being able to pick and choose all the girls we wanted- and we did. We spent a fortune on girls just flying them in for an evening of partying. During the cocaine days it was always a party, even on tour. We'd party all night and sleep all day. When it would come time to do the show, sometimes Merle wouldn't want to go on. Everybody in the crew: Biff, Lewis, Deanie Bird and I – would talk with Merle till he would finally go on. But then sometimes he would only do about 45 minutes, then close the show. That would leave the audience pissed off and the promoters raising hell. Merle would then get mad himself and threaten to fire everybody in the band and go home. After Merle and I had been doing cocaine for a couple of years, one day, Merle just came out of nowhere and said, "Freddy, you're the biggest asshole I know when you're doing cocaine." I turned to him and told him, "You are too," and that was the end of cocaine for me, and as far as I know, Merle hasn't touched it since then either.

Pot's about the only "drug" I put in my body after that. The government has always tried put marijuana in the same category as cocaine, heroin, and speed. They lied so much about marijuana. I thought they were probably lying about cocaine. I did find cocaine to be much more harmful and definitely habit-forming. I have smoked marijuana since I was 21 years old and I have had no problems when I have to do without it or there's times when I just don't feel like getting high. But cocaine is not as easy to just walk away from. Some people can't walk away without help, but I have never known anyone that had to get professional help to stop smoking marijuana. I've known lots of people who have smoked for years and just quit without any withdrawals, not like the government would have you believe.

Even when I turned 75 years old and was still smoking, I felt like I was 40 or younger and I passed for mid-to-late 50s all the time. I know men half my age that are not in as good a shape as I am or as healthy as I am. My doctors tell me all the time they have 50 or 60 year olds that would make me look like a kid. All my friends – men and women- who are my age or close are also marijuana smokers and have been since their young 20s and younger feel young and act young and most of them look as good as I do. And I'm not bragging, its just the plain truth. I see other men my age using canes or worse in wheel chairs, have false teeth and have had several bypasses or hip replacements, or some other health problems. And they damn sure aren't having sex, most of them have been only dreaming about it and living with the memories of sex since they were 55 or 60 years old.

So don't tell me marijuana is bad for you or addictive, and it DOES NOT get in the way of a professional career unless YOU let it. I can't and wouldn't mention any names but I have a lot of friends and acquaintances that are in high profile positions who show up for work every day and lead a normal life and are very successful in their professions. And if anyone uses marijuana as an excuse for committing murder, rape, or any other crime should be convicted because they are the biggest liars in the world. I guarantee you alcohol or speed was probably in every case. Marijuana might make you hungry and kill you from the weight you gain, but 'Murder,' I can tell you no way. I'm not proud of my cocaine days and I'm glad I saw the light before it destroyed me and I ended that part of my life, but marijuana is something both Merle and I kept smoking regularly even after we quit doing cocaine in the mid-80s. Hell, I'll arrive at the Pearly Gates with a joint hanging between my teeth when I finally get to Heaven, a big smile on my face as marijuana has helped me live well past when anyone ever predicted I would.

Chapter 6: "Natural High"

Freddy Powers: Heading into the mid-1980s, we were working pretty hard on tour. We were playing about 15-20 dates in a run, and I was really riding high. Merle got another # 1 on one of my songs, '*Natural High,*' which made two # 1's for me in a row. I got that idea from a great singer named Debbie DeFazio who was always the life of the party even though she NEVER took drugs or drank. '*Natural High*' was not only the name of a # 1 hit I wrote for Merle, but also of the airplane that I built myself out on the Lake.

I found in flying a great form of relaxation, there was something very peaceful about taking off of the water and getting some distance from whatever was going on down below back on planet earth. I had studied flying years back and it was in my blood. I wanted to fly and own airplanes. Deaniebird and I bought a little Gyro but we only went up in it a few times. I had heard about these ultra-light kits that you put together yourself, so I called the company and ordered one. With our celebrity status, they didn't want any bad publicity if something went wrong and I crashed, so they sent one of their mechanics out with the plane to oversee me and make sure I was putting it together right.

Merle Haggard: I watched this man single-handedly build his own airplane on the dock out in front of my houseboat, I watched in amazement. After I watched him assemble this homemade aircraft, I had enough confidence in him to believe he could actually fly that thing and not kill himself because I watched him do it.

Biff Adams: I was with Merle actually watching Freddy build that plane by himself. Freddy was a good troubleshooter whenever we had problems out there at the lake with the boats or whatever; you could bring it to Fred, and he'd usually come up with some kind of useful solution or suggestion, 'Well, why don't you do this...', and I'd normally find myself saying 'Hey, I never thought of that, I think I'll try that'. Sometimes it worked and sometimes it didn't, and with that plane of his, it did. I never trusted the engine on Freddy's plane, it sounded like a lawnmower to me!

Linda Mitchell, Silverthorne Manager: Freddy flew his Ultralight airplane all over the lake! You couldn't hide from Freddy, he'd find you if you were out some place.

Anne Reynolds, Deanie-Bird's Widow: Freddy and Merle had a helicopter they would fly around in that Dean would pilot, because Dean started flying helicopters at 16, and for years, he flew helicopters from Grand Aisle out to the oil rigs during the week. So he was an accomplished helicopter pilot and would fly them around the lake while Merle and Freddy looked down on girls sunbathing on the porches of the houseboats. They were like little school kids, naughty boys, and were always goofing off doing stuff.

Freddy Powers: I originally built the way it came out on wheels. I remember I got out on the runway, and kept taxiing up and down it, just getting faster and faster until one day I just took off and flew. It was a great sensation: here I was flying, flying in a plane I built with my own two hands! Merle probably had more belief in my flying abilities than anybody else. He knew how much I wanted to fly and he believed I could. He said if he didn't believe I could fly and not kill myself, he would have been trying like hell to talk me out of it. So instead he became my air traffic controller. He would be on the dock with a two-way radio telling me what he knew of flying as Merle is a pilot himself and used to fly before I got interested in it. Everything went okay when I flew from the airport, but then one day I was going to land up at Merle's ranch and I lost air speed and crashed it.

Merle Haggard: Freddy wanted to fly that plane and I knew he was serious about it. I have my own pilot's license, I'm a pilot, and understand what it takes to fly, and I told him everything I could tell him about flying and I loved him enough that I would have tried to talk him out of it if I hadn't had confidence in his will to fly it. We talked a lot about it as he built this thing, and before he got his license to fly, I watched him learn how to fly on the lake, and his theory was: 'Well, if I fall, I'll only fall 40 feet, and that water'll be soft!', and that wasn't true, anytime he'd have fallen, he'd have been dead.

We had this two-way radio from the boat to the airplane and I was the control tower with most of the flying experience, so most of the knowledge was on the ground. He did almost kill himself a couple times, and one of those times I remember clear to this day was when he took off in his airplane, got it up in the air, and tried to go out over Box Canyon and the trees were high on both sides, and he got back in there and could only turn that plane so much. Because the pine trees were about 100 feet tall and this was a little peninsula and he got in there and couldn't get out, I think he got the plane high enough to touch the top of the trees, but because it was an under-powered airplane, he had some of the trees hitting the bottom of his plane.

I thought he'd killed himself, and thought I was going to have to go tell people 'Freddy Powers has killed himself in an ultralight aircraft that he built himself and I watched him do it'. But he made it back in, and by some miracle, he finally got the plane up over that son of a bitch, came back around and landed and banged the shit out of the airplane – but he almost bought it that day.

Freddy Powers: I had the ranch hands load it up on a truck and as soon as I got back, I called and ordered pontoons. I decided right then I wanted something softer to fall on if I ever crashed again. I would rather be landing on water than the hard pavement any day. I took the airplane back to the hanger and redesigned the landing facilities, took off the wheels, and put the plane on pontoons.

Damon Garner, Freddy's Flight Instructor/Friend:
I had sold Freddy the plane we did the "Natural High" video with, put it together and had it lettered, and Merle would put him on a private jet and fly him to Carson City and he'd stay with me while he was learning to fly this new little airplane that we built. So it came time, he wanted to get it up to Redding to Merle's ranch, and he wanted to put it on floats eventually, because I was flying on floats out on Lake Taho and he thought that was really cool. So I drove up to the ranch and Merle was there with his drummer Biff Adams, and Freddy and I had talked about where he wanted to land, down by one of Merle's barns, and so we went down and I told Merle and Biff after a quick look around, "Man, this is too rocky for him to land on, he'll blow a tire or something," and Merle said "Well, we'll just clean it off."

So we started moving rocks off this dirt path that was going to be the landing strip, and most of them we moved to the left, and we worked quite a while, a good half hour, cleaning off this dirt road. I mean, it was a job, so Freddy finally shows up and we're kind of waving at him to land on this little dirt road by the barn. Well, from the air, he must of thought for some reason that we were waving him off, but it was plain to see he needed to land on the road.

Anyway, when he came down, he landed right in the rocks!
When he did, he broke off the landing gear, and the
expression on Merle's face was priceless, he turned to me
and said, "We did all this for *that?!!*"

When Freddy was first learning to fly, he just couldn't
get enough, so one morning, he came down and said "I
want to fly out to the dry lake bed,' and I said "Okay, but I
think the winds are gonna be coming up this afternoon,"
because the wind really blows around Reno." So he said,
"I'm just going to fly out by Fallon, do some touch and
goes and then come back," and I cautioned him, "Okay, but
if you feel the wind picking up, get out of there." So off he
went, and I watched him fly off, had a couple students of
my own and so an hour goes by and Fred isn't back yet,
and then two hours pass and he wasn't back. Then three
hours go by and he still wasn't back, and by that point,
everybody at the airport was starting to worry, so we
jumped in our trucks, drove the 20 miles over to where this
dry lake bed was, hoping he was okay.

To my relief, as we're driving, I saw him up in the air,
heading back to the air strip at Carson City, so we turned
around, and when we got back, he'd already landed. When
we pulled up to him, he was just shaking and I jump out
and say, 'Freddy, what's going on??" Well, my eyes went
wide when he replied, "My steering wheel fell off!", and I
said "You've got to be kidding me?? How did you get the
plane back?" With that, Freddy opens the door to the
cockpit and says, "Well, look," and what had happened was,

it came off while he was still in the air landing in one of those dry lake beds and somehow he got it down. Then he walked around in the desert on what he described as a scavenger hunt, found a piece of wire, and he wired the steering wheel back on and flew it home! Next he told me, "I'm lucky to be back here," and we both burst into laughter, partly in relief because we both knew what a close call it had been. Freddy was always adventurous.

Merle Haggard: As Freddy got to be a better pilot, he'd take his plane up and spot fish and women, and I was in the bass boat and he'd tell me where to go to find either one.

Manager Marc Oswald: In his 'Natural High' plane, Freddy would fly over the lake and look for schools of shad that he could see swirling from the air. Then he'd land his plane, and taxi out toward the schools of shad, because wherever the shad are, the bass are, they're just swimming underneath the shad. So Freddy would find a spot he liked, land, shut the motor off, and he would fish right there, and catch fish every time because he could see where they were, it was great! He used to carry fishing poles on his plane, and he would cast right off the plane.

Freddy Powers: "*Ridin' High*" was a song Merle and I wrote. That's just a song, some ideas we had at the time. Merle and I both are pilots and I had a little seaplane there on the lake that lands on water, you know. And I had been flying around that lake all the time. And during the time when I was really hot into flying and Merle was also involved in it, you know, everyone up there was all involved in my big airplane adventure. But during the time we wrote a couple three songs that had to do with flying. That was just where our heads were at the time, but this was the ultimate one of them." 19

Marc Oswald: One day I was out there, just me and Fred, and I got in one of the bass boats and took off fishing by myself because I was killing time waiting for Merle to meet with me to approve some tour dates. So I was just out there all day, and I didn't catch a single damn fish, and I was out there by myself all day until I finally heard an engine coming, and looked up and sure enough, Freddy's circling over me in his plane. Well, he lands on the water in the 'Natural High' plane, and taxis up to this little bass boat of Merle's I'd borrowed, and asks me how I was doing, and I told him the fishing wasn't worth a shit that day. So he says, 'Well, hold on here a minute,' takes off on his plane, and comes back about five minutes later, unzips this little thing on the back of his plane, and pulls out a BIG OLD BASS. So then he flashes that famous Freddy Powers smile, and tells me to follow him, and took me over to this other place on the lake where the fish were biting.

Freddy Powers: So here I am up there flying as Merle had told me, most of the flying knowledge was on the ground watching. But I taught myself how to fly and land and take off on water. Merle's boat, The Hotel Troubadour, was the headquarters and command post for the 'Spree of 83'. It was also the Control Tower for me and my airplane. As I got more sure of myself as a pilot, I ventured out and began flying all over the lake. I quickly saw the advantages of low flying around the lake. Besides spotting the shad for a good fishing location, I could spot the naked women sunbathing. I would radio back to Merle and tell him where the naked women were, and he'd get in his bass boat, come out and meet me and I'd land next to him. Then we'd join the naked women for some sunbathing of our own.

Merle Haggard: He had a hydraulic lift built on the back of his boat where he could pick the airplane up out of the water so it came up about six - eight feet off the water, that sat on the back of the houseboat, sticking off the back end. People could see it for 100 miles. He did all that himself, I just kind of watched it.

Freddy Powers: I had an 80-gallon solar hot water storage tank on the roof of my houseboat and an electric lift Merle's son-in-law at the time had designed and built for me that lifted the plane on the top of my houseboat. We'd go up and spend several days on the Pit River and if we ran out of supplies or needed to make a phone call or something, I'd lower the plane in the water, take off for the marina and get whatever we needed before flying back. My houseboat was the only Aircraft Carrier on the lake.

Manager Marc Oswald: On Freddy's 'Natural High' plane, there were no doors on the plane! So when he would fly it, it had a front nose on it and a little windshield, but was open on the sides. You wore a helmet and a ski-vest when you flew with him in it. But the thing about Freddy's boat that I think was the most awesome was that ultralight lift on the back that lifted the plane up onto the roof, because Freddy would taxi the plane right up to the back of this boat, and the plane would go into this little rack, almost like a jet-ski that you'd pull up to the back of the boat. And it had a cable and an electric motor in it, and it lifted the plane right up onto the roof.

Freddy Powers: Later on, I wanted something a little bigger so I could fly back and forth from Redding to Lake Tahoe. I bought a Cessna 150 and it was a cherry after I had it rebuilt. That one I called 'Air Fred', and it served its purpose for a while. I was making plenty of money then so I later bought a Cherokee 180, which went a little faster than the Cessna and seated four plus baggage. So depending on my trip I would choose the airplane I wanted to fly that day.

By this time, I had a lot of flying experience and had gotten my pilot's license. Merle hadn't flown in a while but wanted to fly over his ranch to look it over, and he wanted to fly my Cherokee. Knowing Merle was a pilot, I had no problem saying yes. So we went out to the airport and took off. Merle was at the controls, and he was making low passes and turning too sharp of turns for that airplane, not to mention we were right on the verge of controlled air space. I kept telling him to get out of the TCA, and kept my hands close to the yolk at all times.

Merle Haggard: I got in his plane one time and was going to fly it, and all it had was a throttle and there wasn't no instruments or nothing, no way to tell when you had enough speed or nothing, I couldn't see anything on there. So I got it out one time, got it ready to take off, and then at the last minute I just taxied back up back and said, 'I ain't gonna fly this plane like this, I'm not going to kill myself today'. Well about a year or two later, I was with Freddy, and he'd never seen me fly, so he didn't know if I was bullshitting him or not. So one time he came out to my house and he was flying his Cherokee 180, we went out to the airport, and I told Freddy 'I want to fly over my house for some building I got going on', then I surprised him and said 'Let me fly your airplane!' He'd never seen me fly, so he said 'Are you sure you want to fly this plane? This thing has a funny break on it, how long's it been since you've flown?' And I said, 'Well, I can fly this plane Fred', and when we got in the plane, I could see had a break that you pulled up with your hand, so you'd reach up underneath the dash, pull this thing up, and it'd stop the airplane.

See, most breaks in airplanes are foot pedals, but this one didn't have that, it had the break up there by the hand, and I said 'God damn Freddy, I've never seen a break like this,' because the break's usually above the rotor, and he said 'No you pull this one with your hand.' So then I asked him, 'Well, what happens if its pulled when you land?', and Freddy said 'No, you don't do that, keep it down…' So we're taxiing out there, and we take off, and Freddy says 'You're too low, you're too low,' and I said 'I want to fly over my house out here.' We were only about 800 feet in the air, flying over my house, and I knew there was another runway across from the main one that was 120 degrees that way, and 300 and something that way, and so we were up over my house, and I just kinda started steering us down, knowing that runway was there- but Freddy didn't know it! So he started screaming and hollerin' in there, 'Hag!', as I'm going toward the ground, and just landed on the runway. I about scared him to death because first we landed on the wrong runway, and I kind of just let it go down real fast and scared him a little more. Then I squeezed it on him, and said 'Look it there,' and he said 'You have scared the *shit* out of me!', and then says, 'My God, you can fly, can't ya!' (laughs)

Freddy Powers: I must say that day scared the 'SHIT' out of me and Merle knows it. I think he was probably just jiving with me, anyway, it did scare me but I do believe Merle is a good pilot.

Merle Haggard: I don't think we ever flew together except for that one time. I watched him fly, and there was about an 18-month period there where he was flying that I wasn't, but I was trying to give him all the knowledge I had when he'd go up. I remember another time Fred and Deanie Bird were flying once over Nevada out there and got into a bad deal where the wings started to ice up in the air, and Freddy got frightened and couldn't fly it, and turned it over to Deanie Bird, who was an old helicopter pilot, so he nosed it over and took it down underneath the ice level, and the ice began to fall off the wings… he credited Deanie Bird with saving his life that day.

Chapter 7: "Looking For a Place to Fall Apart"

Freddy Powers: Even though everything was moving so fast and even in this hectic atmosphere, we were still turning out hit songs. We were on tour coming out of Canada and heading for Nashville to the BMI Songwriters' Awards. It was probably around three in the morning and we had our guitars out. My girlfriend at the time, Sherrill Rogers, was singing in the band. In a joking voice, she said to me, "When we get to Nashville, I'm gonna chase you around the room!" Well, Merle and I picked up on that and it didn't take us long and in about 30 minutes, Merle and I had written the song '*Let's Chase Each Other Round the Room Tonight.*' It was recorded in Nashville shortly afterward and went to # 1 in the Country Music Charts with over one million airplays, remaining on the charts for 14 total weeks! It was amazing how Merle and I could see a song in almost anything you said at that time in our relationship.

When we got to Nashville for the Award Show, we were staying at the Opryland Hotel in two big hotel suites, Merle, myself and Sherrill Rodgers and Debbie Parrott, at this time, Merle's maid and close friend… we were sitting around playing guitars. Merle had just finished writing a lot of songs about Leona Williams. Merle said to me, "I wish I could write a song to Leona and explain exactly how I feel once and for all," and I said, "When are you going to quit writing about Leona? Why don't you write a letter and tell her exactly how you feel, and then we'll try to make a song out of the letter?" He liked the idea of a song where someone would write a letter saying once and for all everything he wanted to say to her and how he felt about the whole affair. He agreed and that's how *'Looking for a Place to Fall Apart'* came about, and it was written exactly like the letter. Sadly, we never saw the letter, some fan at the hotel ran away with it, but we had it on tape. It was also a # 1 song. The letter began: "Dear Leona, I'll probably never see you eye to eye again, and this letter is meant to be my last goodbye. I thought everything was over until your phone call. That call turned my life around…"

Looking For a Place to Fall Apart

I'll probably never see you eye to eye again
This letter's meant to be my last farewell
But you need to under-stand I'm nearly crazy
You need to know my life has gone to hell
Write me back and tell me why it ended
Send a letter that I can show my heart
I'll be somewhere between "I love you" and what you're
feeling now
Lookin' for a place to fall apart
Looking for a place to fall apart
Trying to find a place that I can leave my heart
I need to be somewhere hidin' when I feel the teardrops

start

Lookin' for a place to fall a-part

I can't seem to justify your leavin' me

I'm be-wildered as to how it all came down

I thought everything was fine until your phone call

The call that turned my world around

Send me word and tell me why it ended

I need some final proof to show my heart

I'll be somewhere between "I love you" and what you're

feelin' now (I love you)

Lookin' for a place to fall apart

Looking for a place to fall apart

Trying to find a place that I can leave my heart

I need to be somewhere hidin' when I feel the teardrops

start

Lookin' for a place to fall a-part

Looking for a place to fall apart

Trying to find a place that I can leave my heart

I need to be somewhere hidin' when I feel the teardrops

start

Lookin' for a place to fall a-part

(Written by: Freddy Powers/Merle Haggard/Willie Nelson, 1984

Copyright Sony/ATV Music Publishing Ltd)

Merle Haggard: We wrote *'A Place to Fall Apart'* right here at the Opryland hotel. He got the song title from Willie, brought it up to me, and one day asked me if I'd ever written anything about my divorce, and I said 'No, I don't want to write anything about my divorce, I want to forget it'. I said, 'I'd like to write a letter', and Freddy said 'Well, why don't you sit down and write the letter', and I sat down, wrote the letter, and the letter became the song. That's how it came out. *'Place to Fall Apart'* is a good song, I still do it once in a while and I still do *'Natural High'* once in a while.

Freddy Powers: Merle sometimes showed his affection by writing songs about someone or even giving them a piece of a song's publishing. Unfortunately, as it turned out, we'd have to share the spoils from that song's success with some undeserving participants after our kindness backfired on us and some other writers tried to take partial credit for the song's writing. I wrote the first version of *'I Always Get Lucky with You'* awhile back before I met Merle, and after Merle and I got together, I played the song for him. Merle liked the title right off and thought the title alone was a hit. He took the song and after a few changes, we had a hit. For some strange reason, Merle and I thought it would be nice of us to give part of the royalties we made from the songwriting to a couple of friends and co-workers for all their loyalty and sticking it out with us. Merle gave Tex Watson, his manager at the time, half of his part and I gave Gary Church, my trumpet player, half of my part. Little did we know that would come back to take a major bite out of our asses.

We had been out on tour and pulled into Nashville to see a billboard that read: "<u>Congratulations Tex Watson! I Always Get Lucky With You</u>." Merle and I walked off the bus and directly in to the middle of a party for Tex in his honor for *writing* this number one hit. Needless to say he never mentioned mine or Merle's name, the song's actual writers. One day he was bragging on the song and I finally had enough of it, and handed him my guitar and told him if he wrote the song to play me an A augmented. Well, with that, the conversation was over and I rested my case. Sometimes you have to be careful what you do, because some people start believing their own lies, especially in the music business, a # 1 hit is the kind of score that can corrupt anyone. I think that's one of many reasons why Merle and I trusted in each other so completely as songwriters, because there was such honesty going on in our natural friendship, that it showed up in our creative relationship and songs by natural extension. We shared in the successes that chemistry produced, and the occasional loss when we were taken advantage of by those seeking to get a free ride off Merle's name and stardom. Gary Church had even wound up with his name on a couple of other songs of mine he had nothing to do with writing.

Merle Haggard: '*I Always Get Lucky With You…*' there's a lot to that. We were sitting in somebody's bus, I don't remember whether it was mine or his, and Fred and I wrote the song. Well, there were two other guys there, and being stupid, we gave them part of the song. I said, 'Well, I've got publishing, so I'll just go ahead and give you two the writers' end, and I'll take the publishing.' Well, I got beat out of the publishing in bankruptcy, and when I look down at that song after it was recorded by George Jones, and my name ain't on it nowhere and I wrote most of the song. That's the way life goes sometimes.

Catherine Powers: I never publicly contradicted Merle Haggard before, nothing really serious. I can remember the first time was over the otters and all the destruction they were doing to the house boats and the bass boats and everything up around on the marina. Well, one morning Merle went to shoot at one of those otters and immediately I looked at him and in shock said "What are you doing Merle.?" He said "Ah, those S.O.B.s are tearing up this marina and boats. Just trying to get them off one at a time," and I replied, "What! Wait A Minute Merle, actually, in reality, *you* are the one who has invaded their space, so how would you feel if every time they jumped up they saw us, they shot us off, leaving our children motherless or fatherless as you possibly have just left one little sweet creature out there in the water? You have invaded their space!"

Well, the next morning he showed up with Big Old tears in his eyes, and said it had kept him awake half the night thinking about what I said, and that he wanted to come over and apologize to me, but anyway, back to why I contradicted Merle publicly: when I had read his story about "I Always Get Lucky with You" in this book called Nashville Songwriter, Merle had said in the story that of course he remembered the song because he had written most of it. Well, like I said, I got up at thr Book Release Party, contradicted him and said "Freddy would never take credit for something he did not do, but this is one time I know that Freddy told me the story, and actually used the story when someone would ask him about critiquing songwriting." He would tell them, " I first wrote *I Always Get Lucky With You* back sometime before I ever hooked up with Merle Haggard, but I called it one night at a show and one of my guys said, 'Freddy, Oh No, not that song, I don't like that song!'

So Freddy, without thinking, never stopped to ask why he didn't like the song, instead, he ditched it, never calling it again at a show. We came to find out years later that it had nothing to do with the chords or the lyrics, but the melody because it was full of augmented and diminished and minors and majors. At the time, people were still kind in awe over Freddy's melodies, even Merle would comment occasionally, "Freddy, why do you have to write a song with so many damn chords?"

One morning, Merle walked in and said, "What are you on there Fred?", to which Freddy replied, "Ah, I was fooling around with a song I wrote a while back, I'm thinking about changing the title to it because at the time, it was 'I Found a Rainbow in You.'" Well, Merle – now intrigued – asked what the title was, and when Freddy told him "I Always Get Lucky With You," Merle jumped up and said, "Hell Freddy, that title alone is a # 1!" So YES, they did go to work on the song, fooled around with it and finished it up, but mostly ended up taking out one of what even Merle Haggard later referred to was one of the best verses in the song, which read: "I've searched all my life for that pot of gold and at the rainbows end I found you again and I always get lucky with you..."

Freddy Powers: Luckily, in spite of that stumble, we wound up with three number one hits on the "All in the Game" album, and all of a sudden money came rolling in, and LOTS of it! And we had no problem spending it. Everything from Limos to Jets, still I could see that through the success we were having and all the partying, Merle was a troubled man, it was always on his face. Sometimes he would open up and tell me things that bothered him. He would tell me about personal things, things about his family, the music business, and lots of stories about prison. The better I got to know Merle, the more I realized that his career and his life all has been an uphill fight for him. Growing up in a boxcar, the loss of his father, refusing school, his prison life and being a prisoner of the music business – the very thing he loves most, it's ALL been a battle for him and in some ways still is. You can listen to any Merle Haggard song and tell me how he was feeling at that time whether he was in a sad or happy mood. All his songs tell a story that could fit most anybody's everyday life. Merle is the poet for the common man.

On Merle's houseboat one day, I called my mother. At the end of our conversation, I told her I loved her. When I hung up, Merle said he didn't know if he'd ever told his mother he loved her. I asked him why and he said they just "Weren't that kind of family." Merle decided to call his mother and before they hung up he said, "I love you Mama." When Merle's mother got sick, he and I got on the bus and went to Bakersfield, California to see her in the hospital. We stayed in the parking lot for several days until she passed on. That was a sad time in Merle's life.

One thing's for sure, he did inherit his writing ability from his mother. She wrote her own Eulogy, which was the story of her life and read at her funeral by Ralph Emery. It was the most beautiful and heart-warming story I'd ever heard. With all the rough exterior, Merle's inside is still that of a little boy, with a heart filled with romantic dreams. His songs come straight from his mixed-up past. When Merle was a boy in Bakersfield, he was a restless renegade. He was in and out of reform schools all because he didn't want to go to school. All he wanted to do was get a job and that was against the rules of society. But the reform school only primed him for prison, and he tried to escape from there many times. The prison system almost ruined a life, the life of Merle Haggard. I sincerely believe that if Merle hadn't found success in the music business, he would either be back in prison if not dead. After living nearly ten years next door to Merle, today when I hear one of his songs, I'll remember the story behind it and know what part of his life he's singing about.

Merle had several old friends visit us on the lake over those years, most of them only a few days or weeks, but one woman had always stayed on the scene, Debbie Parrott, Merle's maid and housekeeper. After Leona and Merle finally called it quits, Debbie moved out to the houseboat with Merle and started cooking and taking care of both of us.

Debbie had been with us all the way: she cooked good, healthy things that we needed, she was a mother and sister and a wonderful friend to Merle, and also to me. I could gradually see Merle falling in love with Debbie, but I never believed it was love like between a man and a wife, but more like Merle needed a female friend.

It seemed there for a while we could see a song in everything. Someone would say something and one of us would say, 'That's a good title for a song.' And most of the time, a few minutes later we would have a song. Debbie, she was a great person to be around. She understood we were songwriters. Knowing that, if she saw a song coming on, she would have pen and paper ready and made sure we had peace and quiet. We had a lot of women up there with us that were not so good to have around while we were working. They would do something to interrupt us, like 'Request a song'. I think songwriters have to have people around that understand, and Debbie is that kind of a person and I will always love and respect her for that, and all her devoted care she gave us. And I know Merle feels the same way, as he's told me so many times.

She had a cabin that she was renting just up the hill from the boats. She got to where she seldom ever went to the cabin. She was still Merle's maid, but they just kept getting closer and closer. Debbie did everything for Merle, and was somewhat like Merle. I've seen Merle with all kinds of women, but when things went wrong and he was down he always went straight to Deb. She was what he really needed and would baby him like he was a child, and then sometimes she would lean on him like he was a giant. It was a relationship I have never seen since. Debbie hung on instead of confronting Merle about the other women. Instead, she just worked harder and harder doing things for Merle, so the more Merle would see other women, the harder Debbie would work to make him happy. It was really something to watch her work, but with kindness, and love for Merle, she did something that a lot of women would have liked to do: become Mrs. Merle Haggard.

Merle Haggard: Debbie did a lot of things for us, she cooked for us, washed our clothes, did whatever we asked her to do. If somebody got out of line in the female department, she'd whip their ass and kick them off the boat, whatever we wanted her to do. She took care of that *light* work for us (laughs).

Freddy Powers: In a quiet ceremony at sunrise at Shade Tree Manor, Merle's ranch, Merle and Debbie were married. The wedding was held at Merle's ranch set on top of a small hill outside of Redding, California with a view of Mount Shasta 360 degrees to the north and Mount Lassen exactly 90 degrees to the east. It was a beautiful sunrise you would have thought had been ordered just for the occasion. Dean Reynolds, Steve Van Stralen and myself played a song that Debbie had requested be played at the wedding. It was a song I'd written for Merle, "*Natural High*," and it was so early in the morning that everyone was sleepy-eyed at first. I only cried at the wedding of my daughters, but I must say this one brought tears to my eyes. One thing we had agreed to is that Debbie would never, ever in a million years take more than she had coming from Merle in a divorce, an important topic since divorces had cost Merle so much money (including half million dollar payments he was making at the time to Leona). When the ceremony was over, Gary Church- a trumpet player who'd originally played in my Dixieland band had come with me from Reno and joined Merle's famous Strangers band- stood up and announced: 'The wedding omelet would be served at the ranch house!' Even after he was married, the partying on the boat was still full-blown, and people were often filming there, all the usual fan-fair that goes with being a superstar. I really believe that if Debbie hadn't been there during our party days, always serving good, healthy food and pouring vitamins down us, we probably wouldn't be here today!

"The proudest achievement of my career is to be able to say I have written No. 1 hits for the greatest country singer of our time, Merle Haggard." – Freddy Powers, Sept. 1989, Harrah's Lake Tahoe Resort Casino

"Once I wrote my first No. 1 hit for Merle, people no longer looked at me as 'Freddy the entertainer' – they called me 'the songwriter.' It was like the entertainer part of me got lost in the songwriting. Singers are singers, but poets are forever." Freddy Powers, June, 2006, Texas Music Magazine by Jason Hardison

Photo chapter

Freddy and brother Don Powers Growing Up in the early 1940s in Seminole, Texas

Freddy as a Boy Soldier

Freddy as a Teen Marine in the mid-1940s

Freddy in Service w/ Fellow Marines, late 1940s

Freddy and Don Powers as teens in Freddy's first car, later 1940s

Freddy as Teen in mid-1940s w/his trusty Rifle on Plains of West Texas

Freddy in the mid-50s in Barber School

Freddy out on the town with Marines, early 1950s

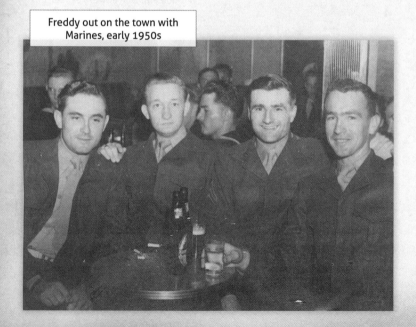

BROTHER PAUL BUSKIRK and his "Little Men"   LIN RECORDING ARTISTS   FREDDY POWERS

Freddy Performing on Stage w/his mentor Paul Buskirk, mid-1950s

Freddy (center) and the Powers Family Band, The W Boys, mid-1950s

Freddy Autographed Late 1950s
Fan Promo Photo

Freddy Playing the Banjo, his primary
instrument for years, in late 1950s

Freddy (center) Playing
Banjo on NBC, late 1950s

Freddy (center) and Willie Nelson (far right) playing Bass in Freddy's Band, 1963 →

Freddy shaking hands w/ Host on The Today Show, 1962 ↓

Wednesday, August 1, 1962   THE NEWS TEXAN   Page 1

Arlington Scene

Scouts Set Ranch Trip

The Scouts of Troop 156 will leave at 2 p.m. Saturday for a trip to Palo Pinto county and the Worth Ranch.

There the boys will get a close look at the ranch and western life.

The troop, sponsored by the Sertoma Club of Arlington, will spend the night on the Worth ranch before making the return trip. Sunday they will attend church services provided on the ranch and on the two – day trip eat all their meals in the ranch house mess-hall.

Saturday night they will sleep in tents that have already been provided.

The troop is a special troop for mentally retarded boys.

Boys making the trip are Ronnie Ellis, Billy Brooks, Gary Curtis, Buddy Strange, Billy Orr and Sammy White.

Men accompanying the boys are Dave Ellis, assistant scout master, P. W. Otts, J. L. Strange, Bill Nolen, scout master, Kenneth Lee, chairman of the troop committee and Joe Houston, institutional representative.

NEW YORK BOUND -- Freddy Powers is shown shaking hands with John Chancellor following a taped segment of the show used on the National network while the "Today" crew was in Arlington. Powers and his band will leave Monday for New York. Others in the picture are Bobby Hollinsworth, and Ralph Sanford. Behind Powers is the groups business manager Arden Powers. --NEWS TEXAN PHOTO.

...and I Quote

BY UP INTERNATIONAL

BERLIN — An American spokesman, commenting on Russian threats to shoot down a U.S. helicopter if it flew over East Berlin:

"We certainly plan to continue to fly in accordance with our rights within the control zone."

AUGUST 10

Banjo Band Sets New 'Today' Date

Freddy Powers and his banjo band will leave Monday morning for New York and their second appearance on the "Today" show. While in New York, the group will also make final arrangements to cut a record album and for

appearance on the Dinah Shore fall show. It was not known if their appearance would be on a special or the regular weekly show.

The local group first gained recognition following an appearance on the morning show "Today" when it visited the S....

ALT Sales

Freddy Powers (second in from left) and Powerhouse IV – Early 1960s

Freddy and company out at the legendary Copa Cabana, 1962

Freddy International Talent Agency Head Shot, early 1960s

Freddy Powers (left) and the Powerhouse IV w/new Tuba Player – Mid-1960s

Freddy Powers (second in from left) Playing Drums w/ his band the Powerhouse IV

FREDDY POWERS SHOW

Freddy Powers Casino Comedy Show – Early 1970s

Freddy's Mother Mary Singing On Stage w/Freddy Playing Guitar in Background late 70s

Freddy Powers (center w/Banjo) Headlining at the Showboat Casino, 1975

Freddy Powers (right) and Willie Nelson, late 1970s

Freddy Powers and Willie Nelson (center left and right) at Gilley's Recording Studio During the "Somewhere Over the Rainbow" Sessions, which Freddy produced, 1980

Original Set of Lyrics to Freddy's first self-penned # 1 hit, "Natural High"

Merle Haggard and Freddy Powers' Houseboats, the Hotel Troubadour and USSF (United States Sir Fredrick) (left to right) moored on Lake Shasta, California, mid-1980s

Freddy Powers (far left) and Merle Haggard (2nd in) playing at Silverthorne Resort Live Club, mid-1980s

Freddy Powers and Merle Haggard (4th and 5th from left) on The Johnny Cash TV Show w Johnny and June (far right), early 1980s

Freddy's USSF Houseboat with his hand-built Natural High Airplane Mounted On Top, Lake Shasta, California, mid-1980s

Freddy Powers (center) at Willie 1984 Pedernales Invitational Golf Tournament

Merle Haggard (2nd from left) and Freddy Powers (2nd from right) at the BMI Awards Ceremony, mid-1980s

"A Place to Fall Apart" – Co-written by Merle, Freddy and Willie – Sheet Music

BMI Congratulations Letter to Freddy Powers for Joining the Coveted "Million-Air" Songwriters' Club after achieving over 1 million plays at radio for songs he'd written

Willie Nelson and Freddy Powers (center) Playing at Freddy's Headlining Gig on the legendary Austin City Limits TV Show, mid-1980s

Freddy Powers' First Pilot License

Freddy Showcasing his Silly Side on Tour with Merle Haggard, 1986

Actor Garner, Freddy's Mother Mary and Freddy (left) at Coach Darrell Royal Golf Invitational, later 1980s

Freddy posing with his airplane, Air Fred, 1986

Freddy's Gyro-copter, which he taught himself to Pilot, mid-1980s

Freddy (kneeling, center) with his Air Fred Band and Airplane in the Background, later-1980s

Freddy and Catherine Powers
Newly Married, 1992

Freddy and
Catherine Powers
on their Harley
Davidson Dyna
Wide Glide with a
Fatboy Front End,
early 1990s

↓

Freddy with
special passenger
Amelia, he and
Catherine's
Sheltie on Golf
Cart, mid- 1990s

←

Freddy Powers and Willie Nelson (center) back home in Austin, Texas on Willie's Ranch Picking for the Cameras, mid-1990s

Rogers and Hammerhead TV Show Set, Freddy and Catherine's Living Room, Austin, Texas, Mid-1990s

Freddy Powers with Rogers and Hammerhead co-host and biking buddy Bill McDavid, mid-1990s

Willie Nelson (far left) with Freddy Powers and Bill McDavid on Rogers & Hammerhead TV Show Set, later 1990s

Freddy Powers (far right) Pickin' with Merle Haggard (center) on the Rogers and Hammerhead TV Show Set, later 1990s

Freddy and legendary Texas Longhorns Coach Darrell Royal
(left and center), mid 1990s

City of Austin

Proclamation

Be it known by these presents that
I, Kirk Watson, Mayor of the City of Austin, Texas,
do hereby proclaim

April 30, 1998

as

Rogers & Hammerhead Day

in Austin, and call on all citizens to join me in recognizing that
the Rogers & Hammerhead Show, an already well known interview series
enjoyed by many people in Austin, has been nominated for the prestigious
CableACE Awards presented each year by the National Academy of Cable
Programming to recognize and promote excellence in cable television programming,
in recognizing that the Rogers & Hammerhead Show, produced by Freddy
Powers and Bill McDavid, also known as Mr. Rogers & Hammerhead, along
with Ingrid Weigand of the Austin Music Network and TimeWarner Cable,
was created to acknowledge songwriters and to give them a chance to talk about
their work, and in congratulating all those involved in the creation and
production of the Rogers & Hammerhead Show which can be seen
in Austin only on the Austin Music Network, Channel 15.

Attest:

Mayor
Kirk Watson

Austin, Texas Proclamation by Mayor that April 30th,
1998 was Officially Rogers & Hammerhead Day

Freddy and Catherine Powers on their Beloved Harley, later 1990s

Freddy and Catherine Powers Out on the Town, later 1990s

Freddy and Amelia On Stage, later 1990s

Freddy and Willie (2ⁿᵈ and 3ʳᵈ in from left) recording in the studio, later 1990s

Freddy Powers w/Nevada Special Olympics Medal Winners

Freddy Performing at the Aftershow to the Freddy Powers Celebrity Golf Invitational

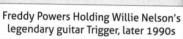
Freddy Powers Signing Autographs for Country Jazz Singer LP, later 1990s

Freddy Powers Holding Willie Nelson's legendary guitar Trigger, later 1990s

Freddy Powers on Tour Bus with his Customized Guitars, late 1990s

Freddy Powers and Merle Haggard
Backstage Together, early 2000s

Freddy Powers and Merle Haggard
Performing on stage together, 2004

Freddy Powers (left) and
John Rich (right) out on the
Town Together, early 2000s

Freddy Powers (left) and legendary Country Songwriter (center) Floyd Tillman on Stage Playing Together, early 2000s

Freddy and Catherine Powers Presenting Check from the Freddy Powers Parkinsons Foundation, 2006

Merle Haggard (center) Roasting Freddy (far right) at his 75th Birthday Roast, 2006

December 10, 2004

Freddy Powers
918 Lauder Drive
Spicewood, TN 78669

Dear Freddy:

Capitol Nashville would like to thank you for your contribution to the new **Merle Haggard's Unforgettable** release. Enclosed please find a complimentary writer's and publisher's copy.

Thanks again!

Sincerely,

Emma Grandillo

Capitol Nashville

Enclosure

↑

Capitol Records President Letter to Freddy for Co-Production Work on Merle Haggard's 2004 "Unforgettable" LP

Willie Nelson (left) and Freddy Powers (right) recording Road to My Heart, mid-2000s →

Road to My Heart
Willie + Freddy 3/6

Freddy and Catherine w their new dog, a piano-playing Russian Toy Terrier, Olga →

Freddy Powers' Bullshitter's Bullshitter Award, April, 2010 ↓

Whereas:

Texans are known the world over as bullshitters without peer, and Texans take pride in the fine art and nuance of Bullshitting, and Texans understand that one can inspire to high morals, ethics and be held in highest respect while remaining a Bullshitter par excelance, be it known throughout the Great State of Texas and all other sovereign countries, that

Freddy Powers

Has been declared and shall heretofore be acknowledged as a

BULLSHITTER'S BULLSHITTER

And from this day forward be allowed to wear his pants tucked inside his boots, the international symbol of the Master Bullshitter.

<u>In witness thereof, this certificate is issued at West Pole Bee Caves, TX, on this day, April 21 2010</u>

- GOD BLESS TEXAS -

Empresatio

Texas State's Center for Texas Music History and the Wittliff Collections honor legendary country songwriter

FREDDY POWERS

April 27, 2011
Free reception
5 to 7 pm

Texas State University
San Marcos, Alkek Library
The Wittliff Collections
512.245.2313

Texas State University Official Invitation to the Prestigious Wittliff Collections' Freddy Powers Exhibit/Archives Reception, April, 2011

Freddy Powers in the later-00s while he could still play Guitar →

Freddy Powers and Merle Haggard in the later 2000s

↑

Country Star John Rich
Playing for Freddy on
the Powers' Bus, 2013

Freddy and Catherine Powers and Country
Star Toby Keith (far right), 2013

Freddy Big & Rich and Tanya
Tucker, 2013

Freddy and Catherine Powers at "Nashville Songwriter" Book Release, pictured w/ fellow legendary country songwriters Neil Thrasher, Sonny Curtis, Bob DiPiero and Kelley Lovelace (top row) and Jeff Silbar and Craig Wiseman (1st and 2nd in, bottom left) 2014

CERTIFICATE
of BAPTISM

This Certifies That

FREDDY DALE POWERS SR.

was

*Baptized in the name of the Father, Son, and Holy Spirit
at La Hacienda Church.*

On,
August 26, 2012
DATE

By:
George K. Grant
PASTOR GREG K. GRANT

Freddy Powers' Certificate of Baptism, Aug. 2012

Catherine and Olga with Freddy Powers on Florida Waters in his last days, 2016

Freddy's Full Marine Honors Burial w/ Handing Catherine Folded Flag, Flora-Bama, July, 2016

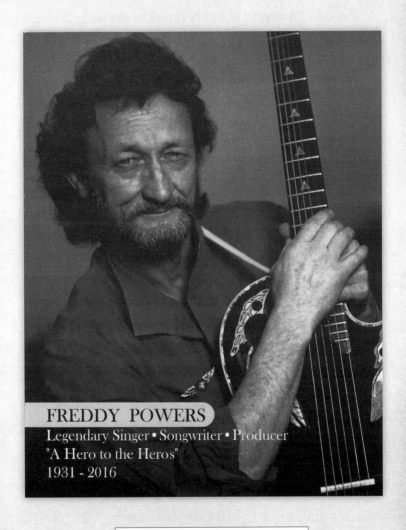

FREDDY POWERS
Legendary Singer • Songwriter • Producer
"A Hero to the Heros"
1931 - 2016

Freddy Powers "A Hero to the Heroes"
In Memoriam Picture, Summer, 2016

Chapter 8: The Country Jazz Singer

Freddy Powers: I am very proud of my songwriting career and thankful to all my friends and to those that I have never gotten to meet that have recorded my songs throughout the years. If I were to complain about anything, it's that after I had my first hit people began to refer to me as a songwriter and somehow forgot I was a singer too. I've spent most of my life as a singer and musician and love the stage and enjoy the satisfaction of knowing people like my singing and my style of guitar playing. After I'd spent a few years writing songs for Merle and producing for Willie, I finally – with their encouragement I must admit – decided that it was time to put together an album that showcased my own musical roots, and *"The Country Jazz Singer"* was born.

Stereo Review Magazine: "Freddy Powers… appears here in an impressive, if quiet, performance of upbeat jazz and country ballads. A dexterous musician and adroit lyricist, Powers dedicates his album to Django Reinhardt, Haggard and Willie Nelson among others, citing their influence on his music. Judging from this outing, however, it looks as if Powers may have been as much of an influence on Haggard as Haggard has been on him…This lovely LP is an eye-opener, revealing Powers as a remarkable country-jazz stylistic and songwriter worthy of far greater exposure on his own."

Freddy Powers: "I never thought about writing songs as to make a living or to make money. I started writing songs because I wanted something to say, you know, in my band. I was a performer long before I was a songwriter. I couldn't believe it when my song became # 1 for the first time. George Jones recorded it…. My sister and I wrote a Christmas song called 'Silent Night, Lonely Night.' I wasn't real fond of it, but Merle was doing a Christmas album, and I got it in there. I was flabbergasted when I heard the song with a big orchestra, the London Orchestra from London. Songwriting is like a habit, like I'm addicted, and I didn't realize this until I got started. Once you write a song and when it's over with, you've finished it, and you've got it all done and you're singing it, then you have a let-down. You need another one; you need another one right now. Songwriters get addicted to the tension of a new song." [20]

Merle Haggard: "He's a genius whispering in the ears of giants, never realizing that he's been a giant all along."

(Source: Texas Music Magazine by Jason Hardison, June, 2006)

Freddy Powers: "When I'm composing, I never sit down to write. I get up every morning, have a cup of coffee and just play my guitar and if I'm ever gonna get an idea, that's when it's gonna come. A lot of songwriters ask, 'How can I get my songs out?', and I say 'If you've got a good enough song, you can't hold that song down. If the song is in the upper category, like *Misery and Gin* and *Night and Life,* that song will escape. Just take it out and play it.' On the other hand, critique is important for a songwriter. If you ask somebody, 'Well, what do you think about that song?', that could just kill the song, he'll drop it right then and there. Just be your own judge. Because I've written songs, played it and gradually a metamorphosis happens. I don't know how many times it has happened to me, and I'll always have a doubt in my mind." 21

Willie Nelson: "You know a Freddy Powers-style song when you hear it… you know you've stumbled onto a good thing – something beautiful." (Source: Texas Music Magazine by Jason Hardison, June, 2006)

Freddy Powers: "The key to songwriting is having a story to tell. To me, it takes one of two things: you have to be devastated by something or overwhelmed by something to start a song. Be totally impressed with somebody or some action, especially over romances. All the good songwriters I know have real bad relationships, or rocky relationships…. You go back and look at the songs from 1900 and they are all saying the same thing as today. They are saying 'I love you,' 'I'm leaving you,' 'I hate you,' 'I've got somebody else' or 'My heart is broken.' You know, there are just a few messages of love that can be portrayed.

I always write the same, I don't write for the modern day, I never did. I never paid attention to what was going on with music. I wrote what I could write; I still do. What comes to me – my emotions or whatever stirs you up…. We write music as we go, and then there is the possibility that after we sing a song for a while we get tired of it. We just change it. There's an incubation period, you know, the song is born, but there's a rebirth. Within a month or so you begin changing the song. I have one song that I wrote yesterday, it will take three weeks or so before it is as I want it. Every day just foolin' around with the words and lyrics – it'll come fine." [22]

Nevada Appeal: "Powers' speaking voice is like music itself. His pronunciation and tone have the lilting, lyrical qualities found in West Texas." (Nevada Appeal, Star Talk, Thursday, Sept 21, 1989, by Pamela Bissell Crowell)

Freddy Powers: "As far as writing goes I guess I like Cole Porter, Johnny Mercer and one of my favorite all-time songwriters, Fats Waller. The stuff that I sing, that's all my style. What I write is reminiscent of that style of music. Most of my music you don't hear on the Country radio station, they're not as easy to pitch because that particular style of music is not in fashion right now." [23]

Country Music Round Up Magazine, London: "Every so often along comes an album that's a little bit

special and as far as I'm concerned, *Country Jazz Singer* is
destined to be my album of the year, sheer musical magic is
the only way to describe it with its deceptively simple feel
due no doubt to the fact that the main instrumentation
comes from the superb guitar work of Clint Strong, whose
sensitive lead guitar on the slow ballads just has to be heard,
while Dean Reynolds on bass adds the necessary depth to
highlight the searing vocals of Freddy Powers."

Freddy Powers: "*Deanie-Bird* Reynolds has been my
best friend, well, since we been kids. He worked with
Willie Nelson years ago with the band. Willie and I and
Deanie-Bird and a guy named Paul Buskirk and
occasionally Johnny Gimbel was working with us." 24

Music Row Magazine: "Powers aligns with a nice
backing trio, including young guitar wiz Clint Strong…The
songs are good, the playing wonderful." (Source: Music Row
Magazine, March, 1987)

Merle Haggard: Fred had a three-piece band and they
recorded and made a really good record. I liked it a lot.

Freddy Powers: "I've always liked performing better
than anything. Performing is where I learned to play music,
and performing is where I learned to write, I guess. It's
better for relaxation, you know. I live out on a houseboat
on Lake Shasta and I stay up there most of the year, and it's

a pleasant life that I'm living, writing. But I got to get out to the people every now and then…. The trio is so pure, we don't use any gimmicks, its all real, pure sound, and you can hear individual instruments. I don't know, it's just so pure, and that guitar player, Clint Strong, is one of the best." 25

FRETS Magazine: "Powers is a gifted songwriter…. The album's sequencing is dictated by tempo, with uptempo swing tunes on side one and ballads on side two."

Freddy Powers: "I've had some albums out over the years, but they were very obscure albums. When I was traveling with the band on the road and I didn't have any national recognition, and we sold them, kinda bandstand albums we'd call them. And I had an old album for Warner Bros. years ago. It was kinda with a Dixieland style that I played. But this is my first big effort in the country music album field of any substance. It was just a lot of fun. It was all in stages, though, I'd written these songs a while back and a lot of them had become hits. Mainly by Merle Haggard, and then I decided, 'Well, I've written me enough hit songs now that I think I'll try to make me an album. So I put my trio together and we made this album…. It's actually a 14-song album, and I did it a little different. I put seven slow songs on one side, my ballads, and seven of those up-tempo country-jazz style on the other side. It's almost like two albums, because you turn it over and you got a whole series of songs in the same style…. It's really an exciting album, and something I'm really proud to be a part of." 26

Country Matters Magazine, U.K.'s first country music magazine: "Some inspired playing back in the mix by Powers and arrangements for the interplay between Powers' guitar and the fiddle work of Johnny Gimble.'"

Freddy Powers: "I have three favorites on there for different reasons. I like the song *'Texas and Oklahoma'* because I was born in Oklahoma and raised in Texas. It's something that I wrote about my memories of Texas and Oklahoma. That's one of my favorites, and then there's one on there called *'I'm Free At Last'* on the end of the album on the slow side. That one Merle and I wrote, and I really do like it a lot. I like the guitar playing on *'Texas Barbecue'* by Clint. It's as good as any guitar solo I've ever heard. Matter of fact, I like everything he did on that album, including his guitar playing. I can listen to it over and over. It's the only thing I've ever done in my life that I've never gotten tired of, and I've been listening to it for two years, before it came out." 27

Reno-Gazette Journal: "After years of opening for Merle Haggard and cutting albums with artists such as Ray Charles and George Jones, Powers brings his special brand of country-western jazz."

Freddy Powers: "I did this album with a strict, 'This is the first album I've ever done with no commercial thought in mind.' I just decided I'm getting to the time in my career where I've gotta do something for my art form for my own self, for what I wanted to do. So I did this album, and it seems I shoulda been doing that all along." 28

Austin City Limits, 1988: "Freddy Powers hosted two songwriter shows: on the first, a bearded Merle Haggard and Willie Nelson joined him, and the three traded solos, duets and trios. The concert turned into an impromptu tribute to Floyd Tillman, present in the audience, whose melodic complexities and popular lyrics had influenced both Nelson and Haggard. 'Pure magic', judged Darrell Royal, 'Pure magic'. The following year, Powers brought back Haggard and Nelson and expanded the circle to include Whitey Shafer and Spud Goodall in a program that crossed the borders between country and jazz…. In the eleventh season, Merle Haggard repaid Freddy Powers' hospitality by inviting him to be a special guest on his own Austin City Limits show – his third."

Pauline Reese: When he played ACL, nobody knew who he was bringing, and he showed up with Willie Nelson and Merle Haggard, that's the kind of guy he was.

Freddy Powers: "The thing that I really like about Austin is that is an acoustic town. Quite possibly the

acoustic musical capital of the world. It could be the
people's ears are just blown up. But it's hard to have a local
music scene when the radio stations do the stuff straight out
of Nashville. It makes it difficult for an area to bust off its
own music scene with that influence hangin' around –
maybe good things are happening. I think people are
wanting to go back to the old country style." 29

Lee Duffy: "Freddy is indefinitely in touch with how
sounds affect the psyche and how lyrics touch the soul.
When you see him perform, you know that he's breathing
with the universe. He can cue the sunset as part of his
delivery." (Source: Texas Music Magazine by Jason Hardison, June, 2006)

Freddy Powers: "When people ask for my opinion of
their song, I always ask them what their opinion of the
song… I always seemed to trust someone else's songs more
than I did mine. If I had any recording to do, a lot of times I
wouldn't trust my own judgment. I'd think it was a good
song, but I'd be afraid to go ahead and play it. I felt I stood
a better chance if I played something that wasn't already
proven. One thing that's helped me more than anything else
with my songwriting is that I was finally able to critique
my own material and not ask someone else to do it…. Now,
I like to critique my own material and I pay very little
attention to what anyone else has to say. That is, until I
perform it. If I play it a few times and I don't get any
response, then I know something is wrong…. The

songwriter who performs also stands a much better chance of being heard." 30

"I do believe there's a lot of great songwriters out there, it's a matter of believing in yourself. Believing, you know, if you think it's a good song, it's probably a good song. You know, believe in it anyway. Believe in what you write. I don't know what to say makes a successful songwriter, but I do know this: when I started believing and letting my own self judge what I wrote, if it's good enough for me to hear, its good enough to play for somebody. Every now and then, I'll write something and I'll listen to it a couple times and it doesn't hit me, so I'll throw it out. But Merle Haggard gave me the encouragement or whatever you want to call it that started me writing, and I try to tell other people as much as I can. If somebody's got a good song, I try to tell them over and over again, because I remember that thing that if the song is good, tell them it's good. Because they need to hear that." 31

Country Music Television: "With the release of The Country Jazz Singer, there was finally a full album devoted to Powers' efforts as a leader."

Augie Savage, Freddy's Keyboard Player: Freddy was real big at the El Dorado Casino, and he went all over in Nevada. I played with him back in between '86 and '91. He would travel up and down to keep the Air Fred Band going. I played keys in the group, and his son was in it playing drums, along with players like Bobby Black, Dave Herscher, Scotty Josh was in the group, and he would get who he could get. B.B. Morse was in the group playing bass, and I tell you, he is a musician's dream, because he sings his verse and then he lets his musicians just go like crazy. He lets them all play and lets them all do a lead, and that's what was so fun working with Freddy, he was a musician's musician. I think any musician will tell you that if they ever worked for Freddy, it was probably the most fun they ever had working, because he would let us play all the time. He completely let the band go, he would sing a little verse and would let the band go.

My all-time favorite guitar player was Django Reinhardt, and Freddy had that rhythm down where he'd just chunk out the rhythm, and it was just so solid, it was absolutely solid. He was probably one of the best rhythm guitar players around, in the Country field, he was absolutely the best rhythm guitar player there was. You couldn't fail, because Freddy was underneath you all the way holding you up. It was very musical, very, very musical. When he had the Air Fred band, we just got up there, held on and played like hell.

Freddy Powers: I've gone to book myself in a club and they'll say 'Songwriter, do you do copy music?', meaning is it played on the radio? I'd tell them 'Hell yeah, just turn the damn radio on.' Sometimes I wonder what would have happened with my performing career as a singer and musician if I hadn't met up with Merle and left it behind for a songwriting career. I was pretty hot at that time and was becoming more well known for my own shows. I had already done several T.V. shows like the Today and Tonight Shows. Before that, I did the ABC Hootenanny Show with Paul Buskirk, and WPAB Serv-All Barn Dance television show with Pat Boone. So I might have been a big star myself, who knows..." 32

Marc Oswald (Merle Haggard's Manager): The Telluride Blue Grass Festival- held in Colorado was one of the biggest Bluegrass festivals in America, and it's still going on today. Well, back during the Spree of 83, I remember we all loaded up on buses from California, and went out to the Telluride Festival just to have fun, we weren't even booked on it. When we got there, Merle wound up deciding he wanted to go home and took off right away, he didn't stay very long, but we stayed for a couple days, and Freddy decided to play a set. Well, in that company, you're talking about guys like Sam Bush and Bela Fleck and Doc Watson, those were the kind of artists that play that show, and are HUGE stars in that genre, and when Freddy went out on stage to play that Festival, he wasn't known as a Bluegrass act. But with his Jazz licks, and all the skills he has on guitar, and the way he sings and all, he was a SMASH!

What made it so cool was, the day he played, the Festival was sold out and there were about 15,000 people there, and so whether Freddy was walking on stage at a Bluegrass show, or walking on stage in a country show, he was always one of the best players in the house. So that day, I remember Doc Watson was over to the side of the stage, and he's blind so of course he couldn't see Freddy, but he was sitting with Bela Fleck and Sam Bush and all those guys were all just transfixed! I don't think they knew much about him up until that point, not coming from the Bluegrass world, but it was just awesome to see, because once again, there was Freddy Powers showing up in a different genre of music, and just smoking the place, because people were going wild!

Freddy Powers: "I'm still not terribly well-known as a singer because my songwriting has overpowered me. Now every article you ever see out of Nashville, they always refer to me as a songwriter. I wonder what they thought I was doing for those 20 or so years before that." 33

Merle Haggard: *'Little Hotel Room'* is a great song off that record. I remember when Freddy was working on it!

Freddy Powers: My proudest song was one I wrote myself that was recorded by Merle and Ray Charles for the 'Friendship Album'. We were in Nashville and Ray was doing an album with some of his friends in the music business. Merle came in and asked me if we had anything Ray could do? I jumped and said 'Yes I do!' I had written this song, and the first time Deanie Bird heard it he said 'That sounds like a Ray Charles song.' So I set beside Ray at the piano stool and taught him my song '*Little Hotel Room*'.

Songwriter Bo Porter: Once you hear a Freddy Powers song, if you listen to it enough, whether Merle Haggard is singing it or Ray Charles is singing it, the way he phrases things, there's just a certain way he can write a turn of phrase. One of my favorite stories Freddy told me came when we were talking about how you cue up the song, where they come from, and I told him I'd been in a grocery store and heard a man talking about how his wife had left him, and the last thing I heard was "I didn't see that coming," and I'd gone out and wrote the story out in the truck.

So next I asked him, "*Little Hotel Room*", how did you write that song? And he says, "Well actually, me and Merle were supposed to do this radio thing up in New York, and I got there and this was back before cell phones, and I just had a piece of paper with a number on it but I'd lost it. But they knew I was going to be at the Waldorf, and at that time, the Waldorf was under construction, they were renovating it. So I figured I'd just go to my room and they'd find me, so I got there and got settled in and decided to order a bottle of wine, called down to room service and they sent it up. Well, this older black man comes up to the room, and he has the bottle of wine and two glasses, and asks me, 'Do you need one glass or two?', and I told him, 'I just need one,' and the man said to me, 'Oh, it's a one-man celebration'."

Then he said, "That started my song, that's the way it starts: 'A one-man celebration, ain't what I had in mind, sitting here sipping on this glass of wine'," and he said, "So I sat in the room, and like I said, it was under construction, and I noticed the plaster on the ceiling was just about to fall, and there was a picture hanging crooked on the wall. And I wanted to be at home, there's no place like home, and its lonesome in this little hotel room." Then he told me, "Everything I needed was in that room, and anything you need to write a song is right there around you, you just have to pay attention to it and be in tune to it." That is the mind of a genius, and one of the greatest songs I think he ever wrote was right there. He was so descriptive, he knew how to describe things, and the way he timed things and phrased things, the air in between words, when I hear that, I know its Freddy.

Chapter 9: Last Days on the Lake

Freddy Powers: Sometime in 1988, I had met this very sweet lady, Ann Pinto, and I introduced her to Deanie Bird. They hit it off right from the start and began dating. They had been together for a while and decided to get married. They wanted Merle to marry them, so Deanie Bird asked him if he would do it. Merle said he would if they found out how to get the appropriate licensing he would need to make it legal. I guess it was Anne who did the research and found the necessary forms you had to fill out in order to become a minister and be able to officiate weddings legally, and the next day, Merle had his people at his office send off for some kind of a certificate to show he was a minister. Lo and behold, the certificate came back legal and all!

Merle took the ceremony very seriously and was very nervous about it. He felt this to be sacred and not to be looked upon lightly. So he put his heart into this and though he has had several failed marriages himself, he married two people who were together till the day they did part by death. It was a wonderful ceremony on the front of Merle's houseboat. The whole crew was there. I remember how happy Deanie Bird looked standing there holding Anne's hand as Merle spoke of the vows they were making, and I played and sang '*Ridin' High*' for them. I was very happy and proud for him.

Anne Reynolds, Deanie-Bird's Widow: It was funny, because years earlier when I'd first met Freddy, he was a little standoffish at first because I don't think he wanted Dean to get interested in me because they were all this stuff with Merle, and I remember Freddy saying to him at one of the shows, "You better watch out Deanie Bird or you're gonna be married!" This was over a microphone at one of the shows, so he was a little bit nervous about me, but Dean and I were head over heels, we were inseparable and never a minute apart if we could help it, so soon, Freddy and I became like family too.

Years later, we were all on the road in Florida and we'd been carrying our marriage license around for like a year and there had never been any time to get married, so Merle called us up onto his bus, and the band only had one more gig left on that tour leg, and he said, "Why don't you guys leave tonight and go on back to Texas and get your things and then fly up to the lake, and we'll meet you up there and I'll marry you on the houseboats." This was the first we'd heard about that, so we flew up there, and he televised it, and it was beautiful. Biff's wife made our wedding cake, and I ordered our flowers and we had a lovely wedding. My older son gave me away and my daughters were my bridesmaids and maid of honor, and my family was there, and all of Dean's older children and our friends. It was quite a big crowd there on Merle's private pier, and even then there were people pressed up against the gate watching.

The day Dean and I were married, after we left, three of my four grown kids were there, and Freddy entertained them as though he was back in the Dixieland era, as a stand-up comedian, for two hours they said, and the whole time they absolutely laughed themselves hysterically to death. They said he was great, talked like a Swede, and was just hysterical funny.

Freddy Powers: Deanie Bird was a special man; he was friends with everybody. Nobody was a stranger to him. He made everyone feel welcome and comfortable like they belonged there. I loved Deanie Bird and so did everyone around him. Anne is also a wonderful lady and still to this day is a very dear friend of mine, though I don't see her much anymore. I know Deanie meant a lot to her and she loved him very much and missed him like I do. I'll never have another bass player that could read my mind and understand my style of playing like Deanie Bird could. And I miss my friend every time I set down to play.

Merle Haggard: I married him and his wife, I pronounced the ceremony. Deaniebird, he played fiddle and upright bass, and he was voted six years in a row # 1 bass player, he was a showman and also a good bass player. He was also a helicopter pilot and built his own steam engine, so he was really an intelligent guy and cooked Cathead biscuits. He was a master at several trades.

Anne Reynolds, Deanie-Bird's Widow: Dean was the
most generous man, he grew four acres of produce when he
came off the road, and would say, "It's just me and the
good Lord on the tractor," grew four acres of produce and
gave it all away. He'd get it all processed and bagged and
then give it to old neighbors and everybody who needed it.
It was his way of getting back in touch with the world. He
was very earthy, there was nothing phony about him, he
was very humble and always kind and happy.

Merle's father was an engineer and he adored his
father, who died right at his feet of a heart attack as a young
boy. He was so close to his father, and that's where he went
wild as a boy, and took off and started riding the trains and
getting in trouble. But he loved trains, and on his tour bus,
he had a train etched all the way down one wall of the bus,
it was beautiful. Not long after he married Dean and I, I
remember one day he said, "Let's rent a train car," and it
turns out you could rent them from a museum up there, an
antique car, and he put it on the back of an Amtrak, and
Freddy and Dean and me and Merle and one of his sons, we
pulled it across from Redding to Reno and then across to
Chicago, and they wrote some more songs, and I was the
cook. He didn't want anybody else to cook, he was very
particular about his food, and so we had a retired General
for a trainman and then a real trainman, and had the most
gorgeous antique car you ever saw. Its lovely, it was crystal
and china and fine linens and rugs that were woven and
fresh flowers.

Freddy Powers: As time went by Merle and Debbie broke up. Strange as it may be they remained friends and she stayed on as his maid and also worked in his office Hag Inc.

One day, this tall blonde showed up on the scene. She was with Clint Strong, the guitar player for both Merle and I. You could tell Merle was taken by her, and before you know it they were a new couple. Theresa Lane is her name, from Sacramento California. She was very quiet with a cute sense of humor. She ran with us for a while and the parties kept going.

Theresa and Merle kept getting closer and closer until they finally married in 1989. This time, Merle had another sunset wedding at his ranch, and believe it or not, Debbie – Merle's ex-wife- became close friends with Theresa and was Theresa's maid of honor at the wedding! After the wedding, she continued to work for Merle in the office for a long time after, but to me, even more beautiful than that, Bonnie Owens- Merle's second wife – also sang at their wedding. I say beautiful because I think it is really great when people can remain friends after a break-up. Theresa had already had their first child, a baby girl. With a baby, it was hard and dangerous to continue living on the house boat, so they moved off the lake and back to Merle's ranch. That ended the boat life as we knew it and the Spree of 83.

Merle Haggard: I moved off the boat to keep from dropping that baby in the water. She started crawling around, and she was six months old and starting to pull herself up on things, and I said 'Well, it's time we get off the lake', so I was looking for a cabin to move into, and somebody said, 'Well, you've got a cabin on your property'. And I said, 'I do?', went up there, found this old abandoned cabin and there was a cow standing inside the cabin when we found it. So we chased the cow out of there, and I said 'Well, this is just exactly what I'll need', so we fixed it up and moved in.

Freddy Powers: I continued to live on my boat for a while, but it wasn't the same. When Merle moved off the lake so did most of the party...

Merle Haggard: I've got a song called 'Favorite Memories' that was a number one song that came out of the lake life. It was very fertile songwriting ground. It was the right period of time in our lives. We were both healthy and both had a lot of experience.

Chapter 10: The Ballad of Freddy and Catherine

Catherine Powers: I fell in love with Freddy and knew in my heart he was going to be my man when I saw his picture on the cover of his *"Country Jazz Singer"* album. I took one look and said to myself, "Oh my god he is beautiful and I am in love, and I haven't even met him yet!"

Merle Haggard: The same time Freddy met Catherine, I met Theresa out there on the dock one day, and Fred had said to me, 'You know Merle, we can't keep these women,' and when I asked why, he said 'Because we're too fuckin' old!' They were young, and everything Fred said that day sounded right because I figured some younger fella would come along and run off with mine over the years, but it hasn't happened, and sure enough, he didn't know what he was talking about because we both still got 'em.

Freddy Powers: "I used to come where she was auctioning off clothes and I'd bring my girlfriends over there to buy clothes." 34

Catherine Powers: When I first saw him my heart felt like it had stopped for a moment and I couldn't breathe and my eyes had to be as big as silver dollars. It was a beautiful day, and Freddy was such a gracious host. He was very polite and I just hung on to everything he said all day (and in a very sneaky way I began to flirt with him, trying not to be obvious to anybody else). Freddy had a girlfriend he hadn't been dating very long, but he flirted back and made his move that evening when he and I finally had a moment alone walking up to the marina to get more beer. On the way back we were talking and walking along the ramp when, all of the sudden, he reached out and grabbed me by my waist and pulled me in close and said, "You and I would make a good couple."

It was a statement that would prove prophetic, but at first, I never really thought it would happen. Freddy's girlfriend was a singer also in the business, so I didn't really think I had a chance. But I was all over him every time he was around without being all over him at the same time (if you know what I mean). His girlfriend was generally with him so I had to be cool. But I think she knew. I'm sure my face couldn't hide how I felt about Freddy. This went on for about two years. Then one night we all went to see a George Strait concert. We all had passes where we could stay backstage or go out front to watch the show, and Freddy had asked me if I wanted go out front and watch the show with him. I agreed, and was lucky everybody else stayed back stage. I had been hoping for a chance to be alone with him. I thought to myself that if I ever had a chance to get him alone in a dark corner he would be in trouble.

We were sitting and talking, people were coming up and getting his autograph and he even introduced me as if I was somebody and they started getting my autograph too. It was fun, but he's a fun guy like that. Anyway we were waiting for the concert to start when he leaned over and whispered in my ear, "I want to feel your panties." Here I was finally alone with him and he's just blown me away with a line I never expected. At first, I moved away and looked at him like he was an old pervert, but then I thought "Wait a minute, this is what I wanted." So I scooched back over to him and said "I hope you do," and he did, feel my panties that is. He invited me up to his houseboat that weekend.

I snuck off up there and it was fabulous, he is such a romantic. I left overwhelmed and head over heels in love. Slowly, everybody began to find out we'd become the new item in town. It was pretty cool: he was an established celebrity and I was well known in the area for the fashion show I ran as the emcee and auctioneer. So I was a bit of a celebrity in town too. It wasn't long and we had moved in together. Our first place was a ski chalet on top of Kingsbury Grade in South Lake Tahoe. Freddy had never been a skier before, but he got into it because I loved it so much. He tried to go out there and just get after it. But he quickly found out it was not quite as easy as he thought. Even with all the practicing on the bed mattress with skis on. The first time out the door on the way to the chair lift – which is only about a hundred yards or so – and he fell so many times, I thought about giving up skiing to keep him from killing himself! Thankfully, he decided to go and take lessons from a pro, and then we were on the slopes almost every day. We had so much fun skiing. Every ski resort had a view made for a romantic ride on the lift, and we were like teenagers!

Freddy Powers: "We traveled all over the world together, and I had a couple of airplanes and we flew all over the country together. I was on the road with Merle Haggard about 15 days a month, and she traveled with us sometimes." 35

Catherine Powers: Freddy was also a pilot with his own airplanes, so if we weren't skiing, we were flying around the country just for breakfast or lunch. We'd fly back and forth over the mountains from Redding, CA to Lake Tahoe all the time. He knew how much I loved flying, and we had talked about me taking a crash course in landing just in case we were up flying and something happened I would at least be able to get us on the ground. Well, one day, right after it had snowed the night before and the roads were still slick I wrecked my car. Being the sweetie he is, he cheered me up by getting me my first flying lesson. Every day just got more romantic and special with Freddy. We lived out on his houseboat for almost three years and those were the most romantic days of my life. He would do things like sneak the houseboat out of dock, anchor down out in the middle of the lake and wake me up with a cup of coffee singing "*Peg Of My Heart I Love You.*"

For all our good times, one of the saddest things about memories I have of Freddy and I together in the early days of our romance, the houseboat days or even times like the day Ray Charles recorded "Little Hotel Room" is that there are no pictures. People didn't walk around with cell phone cameras in those days and most people didn't carry cameras on them. Actually, when Freddy tells me about a lot of days with people like Ray Charles and the houseboat days with Merle, I wish there were more photos. I even have very few pictures of the houseboat years of the houseboat years and all the people we met back then. Even in the early days after we moved back to Texas living on Willie's golf course, technology still hadn't caught up with us. Funny, I remember Freddy and my first cell phone weighed probably 10 pounds and looked like a big box that we left in our van when we sold it, and after all these years, the only thing that probably works on that phone any more is 9-11.

Linda Mitchell, Silverthorne Manager: One of the best things that ever happened to Freddy is the fact that Catherine came into his life, because I had never seen somebody so happy, and the day I met her, I fell in love with her, because it was real. It wasn't a one-night stand; it wasn't anything but pure love. Catherine was the first person I ever saw Freddy with where he wanted to be with her, I mean, literally, it was like the kindred spirits, they just clicked and there was not another man or woman in the world that could turn her face away from Freddy or his face away from Catherine. Catherine was a stable person in his life. I think she grounded him in a point that was just phenomenal. When she came into his life, that was it, that was totally it, and I'd seen the girls come and go but there was just something about her.

Freddy Powers: "We were driving through Lovelock, NV going camping, and I said 'Lovelock, sounds like a place to get married', and we pulled into a Justice of the Peace and got married on the courthouse lawn." [36]

Catherine Powers: Freddy never really asked me to marry him. Actually we both had said we were never getting married again. But we both had friends who were writers for local newspapers and they were always writing about Freddy, especially when he was playing in the area. So the very mention of us as a couple would give them the hankering to announce we were engaged, though we were not. That had never even been mentioned between us (at least not until we went to his cousin's funeral), where with his son standing there he introduced me to his family as his fiancée.

We had moved to Nashville about three years into the relationship when we had an argument and I was feeling insecure with us. He had just given me a white terry cloth robe, but, a few days before he had told me a story about his ex-wife and a white stained terry cloth robe. It wasn't a good story, so I was wondering what he was thinking. I thought he was trying to tell me I reminded him of his ex. So during our argument he just yelled out, "You know I love you," I looked back at him and yelled "Well you've never told me, so how was I supposed to know?", and there hasn't been a day since then that we haven't said I love you at least once a day, generally ten times a day.

We were getting ready for a camping trip to the Ruby Mountains in Elko Nevada with his brother Don and nephew Donnie when he finally popped the question officially. Freddy was mapping out our route when he said "Hey, we're going through Lovelock Nevada, you want to get married there?" I thought he was just kidding at first so I said, "What else would you do in Lovelock?" The next thing I knew, I was out buying a little summer dress to be married in. The next day we were in Lovelock before a Justice of the Peace. We were such hippies about the whole thing: I had gone into the restroom to change into my dress when a lady knocked on the door and told me I needed to hurry because it was going to start raining. We had to get married on the lawn because we had our dog Amelia and I wanted her to be my Maid of Honor. So with my jeans and hiking boots on I slipped on my dress, put my hair up in a French bun and we got married. Just as we were signing the marriage licenses it started to sprinkle which left a memorable water spot on them.

It was beautiful. On the lawn of this old court house, me standing there with a smile as big as Texas on my face and when the Justice told Freddy to take my hand, Freddy put his arm around me, pulled me in close and we looked like we had just been tied into a knot. The Justice of the Peace couldn't even look up at us without smiling. He knew he was marrying us for life. After Amelia finalized it with her paw print on the marriage licenses, we were on our way to join his brother and nephew for a romantic honeymoon up in the Ruby Mountains in Elko, Nevada.

Chapter 11: Road to My Heart

Catherine Powers: My honeymoon cottage was a hundred and fifty-year-old cabin with a dirt floor and half a roof. It was a ten-hour mountain climb that was supposed to be only a four-hour Hike. I thought it was going to take Freddy's life! It was so hard a climb that Amelia, our dog with four–wheel traction, laid down and looked at us like we were crazy and she was not going another step. Freddy gave his brother his backpack, picked up Amelia and carried her up this one steep hill. When we finally got to the top, Freddy said it was like he had stuck a needle in himself and it felt so good pulling it out, but it was worth it, it was so beautiful. We were in what once was a volcano with a beautiful lake and snow-topped mountains and this old cabin. We fished for our dinner that night and for the first time, I ate a fish that was looking back at me. The first couple of bites were hard, but they were so good that the eyes stopped bothering me and I ate at least ten little Brookies myself. He carved "Freddy and Catherine with Amelia 92" on every spot we visited in the ten days we were there. Our trip back down the mountain was a lot easier it only took about four hours to get back.

Don Powers Jr: My dad used to go up into the Sierra Nevada Mountain Range for health reasons every summer, and sometimes he would even stay all summer. So we were up there, and had already been for a couple of months, and Freddy and Catherine spent their honeymoon with us up there. We'd met Catherine only once before this, and it was funny because right about the time they were coming up there, my Dad and I were running pretty low on provisions, and were fixing to have to climb out of there go get stuff, and Freddy and Catherine looked like Santa Clause when they got up there! (laughs)

They come up the hill and here they've got a guitar, food and all of that, and they spent 10 days up there near Overland Lake for their honeymoon. There's around 10 lakes up there in those mountains, and Dad used to go up to every one of them, but you couldn't drive, you had to hike up there. That was the whole idea, we were trying to get out of the Casinos and get some exercise, because you don't get much standing behind Black Jack tables. Freddy brought a solar-bag that you hung up that was supposed to give you a hot shower, he said that was the only thing he'd be missing when he come up there would be a hot shower. Well, there wasn't enough sun up there with so many trees so he never did get that shower! (laughs) Then Catherine, when she first got there, after we all got through hugging and saying hello, handed me a *padded toilet seat*, and she said "I don't mind roughing it, but build me something around this," so we built her a little toilet and put a shower screen around it for privacy.

They had a sheltie dog at the time, Amelia, and she played with our dog, and those two had a ball up there in the mountains. Freddy and them would hike up to the lake and fish, and then come back down to where we were camped on a creek and cook dinner right there over the fire. A funny story, as it happened, while we were up there, a manhunt was underway for a fugitive trapper named Claude Dallas who had shot and killed a Game Warden, so we had our fire going and I guess some of the Indians who live up there saw the smoke from our camp fire and called the Sheriff. So just imagine, we're sitting there one day around that fire, getting ready to cook our freshly-caught dinner, and we're visiting, having a good time listening to Freddy play the guitar when I looked over to my right and here comes two guys with *Shot Guns*. I look over to my left, and there's *FOUR more* coming up the other side, and now they've got us surrounded!

At first, they thought we were this Claude Dallas guy, so Freddy – still holding his guitar – stops playing and says, "What's going on here guys?" So the head Sheriff is still holding that shotgun on Freddy while he's talking to him, and Freddy asks him, "Is that shotgun loaded?", to which the Sheriff replies, "It wouldn't do me much good if it wasn't." So next Freddy says, "Would you mind aiming that thing away from my leg?" Their next exchange was even funnier, because Freddy says "I don't know what's going on but my name's Freddy Powers...", and the Sheriff says "Oh I know who you are," and he had seen Freddy's show at the Casino in Elko, Nevada. We were camped right outside of Elko, anyway, that's the only thing that got us out from under suspicion in a hurry was that Freddy's celebrity preceded him – even up in the mountains!

Catherine Powers: As a wedding present, Freddy wrote me a song "*The Road to My Heart*," which he snuck into my purse as I was going out the door to the store. When I got in my car, put my purse in the seat and saw it, at first I didn't know what it was, then I saw my name on it "*Road to My Heart (Catherine's Song)*". I put it in the tape player and listened to it about ten times, crying every time. For our first anniversary, he wrote the words down on this pretty red material and framed it for me. Then when he recorded it in the studio for the "*Hottest Thing in Town*" album, Willie Nelson did a duet with him as I sat watching and listening. Willie knew it was my wedding song and how much it meant to me so he told me a story about his song "*Half a Man*" which is also a romantic story and how he got the idea for the song.

The Road To My Heart

You're on the road
On the road to my heart.
Just follow that old love light,
That brings you back to me.
You've found the way
To make me want to stay.
Make me want to stay around

And never part.
You read my mind I guess,
You're good at bringin' out my best,
And you're on the road to my heart.
Hey, you read my mind I guess,
You're good at bringin' out my best.
And you're on the road to my heart.
You're on the road to my heart.
... turn right at the mailbox!

I love to watch Freddy when he's writing. There's just something romantic about him when he's all wrapped up in a song. I can see him and I can hear him, but at the same time, it's as though he's behind a glass wall and I can't touch him. I'd sit for hours watching and listening to him play and write and never get tired of it. His music is what he's all about, and what makes Freddy Freddy – and not understanding that, one could never understand him. I am so proud to have someone like him in my life. His creativity is so profound that it almost rubs off on you, and makes you feel as though you could do it too. I have such great respect and admiration for my Freddy.

Freddy Powers: "I've told everybody in the business, don't offer me jobs on the road 'cause I don't wanna go on the road anymore. I'm sick of traveling, I won't even go to Elko. I made those fans when I was out there with Merle, I went out and saw my fans all this time. Now, my fans come and see me for a while." 37

Catherine Powers: When we came home from our honeymoon a friend called to tell us about this little cottage for rent. It turned out to be a little house that had been built in the mid-1800s for a honeymoon cottage. It was perfect, though it needed some work. We grabbed paint and brushes and had a blast fixing it up. We spent the winter skiing Mount Rose, which our cottage was at the foot of. We'd pack a picnic lunch and a bottle of wine or Yukon Jack, which at the time was the party drink of our little crew. We'd ski and drink Yukon to keep us warm {that was our excuse anyway} until lunchtime, then we would find a little place off to ourselves for a romantic view as we ate our picnic. Just about every day in the spring and summer, we rode our bicycles to the two parks on Franktown Road to have breakfast and to feed the animals. We'd stop at the first park to eat and feed the chipmunks and the birds. Then ride to the next park and feed the squirrels. Sometimes we would lay out our blanket and take a nap, or just lay there and talk and listen to the birds singing and the wind blowing through the trees.

We both love animals of all kinds. When we lived on the houseboat, Freddy bought me a rubber raft. I would have all the houseboat neighbors save their food scraps, collect them and as Freddy would get the binoculars and sit out on the deck, I would row myself over to the beach and

scatter the scraps all around. By the time I would get back
to the houseboat, all these animals would come out of the
woods to feast and we'd sit and watch them together. It was
fascinating watching the different rituals and habits of all
these different species of life.

The birds were the most interesting to us. While the
vultures would span their wings and turn from side to side
(we guessed to dry them?), the ravens would fly in, grab a
piece of food, then fly over to the rocks and hide it. We
wondered how they remembered where they hid it, with so
many hiding places. But we were sure that they got more to
eat than the vultures. Besides deer, we also had a wolf that
generally got there first to eat. He was also pretty cool. He
would come out of the woods just a little before feeding
time and come down to shore to drink and watch me load
up my boat and head his way.

Right before I'd get there he'd mosey back to the top
of the hill and watch me scatter out the food. Then when
I'd get back in my boat, he would mosey back down and
feast. I was really known as Ellie Mae around there. I feed
every animal out there including the fish. They'd come up
every night to an underwater light that we dropped down
from the fishing hole Freddy had cut in the living room
floor of the houseboat and eat right out of my hand almost.
We never had to fish in the rain, just lift the stern wheel he
had turned into a cover and set back and watch TV and fish
indoors. Of course, we also had ducks, and if a door was
left open, they would come on in and make themselves at

home. Freddy was asleep on the couch one afternoon and the ducks, he said, must have been hungry, because they came in and got right in his face and let out a quack that demanded his attention. So he got up and led them back to the water with dog food that we bought every week for them.

We lived in the honeymoon cottage for about a year then we found our dream house: a little cabin on the side of the Diamond Mountain range in the Plumas National Forest. I could stand on our front porch with a two-hundred mile view and look back at the Lovelock Mountain range where we got married. It was a small cabin with no electricity or running water. Freddy and I put in the plumbing ourselves, and made our own electricity. We did this out of water from a spring in our back yard. Freddy was so proud of his electricity. He had done this himself in a double door refrigerator he had buried on its back in the ground and with a Pelton wheel and a generator he made electricity. We spent our first three months up there lighting the place with oil lamps and bathing in our wood-heated hot tub. We chopped wood, raised a garden, and I did laundry in a wash tub and wringer by hand. It was old-school and we loved every minute of it!

Freddy and I were a great team all around, whether it be the outdoors or the music business, where we've worked together for the past 30 years. I'll never forget when Freddy and I first got together – the very first day we met – he looked at me and said, "We would make a great team," and it was true, we did, we just clicked right off the bat. I had already been in and around the entertainment business as a fashion model and actress, but as much as I loved being in front of the camera or on a walkway, I found myself drawn with equal fascination to everything that went on behind the scenes to make it happen. I was the type who was always I'm sure driving the producers nuts because I would ask them every technical-type question I could when I'm sure they wanted to say, "Lady, please zip it up and smile for the camera," but seeing I had that spark in my eye, they'd indulge me and eventually, I picked up enough of how a fashion show ran to begin putting on my own. I knew plenty of established and aspiring models to keep the runway busy, and by the time I met Freddy I was putting on charity fashion shows where I was acting as producer and auctioneer and emcee.

So I already had my foot in the door with all these Entertainment Directors and promoters around the West Coast who hired and booked entertainers like Freddy, and so when Merle had his baby girl Janessa and announced he wanted to take a break from the road, Freddy handed me the keys and said, "Start driving mama!" I saw every bit of the star that he was, and versusgoing with some veteran – of which he knew many – he entrusted me to become his booking agent and gave me that opportunity. From that moment on, Freddy and I have worked together on everything we've ever done since, from booking Freddy's solo tours to his celebrity charity events and Concerts to our Pickin' Parties, to the Rogers and Hammerhead TV show and albums we've Executive Produced together behind the scenes for Freddy, Merle Haggard, Mary Sarah, and on and on. Freddy has always been equally considerate and supportive of the fact I still had a career of my own as well in acting and modeling, and whenever I had a booking, he would work his schedule around those dates where he could, and where he couldn't – though we hated to be away from each other or miss any of the other's gigs – he was always supportive of me doing what I had to do.

Whenever we weren't on the road, we were back home at our mountain cottage, which was always an amazing escape because we also had forty acres with mountains to climb, small caves and mountain lions! For my birthday while I was in working on the movie "The Ty Cobb story," Freddy fixed up one of the caves that he had to take over from the mountain lions, and with wine, flowers and the dogs, that's where we spent the night. Freddy and I love the outdoors and love to camp. Every chance we had, that's what we did. Our camping gear was always ready. We have camped in some unusual and some dangerous places. One time, we had been driving out on this dirt road drinking blackberry brandy all day. The next thing we knew, it was getting dark and we hadn't found a camping spot yet and were over half drunk. So we pulled over on the side of a cliff and being too drunk to set up the tent, we just threw the tarp over the car and went to sleep. When we woke up later in the middle of the night freezing thinking it was cold outside, we jumped up to build a fire and found it wasn't really cold, it was the tarp holding in the cold from the night air.

One of our most dangerous campouts, now that we think about it, was in an old abandoned mining town called Masonic. We had been up there a lot and never really ran across too many people, so we decided to camp out there that night. Everything turned out okay, but we were really taking a chance. We didn't even carry guns with us back then and this is miner's country and any escapee hiding from the law "haven". Our funniest story though was camping with bears in Twin Lakes, California. We got there early that morning, and after we set up camp, decided to go for a short hike. We were walking along and Freddy started telling me, "Now we are in bear country, so if a bear shows up, don't run, whatever you do *Don't Run*." Here we are walking along and all of the sudden, I see bushes moving. I stopped Freddy in this conversation and pointed out the moving bushes, he looks up and says, "Oh shit! It's a bear!" He grabbed my hand and tugged tight on Amelia's leash, turned, and did the exact opposite of what he'd just been saying and started high-tailing it out of there. I remember running alongside him in fear, but laughing at the same time, saying, "I thought you said you're not supposed to run!"

Luckily, we looked back and the bear was doing the same thing we were, though running in the opposite direction! That evening, we watched closely especially for

Amelia while the bears walked in and out of the abandoned campsites looking for leftovers. The next morning, I went up to the bathhouse and after I took my shower and was ready to leave, went to open the door to only find {a couple of other ladies and I} were trapped in the bathhouse because there was a bear at the door going through the trash can. We started yelling for help, Freddy heard the screaming and came up to check it out. Here I was standing on the sink, yelling through this small window, which was more like a six slit at the top built that way to keep the animals out.

So now, with all these people yelling, Freddy and the Forest Ranger were outside trying to scare him off with his truck, and the bear just wasn't leaving until he was ready. He sat there on that trash can and ate until there was nothing left. Then, he slowly got off and moseyed on up the hill. Freddy said he'd never seen anything so funny as to see me with my head sticking out of this window screaming like a hyena. We still laugh about that weekend with the bears. Even as I write this story, I can't keep from giggling and at the same time I feel teary-eyed from the memory.

Freddy and I not only loved the camping for sleeping outside, but because hotdogs or scrambled eggs and bacon always taste better on open campfires. As I said, our cabin's property line backed up to the Plumas National Forest. There was this picnic area up there, so we and Amelia along with our hotdogs and buns would go up there and Freddy would dig out the campfire ring and with it snowing, us all bundled up we would have a picnic. While we waited for the fire to get started we danced to the crackling of the fire and the sounds of the falling snow. I got lucky, because most musicians don't dance, but Freddy is a wonderful dancer and loves to dance as much as I do. So we were always dancing. We'd be at parties and while everybody is laughing it up we are over in a little corner dancing all alone and being all romantic. I'll be in the kitchen cooking or cleaning and he'll come up and say, "You wanna to dance?", and I always accept.

We set back and look at some of our camping days back then and thank God we are alive to tell about them, but I wouldn't take a single trip back. We had so much fun and they were always so special. We would dance to no music but the sounds of Mother Nature by the campfire, or sit for hours watching our four-legged little fur doggie daughter explore the area. Amelia was kind of like our engagement ring. We made a commitment the night we got her that we would be together as long as we had her because we knew neither one of us would be able to give her up. It used to scare me, that if something happened to Amelia would our relationship survive (since she had everything to do with us making a commitment to each other). Though it broke my heart to lose her, I now know with all my heart Freddy and I will always be together, and there's nothing or no one can tear us apart. He's the man of my dreams. Freddy always went out of his way to do things that would make me happy or romance me all the time, and he's been that way since the day we got together.

He had a business trip to Oceanside, CA that he really wasn't interested in doing, so he decided we would make this a little vacation and he would show me around since he had been stationed there when he was in the Marines and I had never been there before. He got this little beach condo that had everything a guest would need, including bicycles, and we spent that morning with the accountants, which I thought would surely ruin the day, but we left there and sort of walked down memory lane for him as he showed me Alameda Naval Base. We didn't get to go in because he had not made necessary arrangements you have to get, but the guards knew of him as he had left his mark in guard stand with his military issued pistol. {By accident of course}. It was another one of those times he was goofing around and dropped his pistol and it went off and left a hole in the wall that had been fixed. So he had a reputation there for being more than the ex-Marine that turned entertainer and songwriter.

He'd fallen asleep on guard duty one night standing up leaning against the guard building when the sergeant came by and accused him of being asleep on duty. Freddy jumped to attention and told him, "I wasn't asleep, I was just resting his eyes." The sergeant looked at him and said, "Oh yeah Private, it looks to me like the rest of your body joined in too!" From there, we left and headed over to this bar that he used to play at back then. When we walked in, Freddy said it looked exactly the same, so we sat down and had a drink and he told me stories of those days. After that, we went back to our romantic condo and had an eyebrow lifting evening. {umm bet your wondering}. The next morning after we had breakfast, we rented two of the property bikes and spent the day riding around town. Well, you've all seen the, "Have you got any Grey Poupon" commercial? Here we are riding bicycles when a stretch white limousine pulls up beside us and Freddy reaches over, knocks on the window and says, "Excuse me sir, but do you have any Grey Poupon!" Of course everyone cracks up laughing as they sped away honking.

That evening he had planned on us going out to a fancy restaurant and having wine and maybe some dancing. But I had seen this Der Wienerschnitzel hotdog stand that I hadn't seen since I left Texas. So I persuaded him into going there instead. We got back on the bicycles rode to the Der Wienerschnitzel and had hotdogs, at a picnic table on the street corner. Once again, it turned romantic having hotdogs watching the traffic go by and having a cross between a moonlight and sundown bike ride back to the condo. As the sun started setting in the West, the moon was already full and high in the sky (not to mention this was all with the beach right alongside of us). I've probably had more girl's dreams come true than any other women I know. So many things we've done, most would only be a dream.

Chapter 12: Rogers and Hammerhead

Freddy Powers: After Merle and I moved off the houseboats, I'd moved back to Lake Tahoe and played around Reno and the surrounding area, but that had even changed because the Casinos had begun to feature lesser-known acts who would pay for almost nothing, and most of the classy lounges were gone for more gambling devices. Entertainment became less than important to the casinos, and after trying out Nashville and our adventure living up in the Mountains, Catherine and I decided in 1994 to move back home to the Lone Star state. We set up shop on Willie Nelson's golf course.

Willie Nelson: He lived right there on hole # 7.

Texas Music Magazine: "Their home, the house where Willie Nelson hid out from the IRS when his taxes were just a tad overdue, bears a wall collage littered with enough accolades to satisfy every musician who ever graced the stage of the Grand Ole Opry, including a BMI placard recognizing more than a million radio spins of 'Let's Chase Each Other Around the Room, award nominations for the Rogers and Hammerhead Show he hosted through the '90s; and dozens of awards for hits covered by the business's brightest stars."

Catherine Powers: It was amazing how quickly our life in Austin blossomed once we had settled back in Austin. Personally, I could tell Freddy was excited to be living next door to another of his best friends and clown-around pals in the business, and let me tell you what, like Freddy said, Merle and he were more akin to Tom Sawyer and Huckleberry Finn, and then once you added Willie Nelson into that club, no matter how much older he and Freddy have gotten over the years, whenever they got together, they were all like little boys! By that point, Willie and Freddy's friendship had gotten pretty intuitive like he and Merle's had by that point after knowing each other for so many years, to where Willie could start a joke and Freddy would finish it. And even when he was on tour, and it didn't matter if he was touring the U.S. or somewhere thousands of miles away, whenever he would hear a new dirty joke, Freddy was one of the first people he would call to tell, and they'd go back and forth like that all the time, almost like a competition to see who could tell the newest joke first!

It cost a small fortune too, because I can remember more than a few times over the years being woken up out of a dead sleep at three in the morning to the sound of our phone ringing with Willie on the other end calling from overseas somewhere after he'd just heard a new crack and couldn't wait to tell Freddy! I'm not kidding, because though Willie did a lot of the calling, I can honestly say I've sat back at times and looked at *our* phone bills and had

to shake my head laughing at how many long-distance and
international calling minutes were burned up with those
two calling each other back and forth with new jokes! So
alongside music, throughout the 60+ years they've known
each other, another strong part of their bond has always
been the joke-telling, and they would crack each other up
so hard it was instantly infectious to anyone else sitting
there listening, and I'm not talking where people were
laughing just because it was Willie Nelson telling the joke,
he could always see right through that, but because they
were both genuine comedians. I swear if they hadn't been
musicians, they could have had their own two-man comedy
act!

Don Powers Jr: They all loved jokes, and to show you
how quick a joke gets around, me and my dad used to write
comedy material for Freddy when he was doing Dixieland
Jazz and comedy, so we called up one time and told Freddy
a joke, Freddy told Merle, Merle told Willie, and two
weeks later we heard our joke on the Tonight Show!
That's how quick a good joke got around between those
guys!

Marc Oswald: Freddy's the funniest guy, he called me
one time, and didn't even say hello, so as soon as I picked
up the voice, he said 'Willie's pissed,' and I said 'Fred,
how you doing?', and he goes 'Not too good, Willie's
pissed?' So next he says, 'Willie keeps calling me from the

road, and everywhere he goes, he's hearing another joke,' because everyone wanted to share their jokes with Willie. Then Fred says, 'He's been calling me because I'm sick, and he's been cheering me up, and calling me every day or two with a new joke that he hears out on the road. Of course, I'm home sick here and can't stand it, so I've been out walking around the golf course, and every time I hear a new joke, I tell everybody here at the course the joke, and everybody laughs. Well, then Willie gets home from tour with all those new jokes, starts telling them, and I'd already told every single one of them, so he's pissed!' (laughs) Willie and Freddy are best friends, and that little group of Willie, Freddy and Merle, they're a gang, they're a posse, and do like to help each other out and really care about each other.

Catherine Powers: Whenever Willie was home off the road, being such close friends and neighbors, it seemed like he and Freddy were always together, and I've been there many, many, many times over the years when Willie and Freddy got stoned together where they would pick up their guitars and just pick and play and play for hours and hours, and sometimes days! It's funny too because from what I've seen, there's no real difference in his personality from when he's not stoned to when he is. It's like he has said himself many times, he's been smoking pot for so many years that he doesn't feel like he's stoned even when he is. (laughs) It's the same way with Freddy, except now I

213

notice the difference because of what pot does to calm his Parkinson's symptoms down.

Freddy was at a video shoot years ago working with Big & Rich, Merle and Gretchen Wilson, and Freddy and Gretchen were sitting in the back of the Limo – in fact there was a documentary film crew recording this – and it was funny because Freddy said, "I need to get high" and right there *on camera*, lit up and took a big old hit off his joint. Well, right about that time, Gretchen asked him, "Freddy, do you like getting high?", and he answered her with an expression that has long been a true inside joke among his friends: "If you see me, I'm high," and then laid down out of view of the camera and said, "and if you don't see me, I'm high!" (laughs) With that, he laid back up in view of the camera again, took another big old hit and started coughing, and next Gretchen says, "Well, is it good?", and he leaned back and said "Shit yeah!"

I remember one time when we were living on Willie's golf course when he called Freddy from home and asked him, "Freddy, do you wanna get higher than you've ever been in your whole life?" Well, of course, Freddy's response was "Well, hell yeah!", and Willie said, "Well, come on up," which meant going in our back yard because we were neighbors, he lived behind us. This was when the vaporizers had come out back when they were still these big old machines, and Willie had just gotten one, so Freddy goes on up there and a couple hours later, I get this hilarious call from him saying "Mama, I'm lost..." Now, you've got to remember, Willie lives right behind us up on the hill, and you could *see our house* from his with just a street between us, but still he insisted, "I can't find my way home," and when I chuckled and asked him where he was, in a worried tone, he continued, "I don't know, I just left Willie's and started driving and now nothing looks familiar, I don't know where I am." He and Willie had gotten so stoned that Freddy'd literally forgot where he lived, and he knew that neighborhood well. We still joke about it to this day, and our punchline always gets the biggest laugh: "Now that's getting high with Willie!"

If they weren't playing music for hours on end, they played A LOT of golf, and stoned golf too because I'd be able to see them from our back porch when they were playing on a hole near our house, and routinely, I'd chuckle as I watched little clouds of smoke appear above their golf cart! (laughs) Willie had a pool table up at his house, and they loved to play pool together too. They were REALLY a hoot when they'd get high and had been drinking a little bit together, the two of them were so funny and would sometimes even go out to Willie's World Headquarters Ranch where there's a whole actual main street town designed like it was straight out of the 1800s Wild West where he and Freddy would play cops and bank robbers, they were a hoot!

Anne Reynolds, Deanie-Bird's Widow: The first time Willie and Merle got together to record, they had

215

never been together, and Freddy and Dean and I were there
at the Golf Course, and Merle's bus came in and it was
Thanksgiving, so somebody brought a catered dinner, and it
was all of Merle's entourage – which was a lot of guys –
and I was the only female there, and we were staying at this
one fella's house. So I was the cook, and then the day after
Thanksgiving, we were supposed to be gone by then,
finished with the recording, and we weren't because they
were all getting on so well. Merle and Willie and Freddy
and Deanie were all there milling around the house, and in-
between these hours of what they called *Pickin'*, I became
the defacto cook and made my famous Turkey Soup recipe,
which is all the left-overs from Thanksgiving put in a pot,
and they loved it! Merle even took it on the road when he
left.

Edith Royal: We'd first met Freddy after he and
Catherine moved out there onto Willie's course. After the
children were out of school, we had eventually moved out
by Willie and had a house on the lake out there, so we all
hung out together all the time, and Darrell played golf with
Willie nearly every day. He always went to the studio with
Willie after their golf game was over, and Darrell loved
being around music, and he either met Freddy there or at
one of Darrell's golf tournaments Willie invited him to, but
Darrell and Freddy became fast friends. Then, after the
Longhorn games, we'd always have pickin' parties at our

house, and Freddy was always there for those playing with Willie and the boys all night.

Molly McKnight: Everybody got to know everybody from wherever they'd came from – Oklahoma to California – and James Garner would always play, and Don Cherrie, and Terry Bradshaw and his wife were there, just people who loved music, and what they would do is: they'd play golf and one member of each group would be an entertainer, and they'd be teamed up with famous athletes, astronauts, and we even had a blind guy that played! So the pickers – like Willie and Freddy and Johnny Gimble, who was always there, Floyd Tillman, Sonny Throckmorton, and Whitey Shafer – all got to know all the celebrities, it was just a conglomeration of entertainers playing golf for charity. Then after everybody finished their golf games, they'd have time to come in and shower, then they'd have a dinner, and then the music would start, and once the music would start, Darrell would say "Red light," and everybody whose ever been to a Coach Darrell Royal Pickin' Party knows what that meant: shut up. If they didn't, then Darrell would remove them, no matter how famous they were, that's just how it was. If you were gonna be there, you'd better shut your mouth. Darrell thought it was rude while the entertainers were singing or playing for the audience to talk, and it really is if you think about it, because a lot of places you go to hear an entertainer, a lot of times you can't because the crowd's so loud. But Coach Royal didn't put up with that.

Catherine Powers: Freddy grew close to another true original when he met Bill McDavid at one of Coach Darrell Royal's Golf Tournaments. In that spirit, Coach Darrell Royal was a key to a lot of people's relationships, especially in the music industry. A lot of people credit Coach Royal for helping launch or advance their careers, George Strait being one example. There are so many people who would just have to say if it hadn't been for Coach, they may not have gone on as far as they did, or had the support network that they had.

Edith Royal: Willie moved to Austin from Nashville in the 70s because he couldn't get any gigs, and one time he was here, he couldn't even pay the band, he said, "I'm gonna have to move back to Nashville because I don't have enough money this week to pay the band," and Darrell said "No, don't do that Willie because I'm gonna rent a place here for you, and everybody has to come and pay $25 for a couple, and that will include all the beer they can drink," and Willie said, "Well, I don't think anybody will come. They're not coming to my gigs, so why would they come to that?" And Darrell said, "Well, I'm gonna ask everybody in the Athletic Dept. to come, and they'll come and pay $25," and Willie got enough money to pay his band and stayed. So Willie was just amazed, because he wasn't getting any money from his gigs, but he got a whole bunch of new fans from that, because everybody in the Athletic Dept. started listening to country music after that and coming to his gigs, and his friendship with Coach just kind of grew from there.

Sonny Throckmorton: Coach Darrell Royal was a great influence for music in Texas. He was a big part of Texas Music over the latter 20, 30 years, he had a big hand. He knew all the entertainers, and was always friendly because Coach just loved singer/songwriters, he just loved them and treated them good, and gave them breaks and invited them to do things they probably wouldn't have gotten to do otherwise. In fact, I met Freddy at Darrell Royal's golf tournaments down in Houston, he would come down and entertain and play golf, as we all did, and first they were Coach Darrell Royal Golf Tournaments, then became Darrell and Willie, and then it was a Ben Crenshaw, Darrell and Willie, but those 25+ years of tournaments were all one in the same because they all had Darrell. So I got to be friends with him, and that was probably about 20 years ago. I dearly love Freddy.

Catherine Powers: Coach was a major supporter of musicians and football players, and Freddy first met Coach through Willie Nelson, who was living in Austin, Texas while Darrell Royal was the Coach for the Texas Longhorns. Well, once Willie introduced Freddy and Coach, they hit it off immediately and became very close friends. It was funny, one time, Coach rattled off our home number from memory to someone else who'd asked for it, and that shows you how close they were. Coach was even close with our dog Amelia, who was a singer, and he was fascinated by that, and even brought the current Coach Mac Brown of the Longhorns out to hear our dog sing. Well, as soon as Freddy started singing her song, "*Soldier Girl*," Amelia stood up and started performing, and when she would do that perfect for him and he would show her off, then he'd take her for a ride on the Golf Cart.

Edith Royal: Back when he was growing up in Hollis, Oklahoma, we used to listen to the Grand Ole Opry, that was about the only time we had any music there, and then he grew up in the Church of Christ where they didn't allow instruments, but they all sang acapella without any instruments. So he grew up singing himself in church, and then after we were married, we still listened to Country/Western music, and we listened to all kinds of music. He coached in Durham, North Carolina at one time and Louis Armstrong came to town, and this was a dance – before integration, so the white people couldn't dance, they had to sit up in the balcony and watch and listen to the music. Then when we'd get a chance to visit New Orleans, we always went to hear Fats Domino and all of the Jazz people, so we just grew up loving music of all kinds. We never went to the symphony, but always attended the Jazz and Country Music events any place they were going on, we were there. So then when we landed in Texas and Darrell coached the Longhorns, country music was just a natural fit, and there was lots of it.

So Darrell loved music, and he loved all those guys – Willie, Freddy, Merle, and songwriters like that. They were all very interesting people, and the writing of the songs, he loved to be there to hear how they came about writing something and what it was about, and how it started. He loved all of that, he just loved the music and musicians. After games, they'd come over to my house – including Freddy a lot of times – and I'd have food for them there, and they'd stay playing until we'd go to bed. One time we had Mickey Mantle there, and all of the pickin' was going on, and when it was time to go to bed, we had extra beds, and put them all to bed but Mickey was the last one who wanted to go to bed so we had to make a pallet for him on the floor in front of our bed. That was an interesting night, there were lots of them and it was always fun.

Catherine Powers: We all used to say that his name was the most appropriate name anyone in his position could ever be given, because Darrell and his wife Edith were Texas Royalty. They are more loved and more respected and more well-known than anybody else in the entire state of Texas. You put Willie Nelson and Coach Royal in a room together and you have two of the most famous people in Texas, and Willie's going to get some of the attention, but Coach Royal would get all the attention. I was lucky enough to even have Golf lessons from Coach when he was the Golf Pro at the Barton Creek Country Club when he retired from football. Coach and I are the ones who put on Freddy's 70th Birthday Party. It was a huge roast, and Merle roasted Freddy and were able to pull off a completely surprise birthday party, to where even when Freddy walked in the room, he still had no idea that the party he was at was for him. It took him a moment before he caught on, it was amazing how people played along so well.

One of the characters Freddy met at one of Coach's tournaments was Bill McDavid. They immediately hit it off and became best friends, and stayed close a good 40 years before Bill passed away.

Bill McDavid: "I was out there making money, but I was also hanging out with Freddy for 20 years. I can't remember exactly when we met, but it had to be at one of Coach Darrell Royal's Golf tournaments back in Galveston." (Source: Austin Songwriter Magazine, May, 1997, by Sharon Jones-LeFlore)

Catherine Powers: Bill came to one of our golf tournaments for the Nevada Special Olympics, and bought one of the guitars we were auctioning off that day. Bill had never played before and wanted to learn, so Freddy taught him two chords and spent the weekend picking with him to get him familiar with playing them and switching back and forth, the basics. Well, a few weeks later, Bill called Freddy back up and said, "I've written this song I want you to help me with," and when we hung up, at first I remember Freddy saying "Hell, I'm looking forward to seeing Bill, but he's written this song and its probably not going to be worth a shit, and I won't know how to tell him…" Even I could see he was real nervous about seeing Bill, and next thing you know, we're sitting in the room, and I watched this whole scenario play out first hand: Freddy had a plastic grin plastered on his face not knowing what to expect as Bill excitedly whipped out that guitar he'd won at our auction, and with those two chords Freddy had taught him, shocked us all as he began playing this song. I could tell that Freddy was genuinely surprised by the end, because the first thing he said once Bill had stopped playing was "Holy crap Bill, you've written a great song!"

Freddy Powers: "I was visiting with Bill about two and a half years ago, and someone had shown him a chord on the guitar he had recently bought. I was really happy to see Bill learning how to play a guitar, so I showed him a couple more chords. Next time I saw him, he knew those chords real good, so I showed him a little bit more. In March of 94, I came down here to record and I've been here ever since. I started giving Bill full-time guitar lessons and he's wrote a song, '*Me and My Drummer*', which has now been recorded by two major artists: Willie Nelson and Doug Supernaw…. It's like "My Way," only it's country. I had to march to the drummer in me. Willie Nelson and Merle Haggard said the same thing – it's a damn good song." 38

Bill McDavid: "Freddy was the first person to take me serious, which he did a long time before anyone else did... Willie was the first person I sung 'Drummer' to." (Source: Austin Songwriter Magazine, May, 1997, by Sharon Jones-LeFlore)

Catherine Powers: After that, Freddy was now all of a sudden excited and right there, showed him a few more chords, and Bill – like Freddy – proved to be one of those people who, when he set his mind to doing something, he wanted to learn everything he could and become the best he could at it. He had been a Quarter Horse champion, for instance, and the next thing you know, the very first song he ever wrote based off those chords Freddy taught him wound up being recorded by Willie Nelson. After that, Freddy and Bill started writing together regularly, and as they started going out and playing a little bit together around town, Willie wound up watching one of their gigs and joking around afterward said they looked like a couple of Hammerheads, and was the one to actually give them what became their moniker as songwriters, music publishing company and ultimately the name of their Cable television show. They started writing a lot of songs together after that first one, and even had a couple Christmas songs recorded by the Texas Girls' Choir. Freddy always was very supportive of the Texas Girls' Choir, in fact, we did a fundraiser for them one time hoping to raise $10,000 and wound up raising almost $300,000! What we all laugh about looking back on Freddy and Bill's working relationship is that Bill was 60 years old before he ever picked up a guitar, strummed his first two chords, or wrote his first song!

Freddy Powers: "We were sitting around discussing what to call our publishing company and just talking about songwriting when I said, 'Bill, you and I might turn out to be the next Rogers and Hammerhead of country.' You know, the country version of Broadway. That's where it started. Everybody laughed about it at first, but now nobody is laughing. We've got a TV show going once a week featuring major songwriters: there's Gary P. Nunn, Doug Supernaw, Sonny Throckmorton, Aaron Baker, Ray Wylie Hubbard, Rusty Weir, Steve Fromholz, Larry Gatlin, the Geezinslaws, Merle Haggard, Floyd Tillman, and Willie Nelson." [39]

Bill McDavid: "We started it to provide a place for songwriters to get their songs heard…. We're strong believers in divine intervention because we're not smart enough to have made this happen. I see the Rogers and Hammerhead Show becoming as popular as Johnny Carson. We market ourselves, we've got so many friends in the music business." (Source: Austin Songwriter Magazine, May, 1997, by Sharon Jones-LeFlore)

Catherine Powers: Not long after Freddy and Bill first hatched the idea for the show, we met Randy Willis, who was one of those kind of go-getters there in Austin, and he had quite a resume of production credits from T.V. and Film, and he and Freddy started about doing a T.V. show. Freddy and Bill's concept was simple: invite songwriters to come on and play their songs and then talk about the craft of songwriting afterward, so there was a performance and guest segment for the songwriters, which was a first-of-its-kind format. During the first season, they had a policy where every songwriter appearing as a guest on the show had to have one hit or more under their belt, so the guest would play their song, and then Freddy and his co-host Bill McDavid would ask them questions like, "What inspired you to write that song?" and, "How did you become a songwriter?" and, "How do you write your songs? Do you write your melodies first or do you write the words first?" They talked a lot about structuring, and also talked a lot about the music industry: "How do you get a song out there to be plugged and picked up by a recording artist?" So the show focused on the whole songwriting process and the business of being a professional songwriter. It was an educational songwriting show, and they had everyone from unknown, up and coming songwriters to legends like Willie Nelson, Merle Haggard, the late, great Floyd Tillman, to

Larry Gatlin, Aaron Barker, Steve Fromholz, Doug
Supernaw, and as a matter of fact, the last two shows that
were ever done for Floyd Tillman was the one he did for
Rogers and Hammerhead, and the same for Rusty Weir.
Being a talk show hosted by songwriters, and of course,
those would turn into Pickin' Parties.

Molly McKnight: I was freshly divorced, and had a
little boy named Peyton who was four years old at the time,
and he took to Freddy like a duck to water. He called him
"*The Man With the Stars on His Hat,*" because Freddy
always wore this beret that had four stars on it.

John Rich of Lonestar/Big & Rich: Our manager,
Mark Oswald, along with his brother Greg – and another
guy named Bill McDavid– have known Freddy since back
in the early 80s when Mark, my manager, and Greg, my
booking agent, were promoting Merle Haggard concerts out
on the West Coast.

They got to know Freddy then and all of Merle's band,
and kind of became running buddies with these guys, and
really got to know Freddy very well from sitting around
jamming with them and watching Freddy write all those
Merle Haggard hits, and hearing all the great stories.
Freddy's a blast, Freddy's a party, he's hilarious! And at
that point, stories are still being made, back in the 80s was
when Haggard was probably at the peak of his career. That

was as hot as he ever was, right through there, Freddy and him were hooked at the hip.

So when Mark and Greg started managing and booking Big & Rich, we were down in Texas for a concert, and Mark suggested we go over to Freddy's house, he said 'Freddy lives on Willie Nelson's golf course', to which I replied 'No Kidding!' And he continued, 'Yeah, they live on Willie's golf course, and they have these big jams- let's go over there….' So we rolled over to Freddy's house, and the first thing we saw when we walked in was a giant Neon sign hanging in the living room that said 'Rogers and Hammerhead,' which was Freddy and Bill's band.

I didn't really know Freddy very well at that point, only that he'd written with Merle, and knew Willie and all that stuff. So we sat down, pulled out the guitars, poured a couple of cocktails, and started going around in a circle with everybody playing a song, and what'a ya know, Freddy starts rattling off some of my all-time favorite country songs: *'Chase Each Other Round the Room Tonight', 'Natural High', 'Friend in California',* on and on. And I could NOT believe it! I was just floored, being a songwriter myself, that I was sitting in a room with the guy who had written all these songs.

Past that, watching him play the guitar was really something else, the guy was ripping jazz licks left and right that were Willie Nelson on kill! It was actually probably better than Willie, it was the real, real high-end educated jazz licks in these country songs. So I asked Freddy, 'When did you start putting jazz licks into country stuff?' And he said, 'Always, I've always done it.' So next I asked him, 'Is that where Merle got a lot of his sound and his style?' And Freddy wouldn't take credit for that, but he said, 'Well, we have sat around swapping licks for many, many years', and I was so intrigued by Freddy at that minute that I decided: 'This is a Honky Tonk hero', and that I needed to dig down in him as far as I could and really understand this guy. I just had so much reverence for what he had accomplished in country music.

Pauline Reese: I feel like people think of him as kind of like a Godfather-type presence in songwriting, and they're kind of nervous to go up and talk to him. I've watched other artists around him who are just meeting him for the first time, or are getting to know him or watching him, and they're just so humbled when they're around him that they actually get nervous! I remember John Rich and Big Kenny from Big and Rich, when they were around him, they were just enamored with his presence, every time they were around him – even up through his Parkinson's taking over. They just really respect him and would always listen to what he had to say, there was no talking over Freddy. Everybody listened to what he had to say, and that was another lesson he taught me was, "If you want people to listen, don't yell, don't turn up your amp, don't play louder, play softer, because then they have to be quiet to hear you

because they hear themselves talking and knock it off."
That was a huge lesson he taught me.

John Rich: He played '*Georgia On My Mind*' one
time at a pickin' party, and I'd never seen that many chords
put into that song before. I remember after he got through, I
said 'Alright, you gotta show me how you just played all
that!' So he said: 'Alright, well, here's the first chord,
here's the second chord…' and as he started moving
through it, he lost me after about the third or fourth move.
And I watched him play it, and went 'Unbelievable!',
because he was playing a guitar like people play a piano,
with so many inversions of the same chords, and knowing
how to move them around and create a new atmosphere
around a chord is really something extraordinary that he
does.

Catherine Powers: We wound up on Austin's Public
Access Cable television station, and being that Austin has
as large a musician and songwriter population as it does,
the show quickly caught on and had quite a large viewing
audience each week. We'd film three shows at a time, and
it's kind of funny because if you watch the shows, you will
see how we actually learned how to make a set look better
and how to make the lights work better, more like filling up
the room. It had gotten to where I almost hated to dust in
there because we had so many books, candles and trinkets
of all kinds stacked up on top of each other because it made

the room look bigger and fuller. So we learned a lot about production tricks, those little things that would make the show look more professional, because we were trying to make it as special as we could. In fact, if you watch the first couple of shows, you'll see how the lighting was a little bit dim and the living room doesn't look full, and then as the shows go on, you'll see the room was getting fuller, and then we started panning over to the audiences.

We had three cameras, and would have an audience of 50, 75 people sitting out there – just like the Pickin' Parties – along with all the lights, we were lucky to have a nice-sized living room to pull all that off in looking back on it now. We had a great, big stone fireplace that was part of the backdrop Bill and Freddy sat against as they filmed, and as a matter of fact, whenever tornadoes would come through that part of Texas and tear a house down, those big old stone fireplaces would be the only thing left standing. It was grand, and I would always keep that fireplace cleaned out and ready in case we needed a place to take shelter during a tornado, that's where we would go.

Applause Magazine, February, 1996: "Freddy lives in a big house on the edge of Willie Nelson's golf course. As I entered the room, I noticed Darrell Royal relaxing in a chair and in the center of the room, dressed in a jogging suit with a red bandanna, sat Willie Nelson. I had just entered into that sacred space where Willie jams with friends just because he loves it… Freddy Powers and Bill

McDavid have Hammerhead Publishing Company, and they film a television show in this very living room, a show that features interviews with songwriters."

Catherine Powers: When we got nominated for a Cable Ace Award in 1998, we all loaded up with our production crew and producer from Time Warner, and went to the award show together. Well, when it got to our category, they called out the three nominees, and we were all sitting there like kids waiting for them to announce the winner, and when they said "Louisiana Juke Box" instead of Rogers and Hammerhead, of course, all our faces collectively dropped down together at the same time, and our excitement left, but our table managed to be courteous and applaud the winner. I remember Bill McDavid was really visibly bummed out about it until someone said to us, "Hey, what are you pouting about, you were three nominated out of 500 entries!" So it felt like whether we went home or not with the award that night, that we'd still won.

I learned a lot on that show, because I'd done a lot of movies in Reno and had learned a lot on set about how to be a camera assistant and a make-up artist, and so I was our floor director on the Rogers and Hammerhead Show. Rogers and Hammerhead – you would have to almost say – was a crew of Freddy and Bill and their spouses, Sheri and I, because the four of us always worked together on getting the guests booked, and just every end of the spectrum you can imagine has to be produced running a television show, especially considering that the set was our living room. So really we were all producers on the show, and we all had positions: I did the make-up, I was the floor director, I assisted with the cameras, I wore all kinds of different hats.

We were honored to be the last television show the legendary Floyd Tillman, who had a whole career of # 1s, from *"They Took the Stars Out of Heaven"* to *"I Love You So Much It Hurts"* and *"Slippin' Around"*, *"G.I. Blues"*, *"Drivin' Nails in My Coffin"*, *"I'll Never Slip Around Again"*, *"I Gotta Have My Baby Back"*, *"Each Night at Nine"* and on and on. Freddy was always particularly proud of the fact that Floyd made his last T.V. show appearance on Rogers and Hammerhead before he passed away, along with the distinction of the last show he ever played was being on stage with Freddy in Austin. Our show was also the final interview for Rusty Weir, who was another big songwriter and Texas star best known for *"I Heard You Been Layin' My Old Lady"* and *"Don't It Make You Wanna Dance"*. So that T.V. show, just by the stroke of luck, we had some of the last interviews with major Texas music stars, which was the whole point of the show really, to put a spotlight on Texas songwriting.

Along with our own television show, Freddy also stayed very active playing out on the live scene around town, and he would play shows with Bill, and even took him on tour to Europe with us. One really exciting filmed performance came on the world-famous Austin City Limits television show, where he taped an hour-long set playing with Willie and Merle where they each sang a verse, and one of our favorite moments from that show. You can still see it on YouTube today, the night at Austin City Limits when Freddy sang Bill McDavid's song live on the air. It was very touching to Bill, and I know it meant a lot to Freddy to be able to do that for him, and again, was another example of a great writer with a lot of promise that Freddy helped get started in the music business, something he always felt proud of throughout his career.

Freddy Powers on Austin City Limits, 1996: "My friend Bill McDavid wrote this song, I'm so proud of him because it's the first song he ever wrote in his life. Not only this, but Willie and the Offenders do it as the title song in one of Willie's new movies!"

Chapter 13: The Romance Continues…

Catherine Powers: On our tenth wedding anniversary we went to Paris and with Floyd Domino {a famous Texas piano player and Grammy winner}, went to the top of the Eiffel Tower and with Floyd acting as Minister, we re-announced of wedding vows. I couldn't believe I was in Paris, but to be re-marrying the man of my life I can't help from feeling like the luckiest girl in the world. We also went to Rome and Switzerland on that trip. Actually that was not the first time Freddy and I repeated our vows to each other. We were best man and bridesmaid for some friends of ours that got married in Reno, and as the minister asked them to repeat after him Freddy looked at me and begin lip speaking, silently repeating everything after the Minister as if we were the ones getting married, so I did the same. When he said you may kiss the bride, after they kissed Freddy leaned over and kissed me.

All our anniversaries are something to talk about. We've only had one that we spent alone. Remember our honeymoon was with his brother and nephew camping in the Ruby Mountains, and our first anniversary was none other than camping, this time with his son and new daughter-in-law. Our second and third was with three hundred or so guests we hosted for a golf tournament in Freddy's name to raise money for the Special Olympics. Freddy has been a longtime supporter of the Special Olympics, and for years and years put on celebrity golfing tournaments and performances to raise money for this cause, which has continued to remain especially close to his heart throughout the years.

Reno Gazette-Journal: "You've got several world-famous friends, and dozens of your other buddies are fairly popular across the United States as well. Instead of bragging, or spending all your time schmoozing with your pals, you get them all together to raise money for charity – the Special Olympics. Well, that's what Reno resident Freddy Powers and his wife, Catherine, are doing for the second year in a row. Country music stars Willie Nelson and Merle Haggard will attend the Second Annual Freddy Powers Celebrity Golf Tournament Wednesday through Friday.

"Willie is like me, he's got more stamina than any other human being," Powers said, "It's super that he and all the others are coming here." Powers' primary motivation in organizing the fundraiser stems from his childhood, where he was reared by a mentally-handicapped Uncle…. Other faces some folks might recognize are Darrell Royal, a former Texas Longhorns coach, and ex-NFL star Lance Alworth and Fred "Hammer" Williamson. Tickets for a Thursday evening Texas-style dinner-dance at the Flamingo Hilton Hotel-Casino are $75 per person and $100 per couple. The dance is to feature celebrity songwriters Whitey Shafer, Sonny Throckmorton and Mickey Newbury, plus comedians Norm Alder and Jim MacGeorge."

Catherine Powers: Freddy actually wrote the official theme song for the Nevada Special Olympics. Freddy and I were heavily involved *with the kids*, whether we did Golf Tournaments or Bowling Tournaments, and especially with the Special Olympics. We first hooked up with them back when Freddy was playing at the El Dorado Casino, and there was this couple that came in with their son, who had Down Syndrome. Well, the kid was just fascinated with Freddy, and they ended up becoming regulars at Freddy's shows. The child's name was Tim Young, and one night they asked to meet Freddy so I brought him over after the show and he sat down and got to know Tim a little bit, and he invited us to one of his events.

So we attended, and the next thing you know, I start volunteering, and we started talking to the event organizers, and they asked about us sponsoring an event, and Freddy turned to me and said, "Mama, why don't we do a golf tournament for them and raise some money?" So we started working with the President and Vice President of the Nevada Special Olympics about doing this Celebrity Golf Tournament with Willie Nelson and some other friends of ours.

Freddy Powers: "We got more out of that experience than anything we've ever done. Deaf kids would come up and touch the instruments during the songs and feel the music." 40

237

Catherine Powers: That went so well that we started being hosts at a lot of their charity events, and we would go skiing with them, bowling with them, track with them, Freddy would get his band and we'd go play their dance parties. We got so involved that it became where on a weekly basis, we were involved in one way or the other with the Special Olympics, and we had a lot of the kids that just hung on us and became good friends with us. Freddy was so moved by it all that he decided he was going to write a song for them, and that became the official theme for the Nevada Special Olympics, titled "*Everybody Has a Chance to Win*".

Reno Gazette-Journal, Sunday, May 22, 1994: "Money also was raised through a silent auction that included a golf bag and guitar autographed by event participants. Organizer Catherine Powers coordinated the evening's activities. The Freddy Powers' Celebrity Jam included the Tex Mex of country music Johnny Rodriguez, jazz artist Don Cherry, and members of Haggard's, Nelson's and Freddy's bands. Also appearing were songwriters Whitey Shafer, Sonny Throckmorton and Mickey Newbury, who have 50 or more No. 1 hits among them. The shows and tournaments will benefit the local chapter of Nevada Special Olympics… Powers wrote a song, "*Everybody Has a Chance to Win*".

Norma Powers–Marlowe: Freddy did something quite nice when he did a big benefit for the Special Olympics, that song that Freddy sang was so precious, and he's raised a lot of money for children that are challenged, just out of the goodness of his heart.

Catherine Powers: We ended up taking Merle and Willie and Johnny Rodriguez and George Marriott along with like a hundred Special Needs children and we went into the studio and recorded that song, and had cassette tapes made and would sell them thereafter at all the Special Olympics events we were involved with. Of course, all the proceeds went to their cause, and we had 51 Major celebrities from men who walked on the Moon to Heisman Trophy Winners to Major movie stars to Freddy's usual cast of Major Country Music stars. I remember one of the most beautiful things I've ever seen happen came on the night of the show when we had made up these medals to give to the celebrities, but we had the Down Syndrome group go up and hang the awards on all the celebrities. I'll never forget, the entire stage of 51 people up there, men and women, were all bawling their eyes out, the whole room was all crying. To see those kids and the excitement they were having of putting the medal on somebody instead of receiving the medal was absolutely unbelievable. Those kids just lit up the room with their smiles!

Another favorite time of Freddy and mine came when we were down in Las Vegas for the Summer Special

Olympics, and we're sitting there watching all the events, and Little Timmy was running in this race and Freddy's watching Timmy, and all of a sudden, he's leaning forward and it looks like he's gonna fall over and trip on his own feet. Well, that made Freddy nervous, so now he goes running out there next to the track, yelling and screaming, "Slow down Timmy, slow down," and he gets all the way up there right beside Timmy, "Timmy, slow down!", and Timmy looks back over at him while he's still running and says "Fweddy, I'm in a wace!"

One of the other reasons it touched Freddy, especially the Down Syndrome children, is that he was raised with an Uncle Slim who was mentally handicapped, he'd been kicked in the head by a horse. Slim was in some ways younger than they were mentally, so when we did the Special Olympics, we did all that in honor of his uncle. He wanted to share his love for his Uncle and honor him with the Golf Tournaments. Another time, we were up there with the kids at one of their Skiing events, and we were all skiing together, and whenever Freddy would call me "Ma," I'd say "What Pa," and one of the kids looked up at me and said, "Mrs. Catherine, if his name's Freddy, why do you call him Pa?" So we were very close and very involved with those kids.

On another of our anniversaries, Freddy was playing a gig with Bill McDavid {pre-Sherry} his songwriting partner. On their break Freddy came over to join me and before he could set down next to me, Bill got in between us,

forgetting it was our night. I leaned over and whispered in
Bill's ear to give my husband a kiss for me and tell him I
said Happy Anniversary. That was nothing, the next year
for our fifth anniversary Bill talked Freddy into going to a
Stag party with him. So I stayed home and watched I Love
Lucy and Dick Van Dyke with Bill's girlfriend Sherry. The
sixth he was playing a private birthday party for a friend of
ours. So as everybody celebrated and toasted our friend's
birthday we celebrated our anniversary and toasted to each
other privately. I also spent my seventh wedding
anniversary with Sherry. Freddy and Bill were out on tour
with Merle, so Sherry and I along with the dogs Amelia and
Sugarbam went camping in Spearfish Canyon outside of
Deadwood, South Dakota.

Freddy Powers: "I love traveling and hanging out
with him. We sit at the back of the bus and talk for hours
and hours on the road. If Merle gets on a subject he likes,
he'll expound on it. He's a smart guy and has a lot to say."
41

Catherine Powers: Our eighth we actually spent
alone at a very romantic restaurant not to mention
expensive, which we realized when we got the menu with
no prices on it. But my Freddy never worries about money
until he needs it, so he's always the big spender and just
smiles and says "Momma it's our anniversary, so eat and
drink almost all you want". And we did $275.00 later for

just the two of us. We spent a little larger celebrating our ninth wedding anniversary with my first trip to Europe. We – along with the whole band – went to Amsterdam before going to play a country music festival in Col-des-Roches, Switzerland where we spent four days in this old farm type bed and breakfast with the nicest people, that basically gave us the run of the place. They had a room set up for the band to practice in and served us all the wine, bread and cheese we wanted. They didn't speak English and we sure don't speak Swiss but somehow we seemed to communicate and became friends I'll never forget.

As a bonus, from there, we went back to Amsterdam for a couple more days by ourselves; where I got Freddy on this Ferris Wheel, the tallest Ferris Wheel I've ever seen! You could see the next country once you got to the top, and though Freddy hates rides mind you, it was our anniversary trip and he knew it was what I wanted to do so he ventured the ride with me. It was worth it too because it was beautiful up there, but like I said, it was the highest Ferris Wheel I'd ever seen! I never get scared on rides but this one scared me so bad that I had to hold on and I begged Freddy not to rock it (and with a "No matter what you do, "*DON'T ROCK IT*" attitude). Being the natural prankster he was, Thank God he didn't want it to rock any more than I did. Our hotel room was right on Demark Square and we had two big bay windows that opened up to overlook the square. All the street dancers and musicians were down on the street in front of us while we sat in the windows drinking our special tea we got there and watching all the entertainment wrapped up in each other's arms.

Freddy is never boring. He is one of those types of people who is always witty and has a great comeback that generally cracks you up. I've always called him my personal comedian as he has a thousand jokes. Even though I've heard them all by now and he knows I have he'll tell me again and I'll crack up again. He's always been playful throughout our 30 years together too. I could be sitting there watching T.V. and he'd start walking in circles around the room and every time he'd walk in front of me he'd change his walk into something weird and funny, but all the while would never look at me, acting as though this was normal.

Freddy and I have always kept our natural sense of adventure alive throughout our life together too. I remember when he got a Harley Davidson motorcycle for his sixty-fifth birthday – which I like to joke knocked about ten years off him – I kept telling him if he got any younger, I was gonna have to find an older man! (laughs) We've gone on four-thousand-mile bike runs in twenty-one days: from Albuquerque, New Mexico to Saskatchewan, Canada over to Alberta, Canada and back to Albuquerque! We loved our bike and rode as often as we could before Freddy's Parkinson's started making it too dangerous to ride. Every time we'd get on that bike, he just turned me on. We'd be riding down the highway with my arms wrapped around him and we're kissing while he's patting me on the leg. I'm so grateful to have so many wonderful memories with him.

Chapter 14: Parkinson's Disease

Catherine Powers: Looking back on it now years later, its kind of strange because now that I know about the disease, Freddy's had Parkinson's ever since we got together. There were early signs, I remember one time he was sitting on the houseboat, and he had his leg propped up on a coffee table, and I just looked down and noticed that he had this little ripple going down the side of his leg. I remember I reached over and I touched it and it stopped, and I asked Freddy, "Did that bother you?", and totally unaware, he said "What?", and when I moved my finger away, it started again, and I said "That!" And he said, "No," and when I asked him what that was, he shrugged and said, "I don't know, I see it all the time but it doesn't bother me."

Then, every so often when he'd be flying, he'd put his foot on the pedals of the airplane and his left leg would just start shaking, and he couldn't control it. But once again, he didn't think nothing about it because we'd never heard of Parkinson's before, so we never even thought of anything like that. This was before Google where you can look up a symptom on your phone and have an idea right away of what it is, and back then, because it didn't really seem to bother him that much, we didn't go to a doctor or anything where we might have been able to catch it early and at least be aware and slow it down.

Freddy Powers: "When I first got Parkinson's, the thing that scared me was that I got to thinking back to when I first started noticing it, and it's been a long time back that it started bothering me. My left side has always been a little weaker than my right side, my left arm didn't have as much circulation, and my left leg was weaker. It was little things, nothing that we considered important." 42

Catherine Powers: When it became clear to both of us though was when he broke his hand on The Tonight Show in 2004 playing with Merle and the Strangers, and when he got his cast off, he noticed his fingers wouldn't move the way they were supposed to, and that the little one had a little twitch, and he couldn't make chords on the guitar like he always had. So he thought at first maybe something had been wrong with the way it healed up, so Freddy went back to see his hand doctor, and when he showed the doctor what was going on, the doctor looked at him and said, "Freddy, you need to go have an MRI," and that's when they discovered it was Parkinson's.

Freddy Powers: "At first, it didn't dawn on me just how serious it was, you know? When we finally came around and realized what it was, the impact was already over with kind of." 43

Norma Powers-Marlowe: We never thought Freddy would live this long because of his Parkinson's Disease.

My father had Parkinson's, and my husband had
Parkinson's... When I found out that Freddy had it, oh My
God, I knew what Catherine was in for, because this is a
disease that bothers you like you wouldn't believe.

Catherine Powers: The first time. was all of a sudden
a light switch went on in my head after he'd been freshly
diagnosed and it was starting to become obvious to others
was when we had Big & Rich over at the house on Willie's
golf course, and when both of them entered the room, I
noticed they both walked where the right leg was the
strongest lead and the left arm wasn't swinging at all, and
joked that it was the "Freddy Powers Strut." I didn't get the
joke at first, because I was like "Freddy swings his arm,"
and then thought about it and realized, "Wait a minute, he's
not swinging his arm anymore." So I turned to Bill
McDavid, and said, "Hey, Freddy's arm swings, right?",
and he confirmed to me, "No it doesn't", and I started
going back and visualizing where his arm had started
slowing its swing and not working like it used to. So that
was a big moment of truth for me, when Big and Rich
showed me the Freddy Powers Strut.

At first, Freddy could still play, he just kind of
changed up his chords, because he always had his special
chords that were complicated, but there's also ways of
simplifying those same chords, so he would change their
structure in order to be able to play the chords. So he
continued to work and continued to go out with Merle and

travel – and even went out on tour with Big and Rich a couple of times – but by the middle-to-end of 2005, Freddy's ability to play the guitar had weakened in his hands to the point where he couldn't make a chord at all anymore with that left hand. That's when he came off the road with Merle, and his condition continued to spread and worsen to where he had to have somebody with him to just do basic things around the house or on stage, and that's when it got to be too hard for him to play in the band any more.

Freddy Powers: "The most disturbing part about it for me is I can't play the guitar anymore. Its very difficult, and my left hand doesn't work real good. There's a lot of things we have to give up and it's kind of hard." 44

Catherine Powers: There was a really sad Thanksgiving around 2006 where we'd gone out to Merle's, and we were going to do the Agatha Christie thing, which we all did, and I was shocked that Merle actually played a part in this Agatha Christie Mystery where we all dressed up in costumes. It was kind of funny because I actually won the best costume of the day, but we all had character roles they give you before you arrive, and you show up to the party in the character you're going to be playing. Well, after the game was over, Merle and Freddy and everybody from The Strangers were all sitting there still in their costumes picking on guitars like they always did, and

Freddy was struggling really hard. He was wanting to play and be a part of it, and all of a sudden, he turned to Merle and said "Merle, I just can't play my guitar anymore…. This Parkinson's is taking the love of my life, what am I gonna do Merle?" Of course, Hag and everybody got tears in their eyes, and that's when Merle reminded him, "Freddy, you can still sing." But it was very emotional for everyone, and you could see it hurt Merle really deeply, and it was heartbreaking for all of them. It was just a big slap in the face to everybody in the room to look at Freddy and realize they'd never be able to play or pick with him again *either*.

Merle Haggard: I can't stand to see Freddy like that, it's hard for me to look at him, I'm sure he don't want to be that way and I don't want to see him like that. I hate that, it hurts me….

Freddy Powers: "I can't play guitar anymore, it's indescribable. It was hard to give that up." 45

Rolling Stone Magazine: "Just a few days before wrapping up their Last of the Breed tour, Willie Nelson, Merle Haggard and Sixties country star Ray Price played a sold-out gig at New York City's Radio City Music Hall. Seeing these three on one stage (accompanied by backing band Asleep at the Wheel) is a once-in-a-lifetime opportunity, and the show itself was a master-class in classic country music. Although the audience provided a

diverse cross-section of the country music fan base --
yuppies in suits and pearls, aging hippies in t-shirts and
cowboy hats -- by night's end, everyone was moving (and
boozing) in unison...

The rest of the evening, Nelson and Haggard, along
with Price and Freddy Powers, tossed lead vocals back and
forth on familiar songs highlighted with instrumental solos
and an occasional jam-out. Together, the group focused less
on tracks from the new disc *Last of the Breed* and more on
popular hits such as Patsy Cline's 'Crazy' (originally
written by Nelson) and 'On the Road Again.' No one
seemed to mind.

After the first encore, Nelson returned solo and started
up 'You Were Always On My Mind' before launching into
a couple of new songs – 'Superman' and 'You Don't Think
I'm Funny Anymore' (which proved to be the most
comedic point in the evening). By the time he got to the
raucous 'Whisky River' (and donned his infamous
bandana), the crowd had loosened ties and inhibitions,
dancing and hollering proclamations of love for Nelson,
Haggard, and anyone else nearby. Closing with 'Blue Eyes
Crying in the Rain,' Nelson sent members of the slightly
blissed-out audience on their way with a wave and a
smile." (Source: Rolling Stone Magazine, Willie Nelson, Merle Haggard & Ray Price
Play NYC, By Amanda Trimble, March 23, 2007)

Catherine Powers: It was very hard on Willie Nelson
when Freddy told him and it hit home that he would never

be able to play guitar with Freddy again. So when he realized Freddy was losing his ability to play, Willie was spending every opportunity he could there toward the end of Freddy's playing to pick with him. Every time he was home, they went back to that routine of almost playing 15 hours a day like they used to in the beginning.

Willie Nelson: He's a lot of fun to play with, and when Freddy was at his best, there was nobody better at what he did. He's a great singer too, especially when he was singing what he was playing, he could accompany himself very well, he could sit down with just the guitar and keep you very entertained. We were always telling each other our latest jokes; we were joke tellers.

Catherine Powers: Freddy had been out of the hospital two days one time shortly after he'd first been formally diagnosed, and we went to see Willie up at his place, World Headquarters, and right there in front of he and I, Freddy had his first seizure. I remember it took both of us by surprise, and as we turned around to look at Freddy, he'd stiffened up in that wheelchair and jerked a little bit and his head just fell completely backwards and he was totally motionless. Both Willie and I thought at that moment that he had just died, and he'd been standing on the opposite side of the bar from Freddy and I, he came running around from behind that bar faster than he'd moved in a long time, because he was already in his mid-

70s by then. We were both on top of Freddy like you wouldn't believe trying to wake him, and all of a sudden, he came to, and looked at us both like, "What's going on?"

Well, both of our faces at that moment had gone totally white with shock, Freddy laughed at both of us, but it was quite a freaky situation. Well, we both just about panicked, and Willie said, "We gotta get him to the hospital..." It was amazing because Willie actually helped me lift Freddy in that wheelchair, down a flight of stairs, and into the car, and as you can imagine, here I'm now concerned about Willie getting hurt too! But I got Freddy to the hospital, and then once we got to the hospital, everybody there in the E.R. knew who Freddy was right away. In fact, this one nurse when she saw Freddy's name on the medical chart said, "Is this Freddy Powers?", and when they told her yes, she started jumping up and down in the E.R. going, "Oh my God, I'm such a big fan!" It was hilarious under the circumstances.

When the neurologist walked in the room, the first thing Freddy asked was before she could say anything, "Am I going to be out of here by Saturday night, I'm supposed to be honoring Ray Price?" Then she said, "We'll talk about that later," and began running him through a battery of tests that day, from things as simple as, "Can you tell me your full name?" and, "What year is this?" to, "Do you know where you are?" Then, after a series of questions that honestly scared the shit out of me because I was worried about what impact the seizure had if any on him mentally, the doctor finally got to "Can you tell me what brought you into the hospital? Why am I seeing you?", and Freddy said, "Well, I was sitting at Willie Nelson's…" and before he could say another word, she politely interrupted him and said "Just a minute Mr. Powers," laid her clip board down on the edge of his hospital bed, got right over on top of his face and kind of straddled him with her arms, and said, "Now Mr. Powers, were you really at Willie Nelson's or are you just imagining you were at Willie Nelson's?" I couldn't tell if she was suddenly star-struck or just thought he'd legitimately been hallucinating from the seizure, and then from behind her, Freddy's guitar player Steve Carter – who'd met us at the hospital – started laughing and said "Oh no ma'am, he's telling you the truth! This is the legendary Freddy Powers, he's supposed to be honoring Ray Price this Saturday night, and was definitely at Willie Nelson's house…."

After hearing that, the neurologist stepped back and said "Well oh my Gosh, who's my patient now?", and Steve proceeded to give her Freddy's history in Country Music, so that was of one of those funny stories that came out of the tragedy, and it was like that at most hospitals we've had stays at over the past 10+ years. I remember in Nashville when Freddy wound up in the E.R., the whole staff was extra-alert – not only because of Freddy's condition – but because throughout his whole stay, a steady stream of country music stars would drop in to not only visit with Freddy but in some cases, play for him too as Big and Rich did when they put on an impromptu concert for Freddy right there in his hospital room!

Following the trip to the E.R., for as strong as he was trying to stay physically and in spirit, in his heart, I knew Freddy had fallen into a depression as he began to see the little tolls his disease was beginning to take on and from him. For instance, while we were still living out there on Willie's golf course, he had already gotten to the point where he was no longer able to drive himself into town, and only able to drive anymore down to the little store. Even then, he was starting to have little, small wrecks, and after a while of this, he got really, really depressed to the extreme that all of a sudden, he was just sitting in the bed, not wanting to get up anymore. The best I could get from him was to get up in the morning, go to the kitchen, get himself a cup of coffee, and then the next thing you know, he was right back into bed and lay in there watching T.V. until he fell back to sleep all day. Well, I let this go on for about four days before I was sitting in there with him one morning and finally said, "Are you gonna get up and live with me?", and he just kind of moaned, and I was like "Freddy, either you get up and live with me, by God, or I'm outta here!"

I continued my protest: "I can't live this way, I'm not going to sit here and watch you do this," and at first, he just rolled over and turned his back to me. I'd just gotten out of the shower, and had my hair still wrapped up in a towel, but I jumped in my flip-flops, grabbed my dog and purse, and walked out the door and peeled off in the car. Well, I got about a mile and a half, two miles down the road when my phone rang and it was Freddy, and when I answered, he said, "Mama, I can't do this without you," and I said, "Are you gonna get out of the bed and live?", and when he said yes, I told him I was on my way back.

Freddy Powers: "I want people to know that the disease doesn't mean I'm dead or dying, and neither is my career." [46]

Catherine Powers: Once I got back to the house, we made a plan, decided to get out of the house and bought the bus we currently live on in cash, and decided that it was more important for Freddy to be out there working and alive and keeping himself going than just to sit there in the house and watch himself wither away and die. By then, though Freddy wasn't fully bound to a wheelchair yet, he'd already started having problems with balance where his legs would randomly buckle under him when he was standing or walking, and was starting to fall down a lot. That was dangerous not only when Freddy was doing something as simple as crossing a street or some other every-day activity he and I both took for granted before this, and equally so when he was standing on stage performing. Sadly, after a while, it got bad enough to where he'd actually broken a couple of ribs during one of these random falls, and hit his head during another so hard it left gashes, and eventually got to where it was so frequent he'd have bruises all the time, and was always getting banged up from falling.

Finally, the fall that prompted us to put him in a wheel-chair full-time came when we were in Nashville staying at the Fontanel, which at one time was Barbara Mandrell's mansion and grounds that Marc Oswald and William Morris had since bought and turned into a museum and concert venue. We were frequent guests when we came through town, and on that trip, once again, with no warning or clumsiness on his part, Freddy had fallen on the bus and this time hit the ground so hard he broke his nose! The only funny part of the whole thing is, for his whole life and the 20 years I'd spent with him before then, Freddy was one of the toughest people I ever knew, and would have bandaged that broken nose up himself and considered it nothing more serious than a scrape on the knee. He'd been brought up in that classic Great Depression-era generation where you only went to the doctor if you had a broken arm or something serious, so I knew it drove him nuts to now have to make so many routine trips to the E.R., neurologists, etc because of his condition.

Well, that day, before we'd even gotten him fully into the ambulance and out of there, I was already being inundated with concerned phone calls from all over town, and remember thinking, "My God, news travels fast." So we got him to the E.R., they sewed his nose up, and they discharged him without anyone realizing he'd gotten a staph infection. By then, we'd gotten so used to hitting hospitals on the road that with Freddy's *"The Show Must Go On"* attitude, there was taking a few days off to recuperate so we'd hit the road for a show in Gainesville, Texas to honor Mickey Newberry. Being the professional he was, he'd gotten right up on stage with a broken nose and sang and everything, but after the show, I noticed he wasn't feeling well, and over the next couple hours kept getting sicker and sicker. So without missing a beat in what had become reflex by that point, I peeled out of there and headed straight to the E.R. in Austin. The only difference in outcome that night once we arrived at the Hospital came when they told me his fever had gotten so bad they didn't think he would make it through the night.

It was the first time since his diagnosis and downward spiral of his condition worsening that I'd been faced with the prospect of losing him, and not over time but so suddenly. By the grace of God and Freddy's own resilient strength and spirit (and a very top notch hospital staff ☺), he not only made it through the night but wound up fighting the infection for the next eight days in the Intensive Care Unit and eventually pulled through. Still, by then, because Freddy was pretty much losing the ability to walk independently and I was now having to literally carry him on my back or assist him where I'd have to constantly walk behind him and help him walk even just across the room. I knew this was taking a huge toll on his independence psychologically, especially coming right on the heels of accepting the reality that he could no longer physically play his guitar, and by the time he'd been discharged from the hospital and entered into physical therapy, it became clear to everyone that the atrophy and everything had set in and he was no longer going to be able to walk on his own.

Joi Vinson Davis, Freddy's Personal Nurse: When he first started going downhill, once his feet started going, Catherine would be his feet, and when he couldn't pick his feet up all the way, she would just kind of kick the back of his heels, so he could walk. Then after that became impossible to do, she would actually hold him and have him walk on her feet to try to keep him walking, then he had to go to a walker, and then he got the motorized wheelchair, used that by himself for a while, then got to where he couldn't control it using that arm, so she would walk beside that motorized wheelchair and take him everywhere he needed to go. Then when he got to where he couldn't use the motorized one anymore, it was just a regular wheelchair pushing him everywhere he wanted to go, up hills and dang near across valleys – wherever he wanted to go.

Then she started carrying him like a baby down the steps of the bus, putting him in his wheelchair, then when they'd get back, she'd carry him back on the bus, then when that became impossible, she started piggy-backing him. So every step, she had a solution to keep him active and that's what kept him going for so long.

Catherine Powers: The day Freddy was being discharged from rehab, another miracle of generosity from his peers when I found out that, initially, they were not going to let me bring him back on the bus because, first off from a safety point of view, they didn't like the way I was having to get him on board piggy-backing him in on my back. Then once the medical professionals came on and saw that his bed was all the way in the back of the bus and that I was having to again piggy-back him all the way back to the bed, and then walk backwards in order to be able to set him down, they immediately told me, "Mrs. Powers, you're going to have to make some other kind of arrangement because this isn't going to work." To my relief, they told me if I could get a hospital bed installed on the bus, he could stay, so I called up this old-boy-type club Freddy had belonged to for years called The Coondicks, which is really a group of wealthy guys who sit around and drink booze, tell dirty jokes and come up with the goofiest reasons they can to have get-togethers.

Well, thankfully, as with so many others, once they heard what Freddy was facing, they raced into action and the *very next day*, showed up with a hospital bed. It was quite a sight, because then, right there in the hospital parking lot, cut off the base of the bed – which was the wheels – built this wooden box up in the front of the bus, brought that bed in three pieces up and put it back together on the bus! It was nothing short of a miracle, because the next day, I was able to bring his physical therapists back on and they were impressed too, because after a quick inspection, they signed off and said, "Okay, you got it," and I was allowed to bring Freddy home. That made a life-changing difference too, because had I not been able to bring him back on this bus, he would have been stuck in a home and his quality-of-life would have ended back then. But because of that hospital bed and his attendants, I have been able to keep Freddy out on the road and a part of this world for the better part of the last decade.

Joi Vinson Davis: Whenever some new medical situation would pop up, I'd get a phone call, I knew something happened when she'd call me and say "Okay, well, they're telling me this, what do I do?" Every time I would just teach her everything I knew about anything that was going on – and she knew more about the Parkinson's than I did and I'm a nurse – but as far as taking care of everything, I would show her: "Well, this is how to do this," and she would improve it every time! (laughs) Seriously, she got it all quickly, and there was nothing that I taught her that she didn't improve ten times better by the next time I was with her and Freddy – and she taught me a lot actually. She was his best possible caretaker because she cared most about his quality of life and care, and it was hard to keep up with all the medical supplies too, she'd have to take oxygen and suction tanks, and pills, and syringes, and extra tubes, but she juggled it all.

Day to day, it was wake up in the morning and the first thing she would do was clean his mouth out, then feeding him, and she went from spoon-feeding him every day – and it took two hours to feed him a bowl of anything, and it was always organic smoothies and fruit – to eventually feeding him cans through his feeding tube in his stomach after he couldn't swallow food easily anymore. Then every 3 hours it was pill time, and every two hours, she would change him, and would roll him over every couple hours in his hospital bed. So it was something every hour: he had to be suctioned, he had to be changed, he had to have medicine, he had to be dressed, groomed, and it would take 15 minutes just to set up to have his teeth brushed for instance, and she did it ALL by herself except when she was lucky enough to have me or Cass or someone come occasionally to give her some relief. But 90% of the time she did it all by herself, from daylight to dark, taking care of him. I've never seen nothing like it.

So our friendship grew as I helped her with him, and now, it's just like they're my family. I never wanted Freddy to miss anything, and if I knew there was something going on and Cass couldn't do it, I would always make sure if there was any way possible she could get him to an event or concert and I could get there to make sure he got there, I was going to do it. And if he had any extended stay in the hospital, one way or another, I got there. One time, John Rich had me flown out to Texas where it was a 16-day stay.

Catherine Powers: Following the reality setting in that he was going to now be hospital bed-and-wheelchair bound for the rest of his life, once that hospital bed was installed on the bus, I would still have carry him like a baby or piggy-back him just to get him on and off the bus everywhere we went, and knew at that point, God and Freddy were both counting on me to stay strong for both of us.

Tanya Tucker: She works so hard! I've seen her lift him up over her shoulders and carry him, and she's just a little thing, she's not any bigger than he is, but I have never seen anybody work so hard and be so dedicated and so loving than Catherine. Bar none, she's got to be an angel, there's a song right there! (laughs) You don't see that kind of love very often. I saw it with my parents and I see it with Catherine and Freddy. That kind of love is hard to find.

Freddy Powers: "We've had a wonderful relationship. Everybody notices it, you know. She does everything for me, and I do everything for her that I can, that's the way it works." 47

American Music Project: "As we leave with Freddy's birth we come upon his rebirth. Not all Parkinson's victims have a savior -someone powerful enough to give them new life. Through Catherine however, Freddy is, in many respects, reborn. Her will power nurtures and preserves him. At a time when he could have quickly passed she united with him closer than before and helped him adjust to a new, dark, foreign world and remain. She is a cell of immense love, energy and light. She is the keeper of his new cell. On the couch inside their camper our conversation carries on and goes deeper. She levels with me, quits with the facts and begins to express the true feelings and emotions she has tied to her husband. In these expressions and in her deep commitment to him she propagates his tale and his spirit. Like a surrogate she carries on his story and his personality with impeccable depth, accuracy and care. No one can ever replace Freddy yet she carries on his flame. True to her name Catherine is his catharsis: his release, purification, his restoration, his chance. In my pursuit to understand Freddy I never expected that one of the most compelling pieces of the story would be his wife."

Catherine Powers: When Freddy was first diagnosed with Parkinson's, we went to several different doctors to get different opinions, and at the top of every one of those consultations, Freddy was very open with them about the fact that smoking Pot seemed to help with his condition more than anything else. Well, these were five of the top Neurologists in the Austin area, and every one of them told him, "Freddy, I can't officially prescribe you to smoke marijuana, but if it helps you, I'd advise you to keep doing so," because off the record, they did know it made a helpful difference. Thankfully, in the last few years, Medical Marijuana has continued to gain acceptance by society and the medical profession at large, and without a doubt, Freddy is an example of a success story there because I can personally give you timeless examples where pot has had a calming effect on his day-in-and-out condition physically.

One recent example that might sound kind of funny on the surface but that in reality proved to be life-threatening came when Freddy got the hiccups, and it got so severe that we thought we were going to lose him because it wouldn't stop, so he wasn't even having a chance to breathe and was turning blue. It got so bad we actually had to rush him to the E.R. and the only humor we could take from the whole thing was, "Oh my God, everybody's going to say 'Freddy Powers died from the hiccups!'" Well, even after the emergency room nurses and doctors saw him, it still wasn't stopping, and once they finally had him situated in a room of his own and we were alone, I was so desperate that I finally decided, "Look, I'm going to try this," and right there in the hospital room, gave him a big old hit. At first, I'd been afraid to try it because he was having so much trouble with just his basic breathing, but within TEN MINUTES, the hiccups stopped!

As relieved as I was and as fast as my heart was racing, I needed a hit too right then, but decided not to push my luck in a hospital E.R. The other thing that makes me laugh looking back was when Freddy's nurses and doctors came back in to check on him and saw the hiccups had stopped completely and couldn't come up with any official medical explanation for it, lol. Then when it started up again after about an hour and a half, I gave him another hit, and it stopped. The kicker was, I had smoked so much of our stash myself over the past three days that I ran out before that next hiccup fit started after the first hit calmed him down and actually had to call in a Mayday from the hospital to one of our friends to smuggle us more weed into the E.R!! (laughs)

Even right now as I write, Freddy has developed a problem with swallowing due to the Parkinson's that had gotten so severe he's now permanently on a feeding tube. He even has a hard time with something as basic as swallowing his own saliva, and because he can't swallow it, it all gets built up in the back of his throat to where he's constantly struggling to clear it. Well, I'll suction him to help, but when I can't get it all out and still hear him gurgling, all I have to do is give him a good ole big hit and he'll give me one good cough and all that stuff comes right up. So ironically, I smoke him up now not so much to get him high for fun as I do for what has literally become real, medical reasons, so it's become medicinal for Freddy more than for the pleasure he always got out of it.

Privately, in the first couple years after we'd received the formal diagnosis, my heart broke every day for and with him as we both absorbed the permanence of our new reality and learned to do the most within the boundaries of the disease's increasing restrictions. Whenever Freddy would have this kind of a breakdown during those early years after he was officially diagnosed, I'd try whatever I could to break it up by giving him simple tasks to get his mind off it, sometimes even the simplest tasks that I knew he could still physically do would give him even the slightest sense of completion.

It was brutal to watch somebody as accomplished as Freddy, who'd always been able to physically do whatever he set his mind to, have a mind that was still so capable but a body that wasn't able to keep up anymore. It tortured both of us, and some of the depressions he went through during that mid-2000s period were very dark. He'd always tell me I was his sunlight, but you never quite feel you're doing enough, and it took a heavy toll on both of us. By now, I was wearing so many hats and juggling so many roles that I was going through a whole learning curve of my own, acting as Freddy's full-time nurse and caretaker, our tour bus driver, his manager (as I was still determined to keep him as active with and around musicians as much as possible), and would even carry him on my back onto stage to set him in his chair to sing!

Freddy Powers: "I've got Parkinson's, but Parkinson's doesn't have me yet. You know what I mean? It affects everything about our lives, but we're not letting it…. We're still doing everything that we do, we're just doing it a little slower maybe." 48

Catherine Powers: "*The Saddest Goodbye*" was a song Freddy started working on before he lost his ability to play guitar, as he knew he was fixing to lose that ability. He could still write and play through the basic chord structure, but every time he sat down to work on that song, he would get very depressed, because it was a reminder of the totality of what he was losing in the ability to translate the music he heard in his head physically into those classic "Freddy Powers" triplet chords on the guitar. It took him three years to finish that song where he would have previously had it written and finished in a quicker time than the length of the song itself!

It was so hard to watch him go through that too, because every time he'd get the inspiration up to sit down and work on it, he'd get through no more than two or three lines before the Parkinson's made his hands shake so bad he couldn't form the chords to keep writing on to the next verse. It was heartbreaking for both of us, because every time I'd come in to check on him once he'd stopped playing, he'd always have these big old tears in his eyes and his head hanging down. As a matter of fact, if it hadn't been for a fellow Texas songwriter and guitar player named Gary Nelson sitting down with Freddy to work on it, that song still would have never been finished.

Once word had spread about Freddy's diagnosis, I think it inspired his friends and fans alike to see him out there on the road and in the world so much, and that led to all kinds of new creative doors opening as Freddy could not only still sing, but speak his creative opinion, which meant he could still produce too. That led us back into the studio for a number of special new projects over the past decade, including Freddy still thank God being physically able to record one more studio album while he was still able to play guitar called *My Great Escape*.

Stomp and Stammer Magazine, 2005: "Freddy's songwriting skills are in evidence on *My Great Escape*, his latest album. Also there are his laid-back vocals – very informal, but very skilled with plenty of jazzy phrasing. His last album, 1997's The Hottest Thing in Town, had a Hot Club of France feel, with its wall of rhythm guitars, classic material (*'I Can't Give You Anything But Love,' 'Sweet Georgia Brown'*), and Grappelli and Reinhardt-influenced soloists. For *Escape,* Powers went ahead and found a guitarist named Django. Django Porter is more than an audacious name – the guy plays remarkably in Reinhardt's style, right down to the tone, and really adds a lot to the album…. The album is the first non-Merle Haggard release on Hag Records... (and) the result is a great batch of songs, from the romantic '*Angel In My Arms*' to the camaraderie of '*Tom Sawyer & Huckleberry Finn*'."

Freddy Powers: "He's a young kid here in Austin I sort of discovered. He doesn't play just like Django Reinhardt, but he's got that fire. He's got a little Hispanic blood in him and I think that's where that fire comes from." 49

John Rich: To feel that Freddy has respect back towards the new generation of country music is pretty unbelievable too, the song 'Escape', Big Kenny and I wrote that, and Freddy heard me sing it one night at a party and asked if he could record it. So to have one of the greatest songwriters in the world want to record something they didn't write, is HUGE, and not to mention you wrote it- to have a guy like Freddy sing something that Big Kenny and I wrote was just one of the biggest compliments and shows of respect you could ever have as a songwriter.

Freddy Powers: "I don't force it, I'm too far along to write something trivial, I try to write something more profound." 50

Catherine Powers: When we produced the "*Unforgettable*" album for Merle Haggard, that was another really special project for Freddy because he'd picked with Merle for years, and written with Merle for years, and performed on stage together with Merle for years and years, and with his condition getting steadily worse, all those abilities to interact with Merle creatively were being stripped away one by one. But *producing Merle* was something Freddy had never done yet and could still do, and we were just so grateful that Freddy got the opportunity to let that side of his talent shine on this record. It meant the world to Freddy to get back in the studio with Merle one more time.

Merle Haggard: "Freddy and I are great friends. We play that kind of music—just kind of sitting around. Freddy's an old Dixieland player; he knew all those old songs like I did. He and I had what we call a sidebar band called the Butter n' Egg Band, and for years we've been guitar buddies; we'd sit around the house and pick guitars like everyone else in the United States. Those songs are some of the songs that we'd started doing in the circle. So Freddy wanted to add two or three new ones and do an album of them all: a standards album. And that's the outcome of it, even after this period of retrieving the record after it being stolen—we would have been first with it before Rod Stewart [whose *Great American Songbook* series has sold millions of CDs], but Rod Stewart got out there while I was chasin' the thief." (Source: AllAboutJazz.com, 2006)

Country Line Magazine: "This new release from Merle Haggard is not only Unforgettable, its unbelievable. One of the most perfect albums I have ever heard, from the vocals that are like fine wine, to the fantastic production that pairs Haggard with legendary singer-songwriter Freddy

Powers. This is a classic gathering of pop standards done like no one else on earth could do them… Intricate, amazing arrangements and tasty compliments from the strings, horns and fiddles, this is a Grammy-bound collection that will go down in the history books as one of the finest albums ever produced by an American singer, Country or otherwise… Four stars and two thumbs up."

Catherine Powers: I remember the first time I heard it playing on the radio, I kept saying over and over out loud, "Oh my God, it's playing on the radio!" I was in shock because I was a part of that, I helped put that whole project together, and all of a sudden, to turn around and hear something I'd been a part of being played on the radio, it was just like so many times I've been sitting there when a songwriter or artist heard their song for the first time being played over the radio. I was just overwhelmed, that was such a beautiful record we all made together. Freddy was very proud of that one.

Billboard Magazine: "Warm, relaxed and laid-back, impeccably performed, and pleasurable to hear… what makes *Unforgettable* work is Haggard's easy, assured delivery. He may not reinvent these songs, but he sings them as if they were his own, making this a small, romantic gem for listeners who love Hag the singer as much as they love Hag the writer."

Chapter 15: Freddy's 2nd Act

Catherine Powers: By 2007, Freddy had lost complete ability to play the guitar at all, but by the grace of God, he was still singing, so we kept the shows going on, and that's when Freddy started bringing his comedy back as part of his act!

John Rich: Freddy's a very visual guy, and he's also a comedian, so he loves the set-up and the payoff, he's all about the set-up and the knock-down, and that works for a joke and it also works for a great country song. And I think you can see the similarities between the way he tells a joke and the way he tells a song, they're really one in the same, its just one has melody around it. Whether it's a sad song or funny song or drinking song or whatever, they've all got that classic set-up and knock-down, like Johnny Carson or some of our greats that we've had in country music.

One thing Freddy has that is really interesting in how he writes is that old Vaudeville thing in his approach to writing country music, which is really interesting, and unless you're part of Vaudeville, or just a huge fan of it, you're not going to write that way. So, I'm a big fan of the rat pack and big band kind of music, and Freddy being such a great jazz player, he almost sings when he's writing a song so that you can almost hear horn parts moving around the chords and the melody that he's throwing out.

Its real simple what he does, but he doesn't come at lyrics in a kitchy kind of way, he comes at them in a real clever way but they still got a lot of class, and that's a hard thing to do. It's hard to be funny and still maintain the class, and not get cheesy with it. So for instance, when you talk about 'Let's Chase Each Other Round the Room Tonight', that's a funny thing to say, but it's also very true and it rings a bell with anyone who's ever heard it, and millions of people now have heard that song. Its written in such a clever way that you don't feel silly singing it, and when you hear those moves and those pockets that he comes up with, its really a classic way to go.

Freddy Powers (from stage): "They call me the human vibrator. The girls love me! When I lay out in the sun, they call me Shake 'n Bake." [51]

Don Powers Jr: The last video Freddy was a song called "Last of the Breed," and it had Willie Nelson, Merle Haggard and Ray Price, and Freddy sang back-up in it because his Parkinson's had started to set in, and in the video, you can see Freddy's hand just shaking like crazy.

As sad as that was, it was a real treat for my Dad when Freddy called us up in Oklahoma, and said "What are you gonna be doing for the next couple of weeks?", and when my dad said "Just staying here tending our garden," Freddy chuckled and replied, "Well, you wanna go on tour with me, Merle Haggard, Willie Nelson and Ray Price?" So he went to check with me and I laughed and said, "What's the decision? I can hold Oklahoma down, go!" They played in Tulsa, and picked up my dad from there and went to Missouri, and he got a kick out of traveling with Freddy one more time on the road and all those guys.

Catherine Powers: Freddy was always so funny! I could be sitting in a chair watching T.V. at home and he'd come walking out into the room acting as normal as ever and then all of a sudden, get right in front of me and moon me or something goofy, and then continue with whatever he was doing like it had never happened. Then if I did mention it later, he'd act innocent as if he had no earthly idea what I was talking about, and say something funny like, "I think you're hallucinating over there!" So he was always a prankster, and just loved to see people laugh and never really could escape that comedian-side of his personality, but in what's maybe a testament to his talent as a performer, it never got old.

It gave him great joy to put a smile on anybody's face, whether he'd known you his whole life or you were a complete stranger, and I loved that part of his personality! Freddy was naturally very witty, and some of his comebacks would just crack me up – or the whole room if there happened to be anyone else present. As a natural entertainer, Freddy loved an audience, which is not to say he needed one all the time, but I loved it all and was his biggest fan. Over the years, I've even used a lot of Freddy's humor and it never gets old, his jokes always crack people up, and I'll say, "I stole that one from him." That's why he was always such a dynamic performer throughout his career too because he was extremely quick on his feet, and always kept his crowds entertained. He was definitely a character. In fact, to this day, our dear friend, songwriter Cass Hunter, has a literal pocketbook full of what she calls "Freddyisms," things she has witnessed and watched through his Parkinson's while she was on the road traveling with us for two years.

Cass Hunter: I started traveling with them the last couple years they got to travel before settling in Flora-Bama, and we'd go back and forth between Nashville and Austin, and down to Perdido Key, pretty much anywhere we could get the bus in without hitting limbs. Catherine felt it was very important to keep Freddy moving even though he was stuck in his hospital bed, and to get him to as many different fans and friends around the country who still wanted to see him, and we would go stay in the driveways of our friends' along the way. If I had a gig somewhere along there, she'd plan around that and take me to it, and when we would travel, a lot of times, we'd take scenic back roads, and one of my favorite trips from that time was when we took Natchez Trace Parkway through Mississippi, Alabama and Nashville. It was a far prettier drive than the interstates, and it was more relaxing for her, less traffic, and we would basically drive for a couple hours then pick our rest stops along waterfalls and highlighted the ones that were 10 minutes or less walk from the bus to the attraction and back because we couldn't leave Freddy alone for more than 20 or so minutes at a time.

So instead of gas stations, we tried to maximize the historic or scenic stops as much as possible when Catherine had to stop and stretch her legs and feed and change Freddy. Freddy couldn't get out of the hospital bed on his own, so he never could come with us unfortunately, so on one of these trips where we stopped at a waterfall along Natchez Trace, and it was literally like an eight minute walk so we were literally back in like 15 minutes. It was the only time he was alone on a 12-, 15-hour bus trip, but when we got back to the bus, as soon as we got on board, Freddy blurted out to both of us: "Good thing you're back, I was about to leave you!" He had a wonderful sense of humor, and he tried to use it whenever he could to put a smile on our faces.

On that same day, she was having to pull the mattress pad thing out from under him, and had to roll him over on his side to get it out, and then roll him over the other way, so she's up on the bed, and went to turn him over again and rolled him over too far to where the side of his face was pressed up against the window. Well, I was trying to make light of the situation and make him laugh, so I said, "Good Lord Freddy, you just gonna let her throw you around like that? Ain't you used to that yet, she does it all the time," and he said, "I'll never get used to that!" (laughs)

One of my favorite Freddy road stories is one I call "Malfunction Junction", which was definitely one of our big adventures, we were on our way to Key West from Nashville, and on the very first night of that trip, on the way down, at a rest stop at the edge of Florida, at two o'clock in the morning, I'm sleeping on the couch beside Freddy's bed, and all of a sudden, I wake up to the sound of someone pounding on our door as hard as they could. Well, Catherine came running through the bus in just her t-shirt and panties yelling "Holy Toledo, holy Toledo!", we open the door, and the cops go, "Get out of here now! Get out of here now, it's a fire!" So we look out the window, and sure enough, the truck parked right next to us was on fire, an 18-wheeler, and the whole cab was engulfed in flames 20 feet high! I've got pictures of this…

This trip to Florida was supposed to be eight days long, there and back, and it wound up being a 17-day trip because the bus broke down right in the middle lane of a five-lane Interstate in Miami. There's Freddy in the bed, Catherine's driving uphill, and when the bus broke down, our emergency brake wouldn't work, and we had to hold the brake down the entire time for hours with our feet in the middle of rush hour traffic. We were getting cussed by everyone, and we had to stay up there at the front of the bus taking turns keeping pressed down on the brake while we waited for help to show up.

They had to block off traffic and eventually got us off the middle of the road and next to a guardrail, and poor

Catherine's a nervous wreck, calling tow trucks trying to find somebody who can tow that big of a vehicle. We had three different companies come, and we were waiting hours in between each of them, and *all three* couldn't do the tow. So this took 12 hours before they finally found one that could tow us, and then they told us we couldn't stay in the back of the bus with Freddy – who bless his heart this whole time is stuck in his hospital bed watching all this chaos happening around him – because they weren't allowed to tow a vehicle for insurance reasons. We even showed them, but it didn't matter, we couldn't ride in the wrecker and we couldn't ride on the bus, so Catherine had to call a cab, which was another hour and a half wait. To make matters worse, the bus was pushed off the road so near to the guardrail that Catherine could barely get out the door herself, let alone get Freddy out by herself.

That girl is strong! She had to carry him on her back by herself when she was alone and needing to move him from one part of the bus to another or to his wheelchair, and when I was traveling with them, to help her, I would hold him up from behind by his knees while she carried him on her back and try to take the weight off of her a little bit. On that bus, you can't get through the door side by side carrying him, so one person had to go after the other.

Here we are these two little girls and there are two big old wrecker guys who refused to help us because of insurance reasons, so we're trying to squeeze Freddy out the door while he's shaking and everything. I was on the other side of the guardrail trying to hold onto his legs while Catherine carried him out by the arms. We wound up getting towed to some dealership in the middle of the night, and the place wasn't even opened anymore! In the morning, Catherine and I went to get a rental car and it turned out the wrecker people had locked the keys on the bus! So she had to climb through a window to get that opened, then to top the whole day off, Freddy wound up locking us out of the rental car, and Catherine had to go find a slim jim to open it! What a nightmare.

Catherine Powers: Freddy was lucky to be able to call on that talent once he couldn't play guitar anymore, because he'd done comedy all those years and every once in a while he would throw in a little short joke in one of his shows, when he'd laid the banjo down, he'd pretty much laid his comedy down. At first, even though he couldn't play the guitar anymore, he would still strap it on and walk out on the stage and make the motions of trying to play the guitar because he didn't feel comfortable singing without the guitar. It was always a part of his show, having either a guitar or a banjo in his hands, so he did use it as a prop, but once he couldn't play the guitar any more, he just felt he needed to add something back in there, and that's when he started bringing his comedy back. That started making it easier for him to stand up there without a guitar and we kept him out there working as long as we could.

The Austin Chronicle, August, 2008: "Perched uneasily still on a stool center stage, Powers delivers his long-familiar songs with the subtle touch only their writer can. His arms jerk in slight involuntary shudders, and his hands tremble as if still fretting across his absent guitar, but Powers' voice unfolds with calm, rich control. With his band supplying gently rippling jazz tones, Powers closes the set with his plaintive '*All I Wanna Do Is Sing My Song*,' echoing lonesome through the wooden theater to a hushed audience."

All I Wanna Do Is Sing My Song

All I wanna do is sing my song
It's the only way to pacify my mind until I'm strong
The very thought of losing you chills me to the bone
And all I wanna do is sing my song

All I wanna do is sing my song
Don't wanna think about the times she done me wrong
I just wanna ease my mind but the memories are much too strong
And all I wanna do is sing my song

All I wanna do is sing my song
Maybe I'll find somebody else to help me sing along
There's something bout the melody makes the nights not seem so long

And all I wanna do is sing my song
All I wanna do is sing my song
And when the show is over I'll be waitin' by the phone
And if the phone starts ringin' with "Honey, please come
home"
Who knows I might sing my way back home

(Written by Freddy Powers)

Catherine Powers: It even got to a point where we weren't even sure any more how well he was going to be able to perform physically at the shows, but both Freddy and his fans still wanted him to be out there, but a lot of venues didn't want to hire and pay him if he wasn't going to be able to play. So I would make a deal with the clubs that, "Okay, you don't have to pay him, I'll take care of the band and will pay everybody, just let me have a place for him to play." That's how I kind of got into the financial trouble that I did, because I was trying to keep the band paid and keep him on the road, putting fuel in the bus, and I kind of made that priority more important to me than paying bills. That's the first time I had to actually call Willie Nelson and Merle Haggard who stepped up and Thank God for them, they paid off all the credit cards, paid our car off, and gave Freddy and I a fresh start.

Of course, I turned around and pretty much did the same thing again, but I wanted to keep him out there working and part of the music world as long as I could, and most importantly, to give him something to live for as his Parkinson's continued to worsen. But Freddy's friends really stuck by him, from Merle and Willie to Big and Rich, I have to say, those two guys have been absolutely wonderful to Freddy and I over the years, especially right after they all started to realize that Freddy's ability to perform was changing, and in bigger picture terms, the reality that we didn't know how much longer he was going to have on the earth with us. Big Kenny and John Rich really right off the bat stepped up to the plate, and wanted to keep Freddy's name going, that's why they included "*Filthy Rich*" on their second record, *Comin' To Your City*.

John Rich: Writing with Freddy is a party! You pour a cocktail, and Freddy, he'll smoke something, and you sit around and you basically just start talking about what's been happening and what's going on, and next thing you know, Freddy's over there riffin' on something or he says something, and everybody just kind of looks and says, 'Yep, that's brilliant, let's follow that', and you jump in and get rollin'. Freddy's direction in a song is unbelievable, and I'd have to think when he wrote with Merle, that it probably worked like that. I'm sure Merle was the bulldog in the song, but I guarantee you he was following Freddy's direction on every twist and turn. And Freddy is a twister and a turner, which makes his stuff really interesting.

When we wrote "*Filthy Rich*" together, I remember me and Big Kenny, and Bill McDavid and Freddy were sitting in Deadwood, South Dakota, and I believe it was Freddy who said: 'Everybody's trying to get filthy rich on somebody else's money,' and we all just laughed about how hilarious that line was- and its true. So we tore into it, and I think it took 45 minutes to write that song, and from there, we put it on a Big & Rich record and millions of fans heard it, so that was a really cool thing to do. Every now and then Big Kenny and I will tear back into that just for old times' sakes, and rip it out.

Joi Vinson Davis: When we went down to Mobile with John Rich and all of them, Freddy had a slew of Marines pick him up and put him on that stage when he was honored by Big & Rich, and that was a really cool trip. All these Marines wanted to take pictures with him, and pushed him up and down the street in his wheelchair, they made a path for him and us going down that road, it was just amazing. Then, after the show, we went to New Orleans for Big & Rich's next show, and John and them got Freddy up to the table, and gave him some chips, and John Rich was helping Freddy put his chips out to place bets because Freddy wasn't quite able to, and every time Freddy would ask him to put down a certain amount, John would say, "Are you sure buddy, you sure you want to do that?", and Freddy would always say "Yep", and he wound up winning like $4000 playing Poker with John!

John Rich: "*Medley of a Hillbilly Jedi*" was another one in there that Freddy wrote on, and "*Let's Don't Say Goodbye*", we wrote that song the same night we wrote "*Filthy Rich*". We were getting ready to leave Deadwood, and Bill said, 'Man, I just hate saying goodbye, I don't want you boys to leave, I hate this part of it', and Freddy said, 'Well, we don't have to say goodbye, just say see you later gator'. So we said, 'Well, let's write that while we're here, let's write a goodbye song', an 'end of the show' song. So we wrote 'Let's Don't Say Goodbye', and once again, it has that Rat Pack – Vaudeville thing in it that really only Freddy can do.

Country Music Planet, Dec 2004: "This past weekend, the William Morris Agency, Muzik Mafia, and CMT were in the Austin area filming a CMT special with Big and Rich. Legendary songwriter, Freddy Powers was a part of the festivities. Big and Rich's next DVD will be focusing on Big and Rich's relationship with Freddy, and Freddy's induction into the Godfathers of the Muzik Mafia. Additional footage featured Freddy and Willie Nelson with Big and Rich at Willie's World Headquarters. Freddy will be joining Big and Rich in Las Vegas and Reno Dec. 8th and 10th. Big and Rich also have a dedication to Freddy on their CD Super Galactic Fan Pak. The title track of Freddy's new Smith Entertainment CD, '*My Great Escape*' was written by Big Kenny and John Rich."

John Rich: What Freddy brings to the table as a songwriter is timeless, it doesn't ever change; the equation of what he does in music is not bound by any time element whatsoever. So any real serious songwriter would want to know as much about Freddy as they could. And whether they realize it or not, they know the man's songs. That's the position I was in all those years ago when I met him, I didn't know who he was but I knew all his songs, and so when I sat down and started getting into the guy, I was just more and more blown away by the minute, uncovering all these things and sitting with the guy that wrote all this stuff that impacted me so much. To know that I sat around as a kid learning all those licks and those songs, and those are his creations, and now you're sitting with the guy. It's pretty unbelievable.

Freddy's melodies move like horn sections, is the best way I put it. There's no redundancy in what he does, he could play the same chord progression 10 times in a row and sing 10 different melodies over it back to back to back, you hear that in his guitar playing too. He's a real jazz guy, and we all know about Jazz: its free-flow and doesn't have the parameters around it that other forms of music do, and that really applies to the way his melodies hit too. It feels free-form, but after you've heard it twice, it's a hook that's stuck in your head.

Catherine Powers: That was one of their contributions to trying to keep Freddy's name out there with the Millennial country fans, and it helped him get some music publishing going to put towards our rising medical costs as his condition worsened and he couldn't perform live on a regular basis to earn a living any longer. They included Freddy too at the top of their hit, "*Comin' To Your City*" music video, and Freddy got a kick out of that! He played the old man who got to yell at the T.V., "Those Big and Rich fellas are a slap in the face to Country Music with all that Rock & Roll!"

His friends weren't all just trying to help him out professionally, they loved to put a smile on his face too, and Big Kenny and John were both always joking and clowning around with Freddy. Then when John Rich cut his first big hit, "Save a Horse, Ride a Cowboy", he was one of those guys – and probably the first one Freddy or I've ever heard of – who went back to all his "Honky Tonk Heroes" as he called it and gave every one of them $10,000! Well, when our check arrived to us, it was like a miracle because we were to the point financially where it was like heaven just opened up its gates and rained down money on us, because he knew that we needed it. That was the first time John Rich ever opened up his check book for Freddy, and far from the last, because there's been several times – I couldn't even start to add up – the tens of thousands of dollars that John Rich and Big and Rich/Merle Haggard manager Marc Oswald have personally taken out of their pockets to help Freddy and I and keep our bus running and on and on.

Tanya Tucker has been another Country Music star who stepped up to help Freddy out and Gretchen Wilson and Susie Cochran, Hank Cochran's widow. All of the financial generosity they have contributed, and its been everything from helping out with a bus breakdown to buying $3000 or $4000 in gas cards they sent me to be able to keep Freddy out on the road, going to songwriter Festivals and concerts where friends like Merle, Willie and Big and Rich would bring Freddy up on stage in front of thousands of fans to sing when he couldn't even stand anymore and was wheel-chair bound. They knew how much it meant to Freddy to feel like he was still part of the show, and still had a place in the fan's hearts

John Rich: When you talk about his illness, there's no crueler way to take a guy like Freddy out than with what he's got, for his hands to go away and his dexterity, and he can't really talk and to be as great a singer and picker as he is, and a great people person, for that to be what takes you out is just a crazy irony to me. It is what it is, but I think the thing about him is: he didn't say a word. They picked him up and set him on my bus the other night, and those old crazy, blue eyes open up and look at ya, and he didn't have to say anything, you just start bustin' out laughing because you know what he's thinking. And if you really know Freddy, you can read him just by looking in his eyes and watching his expression, he's a real communicator even now.

Joi Vinson Davis: Catherine called me the day that he went to the hospital, and she said he was really sick and they didn't think he was going to make it two days, she really needed me there and didn't feel comfortable with what was going on with him in the first place because she didn't feel Freddy was being treated the way he should have been treated by the V.A. hospital staff. So I called John Rich and he booked me a flight to go out there and personally take care of Freddy while he was in the hospital, and I didn't make it there till 10 that night, but I'm glad I did when I did because there was a lot of bad things going on: he was getting the wrong treatments, his doctors were back and forth saying, "Don't trust this doctor", "Don't trust this doctor", so it was just a really, really bad experience.

They'd given him the wrong medicine, the wrong I.V. fluid, and upon laying eyes on him for the first time that night, I honestly didn't think he was gonna make it. So every time a nurse or doctor would come in, I would automatically start researching everything they were doing, because they'd made so many mistakes, and I truly thought we were gonna lose him, but he pulled on through. Freddy lasted a lot longer than most Parkinson's patients do, and it was all because of Catherine.

While we were at the hospital, we were all doing anything we could to get him to do simple things like swallow down his pills and food, and affectionately, I've always called Catherine and Freddy Mama and Papa, and one day during this 2012 trip, they were trying to get this tube down Freddy's nose, and we couldn't get it down. They were trying to get Freddy to bend his chin forward, and when Catherine realized what they were trying to do, she looked over at me and said, "Joi, show Papa your tits..." Well, immediately, every doctor's eyes in the room got really big and they started taking their focus off Freddy, and I looked up at Catherine, and said "Now, Mama?" And so I said, "Look Papa?", and those doctors, Catherine still swears to this day they were all about to lose it, but that tube went right on down! The doctors said it was the first time they'd ever been treated doing a treatment.

Cass Hunter: When they came to Nashville in 2012 when he was hospitalized, and they said he was going and we thought it was going to be Freddy's very last walk, so Joi – who's a nurse and a very close friend of theirs – Catherine and I were rolling Freddy around the hospital and grounds in his wheelchair boohooing, and he could still talk, but it took him a little while to get it out, and a lot of times, he would scream things because he'd work it up. Freddy and I used to tell each other jokes all the time, and he would always know mine, I never could find one that he didn't know already, and so on that little spin around the block at the hospital, and I said, "Tell me a joke Freddy," just trying to get him to talk. So he said, "This drunk was standing on the side of the road, and this lady walked by carrying this goose, and a man walks up and says, 'Where did you get that pig?'" At this point in the joke, Freddy stopped talking and didn't finish the punchline, so it got silent again, and we were all so sad that the mood stayed that way for the rest of the walk, and as we made our way back up the elevator. Well, by the time we got back to his hospital room, we were all feeling super-gloomy, and as the nurses were getting him back in the bed, and Mary Sarah and her parents were now in the room – a whole new audience who hadn't heard him start the joke and not finish it – all of a sudden, out of nowhere, Freddy yells out, "I was talking to the goose!" Whenever he was yelling when he'd talk, he'd look at you beforehand and his eyes would be going crazy because you knew he had so much he was trying to say, and when he was finally ready, he blurted it out LOUD because he'd worked it up so long.

Catherine Powers: There were several of those where he'd start to tell a joke and then freeze up and we'd have to wait for him to finish it all.

Joi Vinson Davis: We were all having a good time one night after that, and Freddy at this time wasn't able to eat anything solid – he could have ice cream and smoothies and stuff like that – so we're all sitting around but he wasn't speaking or anything, and was setting up on the couch, and Catherine said, "Papa, what can I get you? What do you want?" And he was looking at us mad for hours, because he'd kept saying he wanted crab claws for like two days before that evening, and he'd kept repeating, "I sure would like some crab claws, I sure would like some crab claws," and we just kept ignoring it because we knew he couldn't have them. So that night, we're all sitting around, having a good time, and then I said, "Freddy, whatever we can do, what can I get you, anything?", and he finally broke his silence, and said "Can you say FUCKING CRAB CLAWS?!!" (laughs)

Catherine Powers: During that Sept. 12 hospital visit, Joi had to leave in a couple days, and kept saying, "Papa, I'm going to have to leave in a day or so, I really want to hear you talk, I just want to hear you say anything," and just kept on and kept on, and finally, the nurse was coming in to check his vitals and everything, and about that time, Freddy screams at the top of his lungs, "I want some pussy!" You could hear him all the way to the nurse's station! SO of course, Joi turns around and says, "Papa, I wanted to hear you talk, but I wasn't expecting that!" (laughs) The nurse kind of jumped back and stared at me, not knowing what to do, and so I told Freddy, "I'll tell you what Papa, you get yourself better, and we'll get back on that bus and talk about some Pussy!" Well, at the same time this is all happening, Sonny Throckmorton calls Joi's phone, and he's on the golf course out there with Willie, so he hears Joi laughing, and naturally asks her, 'What are you laughing at?' So she tells him the story, he relays it to Willie, and they both hang up the phone laughing their asses off. Well, of course, being the joke tellers they always were, Willie picks up his phone right there on the course and calls Merle to tell him about it, and it didn't take very long to make its way all around the Country Music circles that Freddy's first words after being through this horrific near-death experience in the hospital was to belt out, "I want some pussy!"

Joi Vinson Davis: Then he kept saying it, because he would get stuck sometimes trying to get the same thing out, so for the next 20 minutes or so, that's all he kept saying: "I want some pussy!" I mean, the nurses and everybody heard it, it was hilarious!

Catherine Powers: Then to immortalize it, Merle sent me a video with him and Marc Oswald, cracking up, while Merle says, "Freddy, I hear you want some pussy, but unfortunately I ain't got one so I can't give any to you!".

John Rich: When you play a Freddy Powers song, whether its one we wrote with him or one of his, when you play something with him on it, for the rest of my career, as long as I'm singing, we will tell a story about Freddy Powers, or we'll tell one of his jokes, or we'll do something like we did when we were down in New Orleans recently. We played *'Chase Each Other Round the Room Tonight'* and told the crowd, 'That's the guy sitting in the wheel-chair right in front of the sound board who wrote that, go over and tell him thank you for all the great country music!', and 10,000 people turned around and just started applauding, standing up and going crazy because they understand what he means to country music in a world that keeps becoming more and more shallow and shifting, you got a guy like Freddy who's just an absolute icon.

Catherine Powers: It's so amazing the way people have just come out of the woodwork that loved Freddy and have respected him and what he has given them over the years. Freddy was always such a contributor himself and spent so much time raising money for charity and advancing other people's careers, and even Freddy's Dentist, Dr. Anderson, had appreciated Freddy for all he'd done and would never accept money to get his teeth cleaned! The first time that happened, he said, "Freddy, I would never let you pay me for a single thing I do for you. What you have done for so many people, this is my way of giving back." So because Freddy has done so much throughout his life and career for so many other people, that now they've been happy to step up and help him now in a time of his need.

I remember one particularly-touching time in 2010 where we'd actually been able to arrange through the generosity of his friends for Freddy to fly to Europe and perform, and once we were at the venue, they'd known ahead of time about his condition and had set up this nice, big wheelchair on stage for him to sit in while he performed. Well, bless his heart, but that night, right there in the middle of the stage, he was having trouble sitting steadily in that chair because of the Parkinson's shakes, and it got so visibly bad to both the audience and the musicians he was playing with they stopped the show in mid-song. What happened after that was so heart-warming it still brings tears to my eyes, because next thing you know, all these cowboys and country musicians are taking off their belts and a bunch of the band proceeded right there to fasten Freddy sturdily into that wheelchair so he could continue his performance. Sure enough, he sat up there belted into a chair and finished the rest of the show, and the 10,000 people in the audience went crazy!

Steve Carter: My band Stop the Truck became Freddy's band when we took him to Europe, we took him to France twice, and it was after Freddy was too old to go in a way. Traveling wasn't easy for him, the first time in 2008 he was in a walker, the second time in 2010 he was in a wheelchair, and we played at EquiBlues Rodeo in France. I remember the second time, when Freddy's Parkinson's was getting so bad that he'd started to scoot, so we all whipped off our belts and strapped him in the chair to perform on stage! The crowds loved him over there, they knew the words, and didn't even speak English. We had my protégé Ruby Jane on tour with us, and she was standing on stage looking out over the audience and was stunned that these people adored him and cried because it was one of the best things she ever saw. To top the trip off, Freddy and Catherine renewed their vows at the top of the Eiffel Tower with Floyd Domino performing a Jewish Ceremony!

I became his hands and his voice after he couldn't sing, I'm the keeper of the key. I was always a bass player and guitar player, and a friend of mine said, "You need to go see him," so I did, and I'd seen Willie and Johnnie Gimble and this guy in a Motorcycle hat on PBS shortly before that playing all these old Swing standards out at the ranch, and walked in, and at that point, didn't know Freddy by name. He was that guy from the PBS special that was playing rhythm – and I'm a rhythm guitar player, and its almost a lost art. I don't care about solos at all. So I walked in and my first thought was, "Oh no, I can't do this, this is Jazz, this isn't country songs," and when I auditioned, I literally thought he'd say, "Thanks for coming out son," and send me home, but instead he groomed me and taught me how to play Swing.

For about two years, I played bass for him, and the whole time, I was just watching Freddy's rhythm guitar playing, I was watching him like a hawk and stealing everything that I could. Then, B.B. Morris, who was Freddy's bass player for years, he left the band and I replaced him, and B.B. told me years later that it was good I replaced him because otherwise, they never would have found somebody who would learn Freddy's guitar style. So when he got sick, I was right there doing what he did, and so for the first two years I was playing bass, I was really learning those Swing chords and Jazz chords and how he went from one chord to another, and how he strummed and kept time. I was already a pretty good rhythm guitar player and was about 50 when I met Freddy, but he elevated what I did.

What made Freddy's style of guitar playing so unique is his rhythm was militant, he didn't need a drummer, he wasn't playing along with anybody, and militant's kind of a Reggae term, but it was just kind of no letting up. There was no doubt where the groove was when Freddy was playing, and he even made jokes that "It took me 25 years to get a perfect band, no drummer." (laughs) So he was the snare and the hi-hat and the bass player was the bass drum, and he was very much up on his time, there was never any relaxing, or any doubt about where it was. And by that, I don't mean he was pushing, but it was what we came to call digging a trench. If you dig the trench deep enough, the singer can't get out of it, the lead guitar player can't get out of it, so it's a very high-walled trench that you're creating that gives them the freedom to play, but they can't get out of it. They can bounce off the walls of that trench, but they can't get out, and that's kind of what Freddy taught us. He was a natural band leader, he led from the guitar, not from the things he said.

Chapter 16: Freddy Powers Parkinson's Foundation

Catherine Powers: One of our proudest periods of productivity throughout Freddy's deteriorating condition came with the progress we made in fighting the disease through the Freddy Powers Parkinson's Foundation, which began with the overarching goal of spreading awareness about the disease, because Freddy and I didn't know anything about Parkinson's when he was diagnosed, so that was # 1. But secretly, in my heart, I wanted Freddy's name to LIVE. He had done so much for so many people, and I never want him to be forgotten, and over the years, we've been able to call on Freddy's celebrity friends and relationships to host high-profile fundraisers in partnership with prominent local Parkinson's organizations like CAP (Capital Area Parkinson's Society), which serves greater Austin and Central Texas and make a sizable donation. That was always a huge honor and big thrill for Freddy and I to be able – for as helpless as he felt in many ways because of the disease – to still see we'd been able to succeed in making real contributions to the cause. This gave Freddy one more thing to live for, and some of our favorite highlights from those adventures received major press coverage as well, which helped all parties involved.

Freddy Powers: "I still go out every now and then, but I'm not touring like I did before. Most everything we do is for the Parkinson's (Foundation) now. That was

Catherine's idea. She's the spark plug behind the whole thing." 52

Catherine Powers: So through the foundation, we have been able to help people and bring attention to a disease using Freddy's name, which would mean he'd never be forgotten – that was and still is the most important thing to me to this day. That's why I live on this computer, that's why I spread his name and keep him out there as much as I can at all the Hall of Fame Induction ceremonies and concerts I can, because he deserves it. He deserves to be honored and remembered as much as you would remember anyone else of importance in country music, that's the way I feel, and fortunately, that was a shared sentiment too by how successful a run we had during the foundation's heyday.

Country Music Television (CMT) News, 2006: "Big & Rich, Willie Nelson and former U.S. Attorney General Janet Reno will help Texas music mainstay Freddy Powers celebrate his 75th birthday during an Oct. 16 charity event in Austin. A noted songwriter, guitarist and record producer, Powers has recorded with Nelson and toured extensively with Merle Haggard. As a songwriter, his No. 1 hits include George Jones' 'I Always Get Lucky With You' and Haggard's 'Let's Chase Each Other Around the Room'. Nelson and Reno will appear at a roast prior to a performance by Big & Rich. All proceeds from the event at the Barton Creek Art Center will benefit the Freddy Powers Parkinson's Foundation. Diagnosed with Parkinson's disease in 2004, Powers created the organization to fund research and assist Parkinson's patients in Central Texas."

The Lone Star, June, 2008: "Willie Nelson To Host Benefit Concert. Country Music Legend, Willie Nelson will perform a private concert, Monday, June 30, as a preview to the completion of Willie's Place at Carl's Corner, the new state-of-the-art truck stop located on Interstate-35 between Dallas and Austin.

Those attending the June 30 benefit will enjoy a private concert by Willie Nelson, great food and beverages, and pre-opening guided tours of Willie's Place. Platinum sponsors will also be invited to an exclusive meet-n-greet in the Saloon with Willie Nelson. This exclusive event kicks off a week of pre-opening music and celebrations.

On July 1 and 2, David Allan Coe and Ray Wylie Hubbard will be performing live from 8-12 p.m. July 3 will be filled with live performances by Merle Haggard at 6 p.m. followed by Ray Price at 8 p.m. and Willie Nelson at 10 p.m. These concerts are free to the public.

The private concert is a benefit with a portion of proceeds going to the Freddy Powers Parkinson's Foundation. The foundation was founded in 2006 in the name of the award-winning singer, songwriter and producer, Freddy Powers, who suffers from the disease. The foundation benefits Texans with Parkinson's, as well as their caregivers."

KXAN.com: "Parkinson's Patients Find Relief In New Treatment"

Monday February 11, 2008

Michael J. Fox, Katherine Hepburn, Pope John Paul II, Muhammad Ali, the Rev. Billy Graham, Johnny Cash: All have been victimized by Parkinson's disease.

For musician and songwriter Freddy Powers and his wife Catherine, the journey through Parkinson's disease has been grueling. Parkinson's is degenerative, depressing and deadly. It starts in the brain, where cells that make dopamine begin to malfunction. Dopamine is the chemical messenger the brain sends out to tell parts of the body to move.

"Freddy was really walking very slow, moving real slow and his arm was clenched up real tight," Catherine said. "But the two main things were that he had really lost his smile, and his eyes had become real cloudy and really despondent."

But doctors may have stumbled on a promising new treatment. After only 10 daily treatments with a machine that electronically stimulates acupuncture points, things changed.

"It was like I brought home a new husband," Catherine says. "He went from just, you know, almost not with me half the time, or it didn't feel like or look like he was with me, to all of a sudden, he was back; he was back to my Freddy."

Dr. Donald Rhodes was working on a machine to help alleviate chronic pain in his office in Corpus Christi when he noticed symptoms of other kinds improved in Parkinson's and diabetes patients.

"Diseases that respond to this treatment are grouped together by circulation," Rhodes said. "If we can improve circulation, good things happen."

Freddy's neurologist Rob Izor said the treatment is like acupuncture, but with a kick. Intrigued, Izor followed up with a 30-day pilot study with five patients, each of whom experienced some kind of improvement.

"When I lay on the beach to get sun, they call it, 'shake and bake'," Freddy says.

"He came back home with his smile," Catherine said.

"You got your smile back, is that true?" Swift asked.

"Well, it depends on if you say something funny," Freddy said.

Catherine Powers: Looking back now, as proud as I am of what we accomplished, in the same time, it breaks my heart that we eventually had to shut the foundation down due to overhead costs growing because of its success to the point where we had to hire someone full-time to manage the day-to-day operations, but we did A LOT of good while it was running at its peak. It was amazing, all of the different songwriters and musicians that came out of the woodwork and shadows that didn't even want anyone to publicly know they had the disease but were so inspired by Freddy's example that you don't have to be ashamed or don't have to give up what you love doing, and as importantly, that you can find other ways to make what you love doing work in spite of the obstacles of the disease. That has been one of the greatest pleasures and achievements for both Freddy and I, to see him inspire that hope in fellow musicians facing the same struggles.

Even still today, I will get people on the internet who have been struggling with the disease or equally often, folks who are newly diagnosed and scared out of their minds that will reach out to us – kids as young as 32, 33 years old – who write and say, "I have Parkinson's and I'm gonna be like Freddy and I'm not gonna give up, and I'm gonna keep fighting and working and living until I can't anymore," so that in itself is a true honor that he's become an inspiration to so many. It should ultimately be the goal of any type of organization like ours to (inspire) people to come out and accept the disease and learn to live with it and still lead productive lives – what else could be a higher honor?

Chapter 17: South by So-What &
Freddy Powers Legendary Pickin' Parties

Catherine Powers: The lineage of the legendary
Freddy Powers' Pickin' Parties really runs throughout his
entire career, that's always been a part of Freddy. It's
something he's done all the way back to when I first met
him, even out on the houseboats where he and Merle would
have big pickin' parties where there'd be five, six, seven
houseboats all loaded down with musicians and friends and
we'd go up the Pit River there and have big picking parties
right there on the water! Well, of course, those Pickin'
Parties never stopped, and so when Freddy and Merle both
moved off the houseboats and we came back home to
Texas, it's remained a common past-time with Willie and
all sorts of different circles of musician friends of his. So
whenever he wasn't out there working and was at home, a
steady stream of musicians was always coming out to the
house to play with Freddy, and after a while it sort of took
on a life of its own into what has now become an annual
South by Southwest staple.

We lived in a HUGE house on Willie's golf course
when Freddy threw his first official "Freddy Powers'
Pickin' Party" back in 1995, and we started out just having
smaller, private picking parties that first year. Well, not
surprisingly, as word quickly spread Freddy was now back
in town and we got more and more plugged into the Austin
music scene, in 1996 we opened our doors to the public for

the first time to host the first official Freddy Powers Pickin'
Party. In classic maverick fashion, because our event was
happening during the South by Southwest Festival in
Austin and Freddy wasn't into the tradition of having to go
along with the pay-to-play route where all the local live
venues charge bands and artists/songwriters attending the
Festival to showcase in their clubs, Freddy rebelled against
that by sarcastically calling his event the "Freddy Powers
South by *So What* Pickin' Party!"

It really did set the tone for what to expect whether you
showed up to play or listen. He wanted our Pickin' Party to
be more in the spirit of playing just for playing's sake, no
matter who was sitting next to you in the circle, because it
could run randomly from an unknown songwriter to a
legendary one, or an up-and-coming country artist to a
legend like Willie Nelson and of course Merle Haggard,
Michael Martin Murphy, Tanya Tucker, Stu Cook and
Doug 'Cosmo' Clifford from Credence Clearwater Revival
and always lots of big songwriters, like Sonny
Throckmorton and Monte Warden – who wrote # 1s for
George Strait – songwriters have always been a central
focus since Freddy is a songwriter.

Freddy Powers: "Sonny Throckmorton is one of my
hero songwriters. He has written 15 or 20 No. 1 songs, and
he is very prolific. His stories – his songs are stories you
know." [53]

Sonny Throckmorton: I know Freddy's rhythm playing, every time I've ever heard him play, he's just the greatest player I've ever heard in my life on rhythm, he's amazing. If he was going to be on stage, and you were Merle Haggard, you wanted Freddy. If it was Willie, it'd be good to have him because he could play anything that Willie could sing, he was an amazing guitar player.

He's the kind of guitar player that these young people are not going to get to hear that particular style that he played because there's not many people who can do that, or they don't want to because if they're good enough to play rhythm guitar that way, they want to be a lead guitar. So they're not going to exhibit a lot of that rhythm, where his was concentrated rhythm and it was unbelievable. I know when he dies and goes to heaven, they'll have a real good rhythm player up there.

Molly McKnight: I We all love Freddy, what a talent! If you could have known him back then, he had more energy than anyone in the room. I remember the first time I saw him, he was playing the banjo, and boy he was a wonderful guitar player. He and his guitar player Django Porter would just sit out at a picnic table and sit and Freddy would do a run then Django would do a run, then they'd put it together.

Catherine Powers: Originally, Freddy would sit in the center of a room full of musicians – 20, 30 musicians all sitting around – all pickin' with Freddy giving everybody opportunities to shine, and then when Freddy no longer was able to play, that's when we turned it into a party honoring Freddy. That was a very special celebration of Freddy's signature playing style, because there were so many unknown, up-and-coming guitar players throughout the years that have attended these parties to play with and learn from Freddy, and it was pretty funny because usually when they'd first walk in, they'd be scared to death! He'd invite them to sit down and play with him, and at first, they'd say "Oh no, I can't sit down and play with you, I'm not good enough to play with you guys," and Freddy would coax them out. He would tell them, "Play along, just play along as best you can with what you can, follow my hands," so even during these Pickin' Parties, he was giving lessons to new players all the time.

To create as intimate and stripped-back-to-basics performing atmosphere as possible, we decided to hold the party in our living room, which really succeeded in making everyone feel at home and very respectful of the players performing at any given time. We used to always joke seriously with everyone, "It's the funnest, quietest picking party you'll ever go to," because when a performer was playing, there was *NO TALKING*. In fact, that became our number one rule on the wall. We used to call it the Coach Darrell Royal Rule, because of his Pickin' Parties at his golf tournaments where Freddy was pretty much always the host for many years.

Edith Royal: Freddy used to have a lot of pickin' parties at his house too, and Darrell would always be there, and I remember going to Freddy and Catherine's for those, and everybody would bring a dish. Freddy has had a lot of people who met him at our and his and Catherine's Pickin' Parties over the years, everybody who could get in those rooms would come, if they were invited, so Freddy was well known as somebody who helped whoever he could.

Catherine Powers: It would stay busy the entire day too, because we had so many songwriters and pickers wanting to be part of what was going on that we'd start at one in the afternoon and at four o'clock in the morning were still playing! I think in part because it was structured and themed so differently from everything going on in town, and because of Freddy's legend in Texas looming as large as it did, over the next three or four years, our Pickin' Parties grew from 50 to 500 where they were spilling out of the house because our living room was only big enough to seat around 200 people in that living room easy (which still would have been considered a large audience given the setting). So by the turn of the Millennium, it got so popular that every year there would be people spilling out all over the place, and the vibe was so infectious that out in the yard, there'd be little circles of players picking together everywhere. Then on our back porch we had this big old picnic table, and there'd be groups of people sitting out there smoking and pickin.

Finally, after Freddy was formally diagnosed with Parkinson's and we moved out of the house and moved to the La Hacienda RV Park, where we kept them going for years since to where it's become such a tradition that they honored Freddy by dedicating the venue the FREDDY POWERS PICKIN' PAVILLION after him, where we began hosting the pickin' parties shortly after moving off of Willie's golf course. We'd been invited over by the owner to check the pavilion out as a possible new venue to start hosting the parties, parked our bus, and never left. This is one of the finest RV resorts in the Austin area, and in fact, when word got into town we'd moved over, the Austin Statesman came out to do a story on the resort and featured Freddy and our new home:

The Austin Statesman, 2010: "A few yards away, at a party building, a band is rehearsing in the middle of the afternoon. Freddy Powers, a singer-songwriter who toured for years with Merle Haggard, is preparing his band, Stop the Truck, for an appearance at Willie Nelson's Fourth of July picnic. Powers and his wife, Catherine, sold their house and donated his memorabilia to Texas State University in San Marcos after he was diagnosed with Parkinson's disease. They are now living the RV lifestyle."

Catherine Powers: I get inundated each and every year with fans emailing and calling me to inquire about whether there will be a party this year, and I always say "I plan on keeping these parties going for the rest of our lives, as long as there's a place to have a Freddy Powers party, we'll have one." Thankfully, the new owners of the RV resort have proudly continued on what has now become a proud tradition of hosting the annual Pickin Parties, and so as long as there's a Freddy Powers Pickin' Pavilion standing, there will always be a Freddy Powers' Pickin' Party! It has never lost its lure with fans either, and it's funny because on the day of the party every year, you can see cars lined up down the road pulling into the park looking just like outdoor amphitheaters during the summertime, so the demand has sustained itself.

Singer/Songwriter Lee Duffy: "I met Freddy Powers through Rattlesnake Annie and became an immediate fan of his. I got to go to a picker's circle and hear Freddy do all these songs that he'd written for Merle Haggard… Freddy had moved back to town… and Catherine was very kind and encouraging. I was petrified, she was saying 'You're doing great. Don't let them see you sweat. You look good'. She helped me out…. (She) didn't just open the door for me, she opened the door, put me in the damn car and drove me there. Freddy invited me to Coach Royal's golf tournament with all the best singer/songwriters in the world. Freddy is his side-kick; Freddy runs the Pickin' part of the show. He knew how shy I was… if I'm in front of a microphone, I can't speak. I was petrified that I wasn't good enough.

Freddy was in the middle of singing 'Riding High' from his Country Jazz album. The first line is 'They told us we would never reach the top, they told us we would probably not'. I love it. I had jammed with him a few times at his house because he was just really pulling it out of me. I would show up there every day. He leaves the guitar and microphone out 24/7. He would get up early and play until lunch. I would just ask for every song I knew. Catherine found this satchel of a couple hundred songs that he had written, which they found under a bed in Tyler's at her mom's. He would just sort through them; he'd forgotten about five hundred of them. Like diamonds.

So Freddy knew I would never sing out loud in front of all these people. He's in the middle of his show, in a room of singer/songwriters, trained professionals, and I'm minding my own business talking to Coach Royal, so excited that Freddy was singing 'Riding High'. I heard him introduce me as this wonderful singer and friend of his. I was melting. He doesn't play this in the same key I sing, and I heard him say to the band, 'We're going to change this to the key of A'. He just looked at me and smiled. You can't say no to Freddy, what could I do? I had to sing. (Source: "Women in Texas Music: Stories and Songs," by Kathleen Hudson, University of Texas Press, November, 2007)

Catherine Powers: Freddy and I are especially proud of the fact that through our parties, we've had artists land record deals, songs get picked up by publishers, performers get picked up to go out on tour, so through Freddy's parties, once again, he has opened the door for other musicians to move upward in their careers. I remember one year NPR Radio was covering the South by Southwest Festival in Austin, and the first week of the Festival is all about the movie industry, and then the second week, which focuses on the music industry, so they got into talking all about who was in town and what was going on, and the NPR journalist covering the Festival closed his segment with the following nod: "And *renegade* Freddy Powers had his own star-studded South by Southwest Party at his home!"

Once that caught on, we were having pickin' parties all the time throughout the year, and the other one that has become the most famous within the Austin and broader songwriting community worldwide is the Black Eyed Pea and Cabbage Pickin' Party, because we've actually had people travel from England and Switzerland and France and even as far as Barbados to make their vacation around our pickin' parties. The Black Eyed Pea and Cabbage party got its start back in the 1990s while we were still living back at the house on Willie's Golf course when somebody asked us one year if we were going to have a New Year's Eve pickin' party, and Freddy said "Well, most of the musicians will be out working that night, so we probably wouldn't have a very good party, so why don't we have a party on New Year's Day, and we'll serve black eyed peas and cabbage." So we started hosting those, and they were such a hit that the next thing I knew, we'd moved over to

the Freddy Powers Pickin' Pavilion and people were
bringing their own versions of black eyed peas and cabbage!
(laughs) It was like having a tasting party with black eyes
peas and cabbage and wonderful, talented musicians
playing from all around the world in the background.

Tanya Tucker: I went to a Black Eyed Peas and
Cabbage Pickin' Party on New Year's Day, the one they do
every year, and at this point, Freddy was already in the
wheelchair, and we spent the night out there and I got to
see how cool it was to go to these things. A lot of great
writers show up and sing and play, and you could almost
get your whole new album just from going to one of those
Pickin Parties!

It was so cool, everybody brings something they've
cooked, and there's no egos, everybody just has a good
time, and a lot to drink and a lot to eat, and you hear a lot of
great music: stuff that's never been recorded, stuff that has
been recorded, big records, and you get to see where a song
really came from. That's what I like about it. I love the fact
too that you can go and hear new stuff, because that's what
I'm always up for: hearing new songs and just songs that
I've never heard before, that haven't been recorded or
haven't been hits. It's a great way for an artist to get new
songs, and I have done that for years, gone to events like
Freddy's, that's where we used to write, was with a group
of people that liked each other, were talented, and would
get in a room with a few guitars and start writing something.

Catherine Powers: Those pickin' parties became and still are to this day a huge event, even to where people tell us they book their vacations around our Pickin' Party dates, and still to date, the droves of songwriters especially that come each year to play for Freddy, and it's really quite touching to watch because its really like an event within an event. Where they used to play with Freddy at the parties, now they come to play for him, and often will perform Freddy's own songs for him that he can't play or sing himself anymore. That really has helped us come full-circle with the spirit of what the Pickin' Parties have always been about: a circle of songwriters, playing their own new songs as well as the classics, including Freddy's. Our main goal every year is that Freddy is sitting out there watching and hearing these songwriters pay homage to his legacy and perform his hits, both for him and for the wonderful audiences that always wind up attending year after year, and hopefully still will for years to come. Even now, I take him over to the Flora-Bama, and you can see the energy and light in his face when they play one of his own songs to him, it's quite special now that people are playing for instead of listening to Freddy.

Chapter 18: Mentoring a New Generation of Stars

Catherine Powers: Something Freddy and I do laugh about a lot is that in more recent years, it seemed like girls were coming from out of everywhere wanting to learn from and be mentored by Freddy, and one of our favorite early examples of that was Pauline Reese, I remember the first time she walked up to him she was 15 years old with a little boom box. Well, she set that boom box down and started singing for Freddy, and right there he told her, "Honey, you've got a great voice but if you can't play for yourself, if you can't back yourself on guitar, you'll be a slave to a band, and probably go no further than you and this boom box." So immediately Pauline went out and Molly McKnight bought her a guitar, and she played a little bit of guitar but not much, and before too long came back over that same day to get her first lesson from Freddy, and it was like she almost moved in! She was there every day taking every opportunity she could to just sit there and pick and play with Freddy all day long.

Pauline Reese: I've spent 22 years of my life with Catherine and Freddy, who is like a Grandfather to me, he's by far one of my biggest influences in my career. My friend Molly McKnight, her father was a State Senator from Texas, Peyton McKnight, and she had known Freddy for years, and Peyton was one of those people in Government who got Willie and Merle and Freddy all these gigs with

Government offices, because they just loved that crowd of guys, for good reason. So she introduced me to Freddy thinking that he would help me out musically, I already played guitar, but he really took it to a different level.

Molly McKnight: Pauline came to me when a friend of mine had brought her to me, and she was 15, and I had a son and a daughter, but sort of adopted her as my other daughter, and she was playing just here and there at the time. So we went to dinner one night and I said, "Pauline, have you ever heard Willie Nelson?" And when she said no, I asked if she'd like to, and of course she said yes, so I we went over to where Willie was playing, and of course it was packed when we got there, and she was saying, "We'll never get in," and I said "Hush" and went to find Willie's road manager at the time Pootie. So the bouncer went to get Pootie, and of course he let us in, and Pauline could not believe it! So a little after that, I took her out to Freddy's for a guitar lesson, because Pauline didn't play the guitar at all, and of course, she learned to play the guitar with Freddy, and everybody sort of fell in love with her like I did.

Pauline Reese: So when we met, the three of us fell in love, and he and Catherine took me under their wing and into their house, and I literally spent most of my teenage years going to their house and learning chords from Freddy, we'd write songs, I'd stay the night because it was so far away from where I was living in Leander at the time. My parents knew them, and thought it was great that I was working with this wonderful songwriter who was really taking the time to teach me the craft and about the business and everything else about it. I always wondered what his motivation was to take a 15-year-old girl under his wing, I will be forever grateful for a guy like him, and his wife, I mean what a cool wife to have to say, "Yeah, that girl's got some talent, let's help her out!" And I mean, it just wasn't helping me, I literally stayed at their house for years on and off.

Invariably, Willie would come over in the mornings and have coffee with Freddy, and I would just be a fly on the wall listening to these great stories and them just talking about the business and music, and I was so fortunate to be in a position that I was in soaking everything up like a sponge. Freddy would talk to Merle every couple of days on the phone, and Merle knew who I was because of Freddy, Willie knew who I was because of Freddy, and I credit my duets with Willie to Freddy, because I wouldn't have known Willie the way that I do if it weren't for Freddy and Catherine. He LOVED to play jokes on people, and I think a big part of his and Willie and Merle's friendship was telling jokes back and forth, whatever the latest ones they had heard. So it was just constant joke telling, and I had to start categorizing all of the jokes so that I could keep up! (laughs)

Molly McKnight: So I introduced her around to all the people I knew, but Freddy really took to her and she to him, and it's not hard to like Freddy Powers. One thing led to another, and she called me one day and said, "Guess what I'm doing?", and when I told her I had no idea, she said "I'm playing golf with Willie Nelson, Sonny Throckmorton and Freddy!", and I said, "Well, you're in high cotton, aren't you!" So that's sort of how she got started out in the business, and Freddy was a big part of that.

Catherine Powers: Pauline from those lessons with Freddy learned a lot about songwriting and playing the guitar, and she went on to become a star in Texas. She's won every major award that an entertainer can win, and it's kind of a best-kept secret as a recording star, you don't have to leave the state of Texas to be a star. Texas is its own country, so you can have a huge name and make a living in the state, play large venues that would only be headlined by stars, and Pauline plays all the big shows and gets major radio play, and in fact, she and Freddy had a hit they wrote together, *"One Less Honky Tonk"* that went all the way to the Top 10 on the Texas Music Charts.

Pauline Reese: With guitar playing, he taught me songs that had every chord in the book so that I could play anything, that was really important, and another thing that was really important Freddy did for me during those years is he would come out to my shows and watch and critique and say, "Let's video you so you can go back and watch yourself to see what's going on," so we would do that all the time. And I've gone through every old video tape of his old bands, and Catherine loved it, she loved that I was so into the old days of what Freddy had done, and I think I heard every story about his life because I wanted to know more about him and how he ended up where he is, and how he wrote those songs because I wanted to be a great songwriter like him.

He was a great entertainer too, and he would also say, "When you walk in the back door, you better be walking straight onto the stage," and this is kind of an old-school thought process, but then he'd say, "You don't wanna be talking with everybody and doing all this stuff, you need to be getting on to the stage to perform: be a star and they'll treat you like a star." That was something he was really adamant about, and would get mad at me (laughs) if I walked in to visit with people, which was difficult for me because I love people and love my fans and they've become my friends, so if I was out on the floor talking to somebody before a show and Freddy saw that, he would always come and gently lead me over toward the stage, and say "No no, you get on stage the second you walk in that back door, what did I tell you?"

Catherine Powers: He didn't give a whole lotta lessons, but was never one that gave lessons and then charged for it. I have seen Freddy take two guys, two guys

who never played an instrument before, and gave them a
guitar and six months later, he had them not only playing
guitar, but had them singing and writing songs and
performing with him. He gave them the courage and the
ability to get up there and do what they really wanted to do
all their lives, especially with some of the players that have
come up playing in Freddy's band over the years, from
Gary Church – who was just a 19-year-old kid when
Freddy took him on, and he went on to play with Merle
Haggard, and Mel Tillis and Ray Price – or Clint Strong or
Django Porter. So when it comes to musicians, Freddy has
worked with guys as young as a 16-year-old guitar player
named Tommy Bell, and the Manuel Brothers, they called
Freddy their mentor, there's so many.

Pauline Reese: One thing that I really soaked up and I
think the only two people that really got this were Django
Porter and I, it was the triplets, because Freddy – when he
was in a band called the Powerhouse IV with three banjos
and a tuba – was playing banjo and that's a lot of triplets to
be playing and is a different style. So he brought that style
of playing over to his guitar style, and that's what really
made him stand out as a guitar player, because it was a very
Django Reinhardt type of thing, but even more so because
he played banjo for so many years. My grandfather played
banjo as well, so I was like, "Well, yeah, that's killer,"
because it fits perfectly in swing music, it makes perfect
sense, and kind of mimics the banjo sound. So I do that still,

even in the music I just wrote on my new record, its kind of part of who I am as a player because I heard it in my ear since I was a kid through Freddy. I've even had other peers of mine, like Steve Carter, say "Can you teach me that thing that Freddy does? I never really took the time to learn how to do that", and his style really stands out – comparatively speaking – with other rhythm guitar players because that is its own instrument.

I saw all these guys come along over the years, like Django when he was just coming into his own, when I first met Freddy he was just learning how to play from Freddy, and Steve Carter, who didn't come along till 2001. But I just remember all these people coming along into Freddy's life and just watching him embrace everybody, and what that did for their lives. He really deserves to be acknowledged for that from so many of us he helped along the way in our careers.

Catherine Powers: I can proudly say that out of all 30 years I've been with Freddy, in a business where life-long grudges are made off of a single bad encounter let alone the bad blood that can build between bandmates, etc. over time, I've only run across a SINGLE, solitary example among any of the musicians who've worked for Freddy in bands or business, from unknown artists to superstars. Only one, and it was a situation where we had a former member of the Powerhouse IV – of which Freddy was obviously the star in their heyday as the frontman – back together, and asked this former member to be part of a reunion performance since Freddy couldn't play himself anymore. Everybody in the band had signed on except for this one nameless member, and his excuse was over some gripe he made that he'd called Freddy years ago after he'd hooked up with Merle and claimed he wouldn't help the guy out.

Well, that was just not Freddy because he never met a request for a favor he didn't try to come through on, and I was in such disbelief that I finally called the guy myself, wanting to get to the bottom of what this was all about, and he told me, "Freddy hooked up out there with Merle and I called him one time about a song, and he never got back with me." Well, I had to tell him, first of all, at that time, Freddy didn't have an assistant or personal secretary for himself, and more importantly, he was living out there on his houseboat with no phone! That was part of the point because there was a strong possibility he never even got the message, so next I asked him, "How did you try to get in touch with Freddy?", and he was very ugly – and obviously a little bitter – because he replied, "I don't care if he got the message or not, he never contacted me back." That just ran contrary to history because throughout his career, there have been literally hundreds and hundreds of musicians who have played with Freddy, and every one of them still to this day will pay him compliments for the things he has done for them individually to open doors and make introductions that resulted in their careers getting a lift of some kind, and whether professionally or just musically as a player in what he taught them. They all appreciate it, and have thanked him years later for it because it made such an impact, because Freddy's word has always been gold when he referred a young up-and-coming player to a band for an audition or an artist considering opening acts or a promoter for a gig, it's been endless.

As a matter of fact, Freddy was one that was so loyal to his band that he would even put their name on a song he'd written when they didn't have anything to do with writing it so they could share in the revenues as a writer. He's even pulled his own song off a Merle Haggard album to make room for a writer he saw potential in, and lost money over it. But he never had a bad taste in his mouth or turned his back on them, he continued to help anyone out that he could, even if it cost him money. I've always been proud of how loudly that speaks to his character. He's always been someone who inspired people, whether it was an aspiring songwriter looking to learn how to write a song good enough to shop, or hit songwriters like Merle, who was the first one to see something special in Freddy as a songwriter, enough so to enlist him as a co-writer when Hag had thousands of songwriters banging down his door. Throughout his whole career, he's always been someone musicians felt comfortable enough to come to when they needed advice or guidance or a favor where contacts and making a call was concerned, because they also knew Freddy had enough respect among the live promoters, club owners and band leaders that his referral made a big difference as a foot in the door.

I remember a story Freddy told me about one of his band members who had asked him – with an obvious mix of admiration and envy – "Freddy, I work as hard as you do, don't I?", and Freddy said, "Yeah," and next he said, "I put in as many hours as you on that stage, don't I?", and again, Freddy answered, "Yeah," so then he got right to the point of his frustration: "Well then Freddy, how come I don't make as much money as you do?", and Freddy gave him a constructive and honest response – he was never disrespectful. But, Freddy had told him because I booked the job, if you book a job and hire me then you'll make more and I less, and I remember Freddy said because it was one of those rare situations where at first, what Freddy said didn't satisfy him when he quit the band. He must have let what Freddy had told him sink in, a couple years later, sure enough, the phone rang with an apology from this player, and he said, "Freddy, I never knew what it was like being the leader of the band until I *tried* to be the leader of the band. That was probably the best thing you could have ever done for me, was to tell me that." What Freddy had told him had ultimately turned out to be exactly the kick in the ass he needed at that point in his career.

Moments like that were why many people came to Freddy for advice over the years, first because he always made himself approachable and accessible, and equally and maybe more importantly, because they knew there was enough wisdom naturally woven into his conversational response that they knew they'd walk away better for it: professionally, as a player, and if you want a real measure of all the people Freddy's helped throughout their careers, to this day, I get strangers – to me – calling to check on how he's doing, people I've never met, but even if it was back in the 60s or 70s, there was something substantial enough about their connection with Freddy that it lasted their whole career. I never get off the phone with any of them without them telling me how much Freddy means to them personally as much as he has professionally because he always made time for everyone.

Another one of our favorite mentor moments came when this friend of ours sent us a video over the internet of this little girl who was five years old at the time singing a song of Freddy's, and it turned out as fate would have it that she lived right down the road from us. So we go to meet her at her house, and we're visiting and all of a sudden, she grabs Freddy's hand and says, "Mr. Freddy, I want you to come to my bedroom," which got us all laughing, but she takes Freddy back there, and hanging over her bed are two framed pictures: one was of Floyd Tillman – and how many five-year-olds in their lives have ever heard of Floyd Tillman? (laughs) The other was of Freddy, those were the two pictures of her country heroes she had hanging in her bedroom.

Well, immediately, right off the bat, Freddy tells her dad, "She's gotta learn to play an instrument," and the next thing you know, she gets her hands on a Ukulele and with that ukulele, this little girl by the time she was seven years old, was writing songs, winning songwriting contests with adults in Austin, Texas, and she probably is to this day the closest one who can play Freddy's riffs, even more so than Steve Carter, who became what we have always called "Freddy's hands" once he lost the ability to play guitar. But that little girl's name was Lauren Beller, and she copied Freddy and learned all his songs, and after two years was on T.V. with him doing performances so little Lauren became a pretty well-known household name right there in Texas before she was even 10 years old.

The King of Country Dixie Swing

Vs 1
He came from west Texas
With a pen in his hand
Writing and singing songs so grand……..so grand

Vs 2
A guitar on his knee
He plays a song and sings
Country, Dixie or Swing, hear him sing…….hear him sing

Bridge
You can tell by the company he keeps
He's in a league of his own
With all the greats who come to play with him
Paul Buskirk, Willie Nelson, Merle Haggard, George Jones

Verse
He's got a style all his own
He's got a style all his own
That's why Freddy's the King of Country-Dixie-Swing

Bridge
He's a master with the country sound

I tell you brother that's no lie
It's solid gold on your radio
A Friend in California, Texas, Silver Eagle, Natural High...

Verse
What more can we say
About the King of Country-Dixie-Swing
Well, maybe just one more thing,
Freddy we love youuu Oh,,,Oh.....Yea

Outro Verse
Hey, listen Freddy Powers
The pleasures been ours

Cause Freddy, Freddy,
We've Always Been Lucky With You…………

Catherine Powers: Then out of the blue comes along Mary Sarah, who was discovered by Sharon Dennis and who has always referred to Freddy as her father in the music industry because Sharon's first gig was playing drums for Freddy when she was just 18 years old. So she brought Mary Sarah to Freddy to meet him, and he liked her vocal style and thought he could work with her, and of course, the first piece of advice Freddy tells every girl – which he told Pauline Reese, who is another of his major protégés – is, "Honey, you got a great voice and you'll go really far, but you'll really go far and farther if you can play an instrument. You need to learn to play guitar," and he explained to her that if she didn't know how to play guitar, she would always be a slave to the musicians and would be singing to them, instead of them back to her. So Mary Sarah got her guitar, got some lessons, and is a great songwriter as well, a talent Freddy has also helped her develop over the years.

Mary Sarah: I first met Freddy in Austin, Texas. Freddy and Catherine asked if I could sing the national anthem at a charity function they were hosting. We had breakfast the next day. Freddy was not speaking much at the time but he was able to convey to Catherine... things he wanted me to know. Freddy was adamant about not just being a singer, but being a musician. I would say that I began to take guitar playing much more serious after meeting Freddy.

Catherine Powers: When we first took a meeting with her, it was just to hear her sing and Freddy was so blown away that he came up with an idea of having Merle Haggard do a duet with her, and that concept blossomed into what became Mary Sarah's "*Bridges*" album. Freddy has always said that the greatest achievement and honor for him as a songwriter or producer is to take an unknown and give them their start in the business, and since he couldn't play or perform any more at this point but could still produce, he became the Executive Producer on the project, and helped line up a lot of the major stars she did duets with throughout the record, including Willie Nelson, Ray Price and Merle Haggard, and between Freddy, Sharon Dennis and the Oak Ridge Boys, who also immediately wanted to be a part of Mary Sarah's career and opening doors for her.

We were able to get 12 famous legends of country music, including Dolly Parton, Lynne Anderson, Ronnie Milsap, the Oak Ridge Boys, Neil Sedaka, Big Kenny and John Rich, Tanya Tucker, and she closes the album in a duet with Freddy titled, "All I Wanna Do is Sing My Song". Freddy was the Executive Producer on the album, and I wound up getting a crash course on record production during the making of the album after Freddy's ability to

speak failed him completely, and I had to become his voice
on the album, which included things like reaching out to
the artists and their management on all sorts of different
management teams and personalities, and on and on. It was
a lot to juggle while taking care of Freddy at the same time,
but in the long run, great training for the reality that I was
having more and more to take over speaking on his behalf
in matters of business, medical, personal, and musical
decisions.

Mary Sarah: Freddy and Catherine were instrumental
in pulling together *Bridges*. Without them... the heart of the
project would have been missing. Ray Price, Merle
Haggard, and Willie Nelson agreed to help Freddy finish
this final project. Vince Gill also agreed because he knew
of Freddy's work and artistry! I was humbled by the fact
that he was putting his reputation and his friendships on the
line for me. I know he believed in me enough to reach out
to his closest friends and that faith changed my life. Freddy
also gave my previous album, "*Crazy Good*" two thumbs
up and that gave me the confidence to venture out in to
more songwriting.

Catherine Powers: Everybody involved knew this
was going to be Freddy's last project, his last big go-around,
and I remember it was touching, because Ray had called us
about it to check it out, and said, "Well, I'll do anything for
Freddy", went in the studio with Mary Sarah and they did

the duet together. Mary Sarah's album took three years to complete, and she's still getting major publicity from it, and it's another project that is also bringing Freddy's name back out, because he hasn't worked since 2010 as far as going out on the road, so you have to refresh people's memory, and that will always be my goal, for the rest of my life, is to keep his name and music out there and current. That's why it's also great to have so many fans of his out there re-cutting or singing songs of his for the first time as a cut, like "*Day and Nighttime Blues*", that song had only been cut by Freddy until recently, but now it's being made a favorite around here because it's being performed by Chris Newbury, and so songs like that, that aren't his best known hits are making their way into the public by all these new artists performing and recording his songs.

Country Music Association CMA Close Up: "At just 18 years old, Mary Sarah is making herself known among Country Music legends. After years of performing and growing her own fan base through social media, Mary Sarah… with the help of executive producer, Freddy Powers… was inspired to create her latest project, an album titled *Bridges,* which features duets with some of Country's biggest names including Dolly Parton, Willie Nelson, Merle Haggard and Vince Gill."

Mary Sarah: My favorite song is "*Let's Chase Each Other around The Room Tonight*". I love the playful lyrics and the melody. But I also was honored to sing, "*All I Wanna Do...*" this song more than anything told me who Freddy was without him speaking. We connected in that song because that's all I ever wanna do is sing. Music heals and I could see it in Freddy.

Houston Press: "*Bridges* certainly has its heart in the right place. It's dedicated to Freddy Powers, the longtime Austin singer-songwriter and an old running buddy of Haggard's, who spotted Sarah early on and basically set this whole project in motion. Their tender closing duet, '*All I Wanna Do Is Sing My Song*', could choke up your average stone-faced DPS state trooper. (Now battling Parkinson's disease, Powers is also credited as an executive producer on the album.)"

Billboard Country: "All of the artists recorded live with the singer in the studio – a rarity these days. She says she knows they get tons of such offers all the time, but thanks to Freddy Powers – a longtime songwriting collaborator of Nelson and Haggard, the artists all signed on for the project."

The New York Times: "A salute to the latter, Ms. Sarah's mentor, whose voice has been silenced by Parkinson's disease."

Mary Sarah: I was able to spend many of nights singing to him as the Parkinson's was progressing. In the hospital, on the bus and even in the studio he would cry when I sang to him. His favorite song is *How Great Thou Art* and it was something he requested often. Those times will always remain very special to me. His eyes would light up and by the time I was finished he would be in tears. No doubt it was giving him strength!

Tanya Tucker: The first reason I did it was because Catherine asked me too, and I was glad to do it for her, I'm glad to do anything for her. She never asks much, but when she does, I'm ready to do it, and it was very cool that Mary Sarah was a new artist. You always want to give back and try to help out the new acts come along, and that's the other reason I did it, and they made it so easy for me. So I was proud to do it for Freddy and Catherine. I'll pretty much do anything they ask.

Catherine Powers: Mary Sarah's collaboration with Freddy would even inspire her boyfriend at the time to make him the subject of a truly touching college enterance essay:

It was a Sunday night—September 16, just over a month ago—when I had one of the most influential, touching, inspiring, and emotional experiences of my life. As we walked into the hospital room, my girlfriend, her parents, and I looked at an 80-year old man; he was sitting in his bed, wrinkled, quiet, no more than 110 pounds. This man was Freddy Powers, a talented country artist who has played with many of the legends: Willie Nelson, Merle Haggard, you name it. He was also the executive producer for my girlfriend, Mary Sarah Gross, which is why I was there. Mary Sarah was making a visit, her last visit, to Freddy; he was dying of Parkinson's disease—a degenerative disorder of the central nervous system—an illness that takes you from the inside, one in which you know what you want to do, but you physically cannot do it. I accompanied her because she told me he was an amazing man who had impacted her life greatly, and she wanted me there with her during this emotional time. I made my way over to him, said hello, patted his hand, and walked across the room to a chair. And when I turned around, I noticed something; his eyes, an extravagant sky blue, were still fixed on me. At this point in time, I had no clue why, but I was soon to find out.

I watched as Mary Sarah hugged him, kissed him, and then proceeded to sit down on the edge of his bed and hold his hand. She spoke to him softly, telling him that she loved him so much. But when he tried to speak back, his mouth slowly moved, and no words came with it. She looked at her father, Todd, and he said, "Well, Freddy, Mary Sarah wanted to sing you a song. Is that okay?" His reply, a low mumble, an understood 'Of course.' She sat there, still holding his hand, looking straight into his eyes. Todd began playing the chords of a song which was Freddy's favorite, a

song which touched his heart, "How Great Thou Art."
Mary Sarah began to sing as Freddy stared straight back at
her, and I will never forget when I saw the tears roll down
his cheeks as she sang to him:

> Then sings my soul
> My Savior, God, to Thee
> How great thou art
> How great thou art

He may not be able to speak, I thought, but he can still,
as strong as anything, feel the love of our God deeply in his
heart.

The rest of us listened 'til the end of the song, and
when it was finished, we watched as Mary Sarah leaned on
Freddy's shoulder, as they both cried. Then it came time for
me to leave, and I felt the sadness as I walked towards him,
knowing it was probably the last time I was ever going to
see this man, who, even though I had only known for a
short time, had made such an impact on my heart I could
hardly explain it. And as I walked towards him, I noticed
those giant blue eyes were again fixed on mine. When I
reached the side of his bed, I didn't know what to say. I
mean, I barely knew the man; what all could I say? So I
laid my hand on his and said "It was very nice meeting
you." I turned to walk away, but as I turned, I noticed
something out of the corner of my right eye—Freddy's
hand was outstretched towards me. In complete awe, I

turned my body back towards his and took his hand. As we stood there connected by a handshake, we also connected by a stare, right into each other's eyes. As I stood there, we just looked at each other, and that's when my tears began flowing. He observed my face and seemed to know why I was crying. I felt a small pull by his hand, and so I leaned in close, putting my ear close to his mouth, listening for anything he may have to say. And that is when I heard one of the most touching things I have ever heard in my life. "Take care of her, son." Another wave of tears came racing down my face as I replied, "With my life." As I squeezed his hand, I pressed my forehead against his, and then I said, "I'll see you again someday." And I left.

An eighty year old man with Parkinson's disease...can't hardly move, can barely speak, but he can love. That is what really influenced me that day, when I saw a man going through so much pain I cannot even imagine it, yet he still uses all the strength he has to show he loves someone an unbelievable amount...when I saw a man shed tears at such a beautiful song, knowing and showing how great our God really is. I've been having troubles in my relationship with Christ lately, and seeing this man helped strengthen my heart. It helped me listen for the voice and the love of God I've been striving for a while now. And through just that short amount of time, Freddy managed to influence me to love others with everything I have. He influenced me to never pity myself, to always protect the ones I care about. And on the night of Sunday,

September 16, 2012, Freddy Powers influenced me to always love my God through anything and everything because I know that my God will always love me, and one day, I'll be coming home to him.

Chapter 19: The Flora-Bama

Catherine Powers: When I look back over the last 13 years, I still shake my head because I was 52 years old when all this started, and was still young and strong as a blue Ox. Now that I'm in my early 60s, I've started to feel the weight Freddy's condition has taken on both of us physically, because I've damaged my shoulders and my back from carrying him everywhere so many years, and I can't get him in and out of this bus myself anymore. That's been a struggle in and of itself because it's made us more dependent on others around us to pick up that slack, which is again why I'm continually so grateful Freddy has so many fans, friends and sympathizers around the country that – no matter where we pull in to – are waiting to help us out with whatever we need.

We've had some adventures and misadventures along the way too that these close friends of ours witnessed up close and personal, like Freddy's follies with golf carts! The first one of those happened when it was getting to that point where Freddy shouldn't have been driving. I didn't really have to take his license away from him, because one day when he was trying to back out of our driveway, and trying to turn, every time he would try he couldn't do it until he finally ran into the back end of our neighbor's truck. That's when he realized he didn't need to be driving the car anymore, but he could still get around okay on the golf cart, and by then, we were living out at the La

Hacienda RV Resort, and one day he'd taken our little four-legged fur baby Olga out for a golf cart ride while I'd been working on something else. Well, all of a sudden, my attention was pulled away and out the window to the sound of all these people freaking out and yelling, and next thing I know, they show back up at the bus with Freddy. Well, what had happened was, when he'd gotten to the front of the La Hacienda entrance, which was two big double doors, he couldn't stop the golf cart, and instead of putting on brakes, he floor-boarded it! When he did, he broke right through those two doors, and went through the back of a building, taking down every rack, every shelf on the way out, and they said if that dog could have screamed "Help", she was screaming it, because they'd never seen a dog with eyes the size of silver dollars, after that, we all decided that he didn't need to be driving the golf cart by himself anymore.

Cass Hunter: Back when Freddy could still get around some, he had this scooter at the Beach house at the Flora-Bama, and there was like 10 girls, all of us, walking together, and he hit the gas, and he couldn't control his hands very well, so his hand gripped down and he couldn't release it and he went FLYING full-blast heading straight towards the road! We were all running and going, "Oh God, he's going to run right into traffic", and right before the highway, he suddenly turned, did a U-turn and flung gravel everywhere! (laughs)

Catherine Powers: Another of our golf cart adventures actually sent Freddy to the hospital. We were on Willie's golf course, and Freddy was letting Sonny Throckmorton drive, but Sonny was up on the green, and Freddy decided he was gonna pull the golf cart up to where Sonny was, and once again, he put that foot on the gas pedal and was sitting on the wrong side, trying to do it from the passenger's side. Well, his foot locked up with the Parkinson's, and when it did, he plowed into two golf carts totally destroying them, and if it hadn't been for them, he would have hit a tree head-on. Still, the impact threw him out of the golf cart and left him lying on the ground next to the wreck. So we had an ambulance come right down the middle of the fairway of Willie's golf course, before we'd even gotten out of that parking lot, it was already on KVET Radio that Freddy'd had a wreck on Willie's golf course! After that, I started pushing him everywhere in his wheelchair, it was safer for both of us, ☺.

Tanya Tucker: Seriously, I think Catherine is a real angel, really, I really do. She is just unbelievable and it's so great that Freddy has someone like her, because anybody else, there's no way they'd still be around. There's nothing she won't do for that man.

Catherine Powers: Thank God for the Flora-Bama because Joe Gilchrist and John McGinnis have provided us a place to stay with all of our needs taken care of. I have help getting him out of the bus, and on days we can't get out where its pouring down rain for instance, he's got a view and can sit here and look out his front windshield to watch the dolphins, watch the boats go by, and the Blue Angels when they fly by overhead. The Perdido Key Island, where Flora-Bama is located, is known as the Songwriter's Paradise because there's been a lot of songwriters who have made their home here, or who have their summer homes here, it's loaded with musicians and songwriters who live all up and down this area, and there's been many songs written referring to Flora-Bama as the songwriter's paradise or the musician's paradise.

One thing that really makes this a paradise for songwriters and musicians is that *they get paid.* They get paid down here, where in Nashville and Austin, they're working for tips and for meals or the free drink. Here, they get the paycheck, the tips, the meal *and* the free drink, so its very fair the way they treat the talent down here as well, and they've always been very respectful of songwriters of Freddy's stature, and Hank Cochran, and Red Lane – who's written major, major hits – we're all part of the Flora-Bama Family of songwriters and musicians.

Joe Gilchrist is the founder of the Frank Brown Songwriting Festival. At this Festival, they bring in songwriters from everywhere and again, they're getting paid vs. having to volunteer to play, and they're playing for an actual audience, which is one thing most songwriters don't get a lot of. And a lot of these songwriters, people don't even know them by name, because all they hear is a recording artist singing the song that the songwriter wrote. So when they come down here, they get to perform their songs and play on the same bill with songwriting legends like Wayne Carson – who wrote "Get Me a Ticket for an Airplane" or "Always on My Mind" for Willie Nelson – and guys like Dean Dillon, so it's a great mix at the Frank Brown Festival.

Co-Owner Joe Gilchrist: Freddy has a lot of musicians here that respect his history. For so long, I've been thrown in the middle of such wonderful characters and great music, and I mean, you can't make up people like Freddy and Hank Cochran: 8th grade education but communicates better than most anybody I've ever met with a PhD. Mickey Newbury, who gives words and music a feeling kind of like Ernest Hemingway's "Ill Man in the Sea," where you can feel the rope slide through your fingers. People who can transmit those kind of emotions through their songs deserve to be appreciated, and Freddy is one of those.

With Freddy in particular, and most of these people that create music, they should be appreciated because they are the kind of folks that make the burdens in life more bearable. So what I like to say is, "These folks express my feelings because I don't know how to", so when I listen to certain songs that affect me, I say to myself how fortunate I am to have people who can express emotions I wish I could express better, and Freddy's one of those people. Its infectious to have people do things that make your life more fun, not to mention more mentally stimulating, and I just feel fortunate to be a friend of Freddy and Catherine's. What could you want more of in life, than to sit down here on the coast with people who make the world a better place to live.

Catherine Powers: As a matter of fact, Freddy's final show was here at the Flora-Bama in 2012 at the Frank Brown Songwriter's Festival, which was also sadly during the time when Freddy was starting to lose the ability to have the wind to be able to completely sing a song or tell his jokes. So even though Freddy would get most of the song out, most of the line out, then he would kind of fall off. But the audience, who'd been hearing and listening and watching Freddy for so many years at the Festival, that when Freddy was falling off on his words, the audience was picking him up and helping him. It was really a beautiful thing to see that audience connected with Freddy so well that they all knew the words to his songs. With the jokes, he still had the wind for talking soft, but his jokes were getting softer and softer, but the audience quieted down to hear every word he said.

At the end, I remember that crowd stood up and gave Freddy one of the most beautiful standing ovations, it wasn't just your standard stand-up-ovation and applaud – if there had been a roof, they lifted it. It was just so special.

Freddy's a legend on this island, and he's highly respected and loved and looked up to. He's considered a hero, and the songwriters play his songs for him: Jack Robertson does "*Natural High*", and it was even the first dance at their Wedding; The Perdido Brothers, that's with Pat McCann who was one of Freddy's guitar players, they do several of Freddy's songs, including "Little Hotel Room" and "Daytime/Nighttime Blues"; and Chris Newberry, whose father is Mickey Newberry, who performs "Always Get Lucky With You". There's a lot of artists here on this island, and when we go in the room, they make a major deal and let everyone know that Freddy Powers is in the room.

Gulf Coast News Today, April, 2013: "Wednesday night was cause for several celebrations at the Flora-Bama. The iconic Lounge and Package Store marked its 35th year of existence, founder Joe Gilchrist celebrated his 71st birthday and a tribute was put on for legendary songwriter Freddy Powers. Perhaps Powers' most popular hit was, "I Always Get Lucky With You", which was a smash hit for George Jones and Merle Haggard. Powers wrote numerous songs for and with Haggard. Another fellow who knows a thing or two about songwriting was also in the house, Wayne Carson, a member of the Nashville Songwriter's Hall of Fame. He penned the smash hit, "The Letter" for the Box Tops that reached No. 1 in 1967 and was subsequently redone by several famous artists. He was also a co-writer on "Always On My Mind" made famous by Willie Nelson but also recorded by numerous other artists."

Catherine Powers: He doesn't even have to be in the room over there, and someone will play one of Freddy's songs, and they'll make a big deal out of Freddy, even though he's not over there. They talk about Freddy as if he were there, and the audience knows all of his songs. That's what was so amazing with Toby Keith and Scotty Emerick, they were playing obscure songs, down deep cuts in the albums, not normally known by many, and songs that no one would normally sing. When other peers of Freddy are playing, someone like John Rich, would say, "This is a song Freddy and I wrote together", and tell the audience about Freddy, and writing with him and what a great experience it was.

As a matter of fact, the last song Freddy wrote, was right across the street at the Metropolitan, and he and Mary Sarah and Mark Sherrill wrote it together. By then, Freddy had lost a lot of his ability to talk very well, but when he got over to that room and they started setting up to write, Freddy just started spilling out words, and Mary realized what Freddy was doing and grabbed a paper plate and a pen, which was the closest thing she could find. Well, Freddy started spilling out the words so quickly, that they were all just writing them. Then, when it was all done, and Mark and them called me in there and asked if I wanted to hear it, all of a sudden I realized I'd been hearing some of those lines in the days leading up to that write. Freddy would just blurt out, and I'd say, "What are you talking about?", and he'd go "I'm just thinking". So when I heard that song, I realized then, "Wow, that's what Freddy's been doing. He's been lying over there in that bed, unable to speak very much, but he was still *writing a song*."

Mary Sarah: Writing "*Dreamin'*" was a very supernatural experience. Catherine would tell me he would try to talk and some of the lyrics to "*Dreamin'*" came out. She told him I think you have at least one more in you. I had made a trip to the Flora-Bama for songwriting with Mark Sherrill and the next thing I knew... we walked in the door of the condo and I had to grab paper plates to write the lyrics down because he was just saying everything so fast. He was mumbling but yet I could hear him clearly. It was an amazing night. Catherine confirmed when she heard what we wrote that he definitely was telling her he had one more song!

Catherine Powers: They just had the Mullet Toss down here, which drew 30,000 people down to the beach to throw dead fish, that's a big huge event here, with boats stacked up all over the ocean and the Old River Bay and Gulf. Then they have the Shin Dig on the Beach, and Mary Sarah will play that, then they have Bulls on the Beach, and the Barefoot Ball, where everyone dresses up in Evening

Attire but wears their flip-flops, so it was a Black-Tie affair beach-style.

Musically, there's a little bit of everything playing. In the dome tent, they will have anywhere from a single-to-duos to full band, and music starts in the morning, usually single songwriters or a duo, and runs all the way through the evening with the full bands playing. Then upstairs is basically the Listening Room, where songwriters exclusively play, and they will have singles, duos, or a round of writers playing together, then there's the tent stage, where the kids go to hear Rock & Roll. So the dome stage and tent stages are where you see the dancing happening, but it could be everyone rocking to country in the dome, and then over in the tent it's straight rock or Reggae, etc. Then you have to bring it all the way across the street where they have two stages at The Flora-Bama Yacht Club, where they'll have either music playing on the inside or during the day outside on the beach stage. Then when you go over to the Flora-Bama Old River Bar and Grill, they have another two stages, one upstairs and one downstairs, so on this Island, just within this little conglomerate of clubs. I call it our compound: we have a total of seven different stages where music could be going on all stages on the weekend at the same time.

Co-Owner John McGinnis: Joe Gilchrist and I have been friends for a long time, probably 20-something years, and we worked a lot in the community together, and years

ago before I got involved, he'd invite me for years to the
songwriter festivals at the Flora-Bama, and I didn't go
because I didn't think it'd be any fun. Then finally he drug
me in there one day and I sat there for two days with him
listening to songwriters and I fell in love with it and for the
first time in my life, learned to listen.

Joe Gilchrist taught me how to listen, and from there,
we became partners in the Flora-Bama, which holds the
annual Frank Brown International Songwriter's Festival
among others and has become world-famous over the last
50 years for hosting and being home to so many
songwriters. We've been ranked the # 1 bar from Playboy
to Maxim, CNN to Yahoo, and has the stamp from Jimmy
Buffet, Kenny Chesney, and people think it's because of
the parties and the fun that people have, and that's all great,
but what made the Flora-Bama famous was all the
musicians and songwriters – that's the secret sauce!

Catherine Powers: If you take Nashville or even
Austin, who consider themselves big Music industry towns,
the musicians and artists cannot make a living in these
towns because they have to work for tips or they're getting
a free meal, and so that's why when you mention the Flora-
Bama to these folks, they refer to it as the "Songwriter's
Paradise" because they can come down here and play and
get paid a living wage and also get shown respect, and it
doesn't make a difference whether it's a famous songwriter
whose got 100 hits or an unknown, up and comer – they are

all treated equally. So it's the music that brings people here, without the music, what would they do?

John McGinnis: That's the feeling you get, that the people on stage here love the Flora-Bama and love living here and playing their music and telling stories behind their songs, and the audience falls in love with that and feels like they're part of the show. And if the musicians and songwriters did not feel the way they do at the Flora-Bama, and weren't treated the way they are treated, the Flora-Bama would be another beach bar that maybe you'd heard of. But because the musicians and songwriters are the heart of it, that's why people come here, because they can't experience that anywhere else. Joe told me when we first partnered up together and I was excited to be diving into all this new expansion, he said, "Look, this is all important, but you gotta understand one thing: The Flora-Bama is a shell with a bunch of great memories. That's all this building is, the people are the Flora-Bama."

People feel a sense of freedom when they come to the Flora-Bama, they can be themselves, they don't get to play what they want to play when they want to play it anywhere else in the business, vs. having to play hours of cover songs for tourists, down here, Joe Gilchrist created the opposite, and so they are encouraged to play their own original songs or if they are covering somebody, its one of their fellow songwriters most of the times.

Joe Gilchrist: So when Freddy is able to come over to the Flora-Bama, they will play some of his songs, and though we know he can't communicate, we know he's listening – anything that shows some respect to him given how many great songs he's written over the years.

John McGinnis: So with the musicians being in charge at the Flora-Bama, again, they pick their set-lists, how they want to play it, and they're in charge of entertaining the crowd and making everyone feel like they're hanging out together. We've expanded a little bit here because there's an extra four million people down here, and it's not as much about making money as it is providing people a good experience when they come here with all the expanding we're doing. So we have two restaurants now across the street, you don't have people waiting in the street anymore that drove here from Wisconsin because they heard about the personalized experience. We don't want to feel like we're moving cattle, and it's the same with the songwriters we employ. We've got 400 employees now, and of course, more buildings mean more stages for that many more songwriters to play on, and we want everyone to feel like we care about each and every one of them when they walk in the Flora-Bama, from the customer to the performing songwriter to veterans like Freddy, who have been around as long as guys like Joe supporting the songwriting community.

We even have church services down here at the Flora-Bama on Sundays! Right about the time I got involved here, the Perdido Methodist Church down the street came to us and said they wanted to do an outreach and start a little church service in the tent out on the beach every Sunday. So I was thinking 10, 20 people every week, and the first weekend, we had 50 people, then the next week, 200, then it went to 500, and now it's up to 1400 attendees with two services every Sunday.

So it's totally transformed our community, you had all these people who were unchurched and who were not treated right in church or church tried to get in between their direct relationship with God, and they just felt welcome down here and unjudged – tattoos and all, whatever! And if you want a Blood Mary, Mimosa or Bushwacker, you can have that too, but it's a no-judgment zone and we come and have a party for God and Jesus every Sunday, and everybody leaves high-fiving each other. You'll find a lot of songwriters and audience members in the audience together, and this is now the largest attended church anywhere down here at the beach, and on Easter Sunday they had 3000!

Catherine Powers: The Flora-Bama really is a miracle, the way they saved me and saved Freddy, and given us a life, a good quality life. There's never any way I could ever repay them for all they've done for us.

Co-Owner John McGinnis: Catherine often jokes about the Lord blessing them with this place, and I feel like the Lord blessed us with them. She's a good, loving woman with a wonderful man who used to come down here and support this place and treat us like we want to treat them now. Freddy and Catherine treated the Flora-Bama for years like it was their second home, and now it is their home! We want Freddy to have that final chapter living at the beach in a songwriter's paradise.

Conclusion: Guitar on the Wall

Catherine Powers: I have to tell you, I feel like the most honored and blessed wife ever because Freddy and I have led such an amazingly interesting life together. Not just being married to a songwriter and performer, but actually being a center-focus and a part of it, not only for the love and friendship Freddy and I have had, but to have been truly a part of all of this has been overwhelming for me.

In the music industry, when we got together, Freddy already had that reputation and was pretty well known but there's something I always remember that I kind of go by as my edict, and it's kind of a sad thing today is, Floyd Tillman, that was one of Freddy's major heroes, and when Floyd died, there wasn't any mention of him, not even on our local radio station. It was like he died and that was it, and Freddy looked at me and said "Mama, I don't want everything I've done to just disappear overnight and never be spoke of or played again," and I promised him, "That will never happen." I was fortunate while he was still able to perform that I was acting as his manager and doing all his bookings and dealing with the music publishers because when Freddy and I first got together, I did work as his booking agent and his promoter out there on the road, and he trained me well with booking and promoting. So I was lucky to be able to draw from that real-music business experience in the more recent years since I've been running our business full-time.

Biff Adams, Merle Haggard's Drummer: I knew Catherine before she met Freddy, and over their years together in the business, he's made her into what she is, and she works her butt off for him managing his catalog now that he's medically unable to any longer. They really deserve each other, and my wife – who got to be friends with Catherine when we were all up there on the lake together – used to say, "Now that's a devoted lady!" From the time they first got together and since, she's definitely dedicated herself to Freddy, and anybody that's ever around him can see that.

Catherine Powers: I have to say, when the computer came along, that connected us with the world, and has been a huge tool and invaluable resource for me in utilizing social media and the digital music community to keep his name out there probably bigger than it's ever been before, especially with the arrival of Facebook, etc., we've been able to not only keep his classic fan-base together, but also introduce his music to a whole new generation of Millennial fans. So I give the main credit for that not to myself but to the computer, because we've been able to keep in touch with so many old and new fans over the years, many of whom have become like family to us.

Tanya Tucker: I see how Catherine works like a little bee, she's always buzzing around!

Sonny Throckmorton: I'm amazed at what she does, and she's always been in Freddy's corner, she's always been there for him. She's the # 1 promoter, and # 1 everything for him, she's a jewel.

Catherine Powers: Freddy's legacy has started to catch up with him the past few years, as he's been honored with inductions into the *Texas Country Music Hall of Fame, the Western Swing Society Hall of Fame and the Texas Heritage Songwriter's Association, recipient of Lifetime Achievement Awards by the Nashville Songwriter's Association International, the Texas Music Academy,* and *the Texas Guitar Association*. Gibson Guitar Company has also honored Freddy with his own signature guitar in acknowledgement of the unique Dixie-Jazz style he is largely credited for first introducing into country music. Freddy's legacy is distinguished and historic enough back home that Texas State University gave Powers his very own archives museum as part of their esteemed Witliff Collections in conjunction with the Center for Texas Music History.

Austin American-Statesman: "The first two inductees into the Hall of Fame were Sonny Throckmorton and Freddy Powers, not household names exactly, but between them they crafted hits for Merle Haggard, Kenny Rogers, Willie Nelson, George Jones and Big and Rich."

Texas Heritage Songwriters Association: "With five solo albums under his belt in addition to his production and writing, Powers' career is unparalleled in country music.... His award winning songs and production work are behind-the-scenes testaments to his talent and success."

Freddy Powers: I have always had great musicians working with me throughout the years. Guys like Gary Church, Paul Buskirk, Milton Quackenbush, Red Allred, Alan Barnes, Stu Landing, Joe Lynch, Tony Savage, Jay Thomas, Spanky Jones, Ben Wilhorn, B.B. Morse, Gary Xavier, Clint Strong, Tommy Roberts, Steve Joyce, Bob Minnette, Bobby Black, Tom Herzer, Django Porter, my son Freddy the 2nd, and my beloved friend Dean Reynolds (Deanie Bird), who passed away in 1996.

John Rich: When a guy like me gets to hang out with a guy like Freddy, its always rarified air. That is a place that... not many people can say they know a guy like Freddy, and really know him, and really have written with him, and really understand him. Freddy's songwriting and artistry is bigger than country music, its truly American music. When you meet somebody like Freddy, you go out of your way to find times and find places to make sure you reconnect with him, because you know he's only going to be around for so long.

Freddy is a really unique combination of things: he's a very low-key, behind-the-scenes kind of guy, but at the same time, I call him a quiet rock star, it's what I call him. Because he plays guitar like a rock star or country star, and he's hilarious, really edgy and has hilarious jokes, and always has one joke after the next after the next. But then he has such substance with the stuff that he's written and where he's been and what all he's done: he's been in the military… I mean, he's done a lot of things in his life that have a lot of gravity. So he's a real unassuming megastar in my mind.

Marc Oswald, Merle Haggard's Manager: I've never met anybody like Freddy, he's singular, and I think first off, as a rhythm guitar player, he was one of the greats. Everybody appreciated his skills, from his history of Vaudeville and his capability with all the stringed instruments: banjos, guitars, basses, anything with strings on it. And with his comedy capability, he's a comedian, a Vaudevillian, a jazz guitar, a multi-instrumentalist, a songwriter, when you add all that up, guys like Merle and Willie and the people Freddy has worked with, George Jones, Kris Kristofferson, it goes on and on, they fall in love with him and he's so humble. He's always the most humble guy in the room, but he was always the star's star, I always thought of Freddy that way because our stars in

Country Music in that period were Merle Haggard, Willie Nelson, Hank Jr., Waylon Jennings, they were the stars to us. Well, Freddy seemed to be the star to them. He was like at a different level in terms of being the guy that they followed and that they were fans of Freddy, all those mega-superstar country artists, and some other artists as well, were fans of Freddy, while we were all fans of them. It was just the strangest thing, and I think it was because he had a combination of all those skill sets, and his humility and his sense of humor. So I think it all started based on mutual admiration between those guys.

Freddy Powers: There are so many other great musicians that I've played with from time to time. I wished I could list them all. I have always had a great respect for really good players and those that knew how to swing. I will always be thankful to them for sharing part of their musical life with me. I can't imagine my life without music. Most of all, the people I love best are musicians or people who solely love music and have respect for it. As for my songwriting, I owe much of it to Merle and my sister Mary Lou.

Merle Haggard: Fred and I can drive 300 miles and never say a word, we don't have to talk.

Willie Nelson: I enjoy playing music with Freddy, he's a friend and a good musician.

Tanya Tucker: I know he knows me when I seem him because his eyes just light up and I can tell he knows exactly what I'm saying to him and we'll have a conversation. It's such a great feeling to know that he knows who I am. He's like the Energizer Bunny, he just keeps on ticking, it's amazing.

Edith Royal: They have a music festival here every year at the start of Football season, and they always had a Pickin' Party the night before. Now, it lives on as a fundraiser for Alzheimer's Disease and the money goes up to Dallas to a medical hospital there where they study how to treat it, it's an Alzheimer's Fund, and Freddy and Catherine always came to that party on the campus, all the way from when he played at them up through recently when Catherine was pushing him in a wheelchair. It was a little funny in spite of Freddy's condition, because they had him in a little roped-off area so people couldn't swarm him. They could come talk to him but not for a very long time because he had a lot of fans and only so much energy. Freddy is very recognizable in Texas.

Mary Sarah: Freddy's ability to touch you with his melodies and lyrics is a gift, something he practiced his entire life. If I was to describe what I know of Freddy... He is sweet and sassy!

Steve Carter: The word that really comes to mind is just trust, he trusted me, and never had to tell me do it this way or that way, he trusted me to do that, and it was from playing in the living room with him, asking "What's this chord? What's that chord? What are you doing there?" So he was like a father to me, really, I call him Papa, and made sure to be in touch with him on Father's Day, so it was that kind of a relationship for me. My Dad was gone at an early age, and Freddy was as dear a Dad as I could wish for. I think he'll be remembered as the Best Rhythm Guitar player in Western Swing in modern history.

John Rich: What you realize is that what Freddy is is he's a Great Grand Daddy of Country Music. He's an innovator that now, for generation after generation of country singers – including myself – has been impacted by his songwriting and playing, whether they realize it or not. Because what Freddy did with Merle back in those days, there's not one country singer out there that won't count Merle Haggard as an influence. And when you find out that one of the main men behind the curtain was Freddy Powers, well then you have to count Freddy Powers as an influence and just as important as Merle. And you have to wonder: would Merle have even written those songs had Freddy not been sitting there with him? So that makes a guy like me just blown away because it's like your sitting there with somebody that should be on Mount Rushmore, I mean, that's Freddy, but he's an unknown, pretty much faceless,

nameless guy to the general public pretty much. And even
to a lot of artists really, if you say Freddy Powers, they kind
of look at you and go, 'I'm not exactly sure who that is.'
Then you start listing off the songs and their eyes bug out
of their head! Then they want to meet him, then they want
to jam with him, you know, so he's a really interesting cat
that he's remained so off the radar and had so much
massive impact and success.

When I think about my favorite Freddy Powers' songs,
I think right off the top of the list would have to be
'*Natural High*', because first of all, it's just an absolute
ridiculous melody, and in true country fashion, it gets right
down to the heart of the matter, right off the top of the song.
'You stay with me through thick and thin, you watch me
lose, you watch me win,' just real simple lines that cut
really deep and ring really true. That's a really great
example of Freddy Powers' incredible medley coupling up
with a real simple country lyric and how impactful that can
be. I think '*Always Get Lucky With You*', that's just
unbelievable that song. 'When I'm down to a phone call,
I'm minus a dime,' that line just blows me away, every
time it gets to that one, I have to say 'God, what a line!'
You could talk about a lot of Freddy's songs that way, but
those two probably hit me as hard as anything I've ever
heard in country music. Matter of fact, some of his songs
could have been recorded by Frank Sinatra or Dean Martin,
they're on that level. He is a jewel, there's nothing like him
anywhere out there. His mind is still current and still fresh,

and what he's about musically is really ageless. The definition of a classic is something that was loved when it was brand new, and the older it gets, people love it even more, and I think that's Freddy to a T. He is the definition of a classic.

Tanya Tucker: I had to call Catherine once to figure out where I met her because I told her I could always remember when I met an asshole, but I can never remember where I met my best friends. I put her in that category.

Pauline Reese: Something I did for them on my new record was write a song for them called "*Wanderlust Fantasy*", and its about Freddy and Catherine and their life and the way that they love each other.

Wanderlust Fantasy

Vs 1
I feel the sunlight on my face
The wind is blowing like a race
My feet are on the ground and I
Can't hear a sound, all I see is you

Chorus:
You haunt my days
You haunt my nights
Wanderlust fantasy

Give me your love and you'll be
Living a life of ecstasy
I would be your Queen
And you would be my king
Wanderlust fantasy

You haunt my days
You haunt my nights
Wanderlust fantasy
Come run away with me
Don't hide those feelings
We can't fight

I would be your Queen
And you would be my King
Wanderlust fantasy

Vs 2
Take my hand and you will find
There is no love like yours and mine
You will rule my world
And I would be the girl
To make you feel like home

You haunt my days
You haunt my nights
Wanderlust Fantasy

Vs 3
Take my heart and follow me
We'll build our kingdom you will see
Dancing on a cloud
Living life out loud
Wanderlust fantasy

You haunt my days
You haunt my nights
Wanderlust fantasy
I would be your Queen
And you would be my King
Wanderlust fantasy
I would be your Queen
And you would be my King
Wanderlust fantasy

Catherine Powers: If you look closely at Willie Nelson's beloved guitar Trigger, you can see Freddy's name etched into its hallowed body, just as permanently as his name is forever etched into Country Music, and we're truly grateful for the amazing journey this life in the music business has given us. Its given Freddy his legacy, but I know he's equally proud of being able to give back to his fans and friends, through the Special Olympics and with all the musicians he's helped get started in the business, keeping in the tradition of forefathers like Paul Buskirk who did the same for Freddy and Willie so many decades ago. Willie is still with us, still touring on the road, and whenever he comes through town and Freddy's able to see his old friend still up there doing what he loves, I know it brings a big smile to his face. It's nice to see how loyal those two old friends are to each other.

We lost our dear friend Merle Haggard earlier this year, and the loss was devastating not only for Freddy and I, but for generations of Country Music fans who grew up on Merle's music, going all the way back to the early 60s. Freddy told me many times that his years writing and playing with Merle were the happiest of his life and career, and Merle has said the same. They truly were brothers in every sense of the word, and remained that way through Merle's passing. Freddy has outlived so many of his siblings, countless medical expert projections, friends and musicians he played with throughout his life that have left us, and we both feel so thankful for that – especially as we've fought through Parkinson's Disease along the way. Everybody who has crossed Freddy's path over his 84 years on this earth have all said they fell in love with him within moments of meeting him, and it was the same for me.

If I have one wish I hope has been fulfilled by the time someone finishes reading this last page of our story and closes the book, it's that they do so with a feeling of completion, of coming full circle, because that's exactly what we've done with it. I'll never forget, four years ago when we really began working in earnest on this book,

Freddy had just been baptized for the first time in his life, and 10 days later, he wound up on life support at the V.A. Hospital in Nashville, TN. So here I am, crying and praying over him, "Please Lord, don't take him from me, I'm not ready," and all of a sudden, Freddy was able to open up his eyes and look up at me and say, "Mama, I just got baptized, I'm not going anywhere…"

Guitar On the Wall
(Written by Freddy Powers, Gary Nicholson)

Vs 1
My old friend quit the cigarettes
And cut way back on the booze
But there's some habits of a lifetime
Ain't that easy to lose
He'd been pickin' guitar
Since he was just a kid
Then one day the doctor told him
He'd never play again
And the saddest good-bye of all
Was when he had to hang his guitar on the wall

Vs 2
If that six strings could talk
Lord, the stories we would hear
It was there to bring the songs to life
Through the laughter and the tears

Now he knows his old guitar
Has made its final curtain call
And the saddest good-bye of all
Was when he had to hang his guitar on the wall

Vs 3
We've all lost things we love in this life
We've all said our share of good-byes
But the saddest good-bye of all
Was when he had to hang his guitar on the wall
Yeah, the saddest good-bye of all
Was when Freddy hung his guitar on the wall

Epilogue: June 21st, 2016

Catherine Powers: Freddy passed away on June 21st, 2016 with loved ones by his side. I was too distraught to remember much of the day, but felt fortunate to have family like our daughter Karen, dear friends Robin Harpster and Freddy's nurse, Joi with me that day…

Robin Harpster: I've never been through anything like that. It was a Tuesday morning and I was on my way to Bible Study at the Flora-Bama Light House, and I texted Catherine to see if she wanted to join me, and she texted back and said, "Robin, Oh My God, Freddy… It's an emergency, when you get done, please come over here." So I went over to the bus right after Bible Study, and it wasn't good at all: Freddy was having a hard time breathing, and she made a phone call to our Pastors Joe and Dan to come over and administer final rights, which was a very difficult call for her to make. Her strength was always amazing with Freddy, but especially that day, because when the Pastors both showed up, we all knew it wasn't looking good.

We were all talking to Freddy, telling him we loved him, and reassuring him Catherine wasn't alone, and at that point, she asked us all to pray for Freddy because I think in her heart, she knew he wasn't going to last much longer. After we all said prayers for Freddy, their dog Olga all of a sudden jumped up on top of Freddy, and you could just feel something in the room at the time. So Olga was looking at him, kind of barking, and then we all looked at each other and you never know when something like that's going to happen, but it was time. There was a lot of tears and hugging and silence and sadness, just a lot of emotions, and she was shaking and beside herself, but at the same time, you felt this spiritual presence in the room. It's hard to explain, but after we'd said the prayer together, we saw something in Freddy where he seemed at peace, and suddenly had a different breathing mechanism, and we'd told him, "Its okay Freddy, if you go, we're going to take care of Catherine, you don't have to worry about her." That's what portions of our prayer was about, and you could just see he was relieved, and he passed shortly after that.

I was supposed to be at work that Tuesday but had just left that job the day before, and I feel like it was God working in our lives for sure, because had I gone to work, I wouldn't have been able to be there with Catherine. I know there was reason why everything happened the way it did, and being able to be with her at that moment meant the world to me, getting to experience that with someone so special in my life. She likes to joke now that Freddy and Merle were having a Pickin' Party for Jesus up in Heaven, and we all knew he'd gone on to a better place.

Joi Vinson Davis: I'm so grateful when Catherine called me and told me Papa wasn't doing good, I was debating on whether I needed to leave right then, and said,

"No, I'll wait till tomorrow," and when I called her the next morning, she told me it wasn't good, so I threw stuff in a bag and took off and was about two hours into my six-hour drive when they called and told me Freddy had passed. I lost it of course, and about 30 minutes later, Catherine called me, and she said, "How far are you?", and I was still probably four hours out, and I got upset and said, "I'm not going to get to kiss him bye, I just want to kiss his face one more time," and she actually left Freddy there on the bus till I made it there, which wasn't till nine o'clock that night, but this beautiful, beautiful woman kept his body there so I could kiss my Papa bye one more time. That really meant a lot to me.

Catherine Powers: We celebrated Freddy's life on July 28th, 2016 in the place we'd both come to call home in our hearts, the Flora-Bama, with a full Military service by his fellow Marines, and comical stories and songs about and by Freddy from his friends and admirers.

Paster Joe Brantley, Worship on the Water Campus Director: We're honoring Mr. Frederick Dale Powers, born October 10th, 1931, in Duncan, Oklahoma. He was raised in Seminole, Texas, and he died June 21st, 2016. He's survived by his wife, Catherine Allen Powers, his 5 children, 10 grandchildren, 2 great-grandchildren, and 1 sister, Ms. Norma Marlow, and many nieces and nephews. So he's surrounded by not only a large family, but also by a large community that stretched all over this country who dearly loved Freddy Powers.

Catherine wanted me to read a funny scripture, and the only one I could think of is, in Numbers 22, when *Balaam*'s Ass talks, he was riding on his Ass and it started talking to him. So I was thinking what better way to segway into Catherine talking, because she's been riding Freddy's ass for years, right? (Cheers from the crowd)

Catherine Powers: That's just a little taste of what you're in for today, because like Freddy said, "Mama," because he always called me Mama – so does half the people in the room – "I don't want no celebration of life where people are standing up crying and talking about how great I am – because I already know that!" (laughs) He said, "Mama, I want y'all to throw me under the bus, and make me and the Lord laugh so hard that we're falling off the clouds."

So today, we're actually going to be roasting Freddy, and I'm going to start with the story I'm going to roast my sweetheart with: I found out and I realized how crazy he was and what kind of ride I was going to be on when we hadn't even been dating a couple of weeks and I'm following him home from the Casino, about two or three in the morning, and we're driving down Main St. in south Lake Tahoe, and if you've ever been there, you know they only had one street when all of a sudden, he just stops in the middle of the street! He gets out of his car, and I'm rolling my window down thinking he had something he needed to tell me, when all of a sudden, he gets to the back of his truck, drops his pants, turns around and moons me, never takes a look back, gets back in his truck, and drove off… (crowd laughs) I knew right then I was in for one heck of a ride. I didn't know exactly where we were gonna go with this, but I knew I was going somewhere.

Then I found out another little thing about him, he was a liar, he could lie good. What he actually did was let me believe he was 49 years old. I was 31 at the time, so he just led me on and kept letting me assume that he was 49. Well, I went to the Doctor's office one time for his physical, and the nurse came in and was doing all his vitals and she says, "Freddy, how old are you?" And I saw this funny look on his face when he said, "It's in my file," (laughs). So the nurse persists, "Freddy, I'd have to go in there and dig it out! So just tell me how old you are?" This time, he's got a very stern, mean, ugly look on his face when he repeats it, "I said, it's in my file…" So she goes into the file, comes back out and says, "Hey Freddy, you've got a birthday coming up October, 1931," and I looked at him, took a deep breath, and said "My daddy was born in '34!" (crowd cheers) Well, lucky for him, by this time, I already knew I was in love with him – from the first time I saw a picture of him, I hadn't even really met him yet, but saw a picture and was like, "That's the man I'm after!" So, 18 years, 23 years my senior, what did it matter, I was already there…

Then I found out he thought he was brave, and we were out on this camping trip and staying up in Bear country in the woods in Northern California, and we're walking on this trail as he's telling me what to do if a Mountain Lion or a Bear was to come up to us. So he tells me, if it's a Mountain Lion, make yourself really big and get loud and run them off, but if it's a Bear, whatever you do, do not turn away and start running. Just fall to the ground, roll up like a ball and they'll think they've already killed you and won't mess with you, and about the time he's telling me this story, I see the brush moving and I pointed us over there and said "I wonder what…" Well, about the same time I got the "what" out this big, old Brown Bear stands up, Freddy grabs me by the arm, picks up our dog Amelia and takes off running as I'm running alongside him going, "I thought we weren't supposed to run!" So to myself, I'm laughing thinking, "Okay, he's brave…"

Then I found out, he's a wimp! He's a chicken. I go to the grocery store one day and I come back home, and walk in and have two guys – he and Sonny Throckmorton – setting in these red, lazyboy chairs, and I'm looking at them as they have this strange look on their faces, and Sonny's going, "I'm not gonna tell her, it's your house, you tell her…" So I'm like, "What??" So Freddy goes, "Mama, I don't know what it is in here, but you need to go up in my bedroom, we've got this big old long, worm-looking thing crawling around the ceiling." So I go in the room, look up, and sure enough, there was this really big, huge red centipede about 6 inches long with a million legs, and guess who got it off the ceiling and got rid of it? Because neither one of those boys could to it!

So like I said, it didn't take me very long to find out what I was going to be marrying into, because Freddy Powers was someone who always wanted to keep people laughing, and I was his first audience always. For years, he was a stand-up comedian, and did what they call *slap-stick comedy*, with three banjos and a tuba, which got him on the Today Show, that's all he cared about! He got on the Today Show and followed by the Tonight Show, and before too long, had his own little T.V. show there in Ft. Worth, Texas on (WBAP?) T.V., but Freddy always loved to make people laugh. One of his favorite in recent times was the Freddy Powers Dirty Joke Night! (laughs)

I'm going to tell a funny one on Freddy and Gretchen Wilson, because most people know that if you were friends with Willie Nelson and Merle Haggard, it kind of just goes together that you do... to, so when I explain this, you'll go "Oh!" So one time, Freddy was sitting in the back of the Limo, and he and Gretchen had just met at Merle's, and somebody said "Freddy, you want a hit?", handed him a joint, and Gretchen laughed and said, "Freddy, you like that stuff?" So Freddy looks at her – and this is on film – and says to her, "If you see me, I'm high," then ducks down and says, "If you don't see me, I'm high." Okay... Here's Mr. Bo Porter and Mr. Chris Newbury!

Bo Porter: Catherine and Freddy lived just a little bit down the road from me at La Hacienda R.V. Resort, and there were times that Catherine had to go out to the grocery store or Doctor's or something, and Freddy was still at the point where he could communicate, talk to you and he could walk with assistance. But he still needed someone there with him, so when Catherine called me one day and told me she had to go to the Doctor and asked if I'd please come sit with Freddy. So of course I said "Sure," headed down, and on the way there, I got to thinking of all the times I've spent with him and played music with him and talked, I'd never told him what he'd meant to me. So I just decided this was the day for me to tell him what he's meant to me, and when I got there, went on to tell him about how much he'd taught me about songwriting, he'd coached me a bit in that. And he taught me a lot about the music business, and about how to dress and how to respect an audience, and how to be a good bandleader, which was one of the big things he taught me.

So I'm just gushing on him, and I finally told him, "Freddy, you're just one of my heroes, and I want you to know that." So he told me thanks, then a few minutes later, looked at me with this sheepish little grin on his face, and says "I gotta shit." (laughs) So I said, "Well by God, let's get it done!", and I got him up and helped him down the hallway, got him slipped into the bathroom, and I remember he's hanging onto my shoulder, and looks right at me and says, "Well, you gotta pull 'em down." So I said,

"Oh, okay," and pulled his pants down for him and got him settled on the toilet, and Thank God, next he says, "Bo, I can do everything else."

We both laughed, I shut the door and went and sat up front waiting on him, and a few minutes later he knocked on the door and I went back and said, "You ready?", and he said, "Yeah", so I opened the door, and he's sitting there on the toilet. So I bent over, got him over my shoulder and off the toilet, and then he says, "Well, you gotta pull 'em up." So I said, "Okay," and of course, about the time I bend down, I get into about the bathing suit region, if you will, and he says, "Hey Bo?", and I said, "Yes sir", looked up at him, and he said, "What do you think of your hero now?", and we both just busted up laughing! That was just Freddy humor, and he was good about that, setting up a punch line: his comedic timing was just the best. He probably sat there on the commode thinking about what he was going to say to get me. (laughs)

Chris Newbury: Thank You Mama Catherine! Okay, this is a roast, so I'm going to try and say something… but its hard because this is a Hero of ours, all of ours, and I don't know if y'all know but Freddy started out on Banjo. He wasn't really a guitar player to start out with, but he really was one of the greatest guitar players in Country Music. So I have one story to tell, and fortunately, it looks like there are no kids in the audience, so I can use the real words because its part of the punch line. But we were out partying one night over in the bus, and this is when Freddy had already been incapacitated for quite a while and couldn't get up and move around, but could still speak. So we were all laughing and having a good time, but apparently, he wasn't feeling so good because he'd already made a couple of comments about Jackyls or Hyenas laughing, then after a couple hours, his nurse Joi says, "Papa, is there anything we can get you?", and Freddy says "Yeah, I'd like some fucking Crab Claws!" He'd been asking for hours, and we were like, "Papa, we're sorry, we've been partying and can't drive…" So I sobered up a little bit in the middle of the night, went down and got them, picked them up at the Shrimp Basket, came back, and said "Alright Papa, here are your fucking crab claws!" (cheers)

Catherine Powers: Alright, I'm ready for you Bo and Jo!

Bo Roberts: I think everybody knows that everybody in the world would probably love to have a Catherine Powers! (cheers) She's priceless… Okay, I'll tell a quick one, I met Freddy back in the '60s when he was playing the Showboat in Las Vegas and we were I was working with an old Cowboy by the name of Eddie Dean. He was playing Banjo at the time, and he told me, "I got sick and damn tired of those banjo jokes, and I figured I'd be a guitar player." So he went down to the store, and said "I want a Stratocaster, I want a Marshall amp, stacks, effects, picks, strings, the works…" So the guy behind the counter looks at him and says, "You're a freakin' Banjo player!" (laughs) So Freddy said, "How the hell'd you know that?", and the guy behind the counter says, "This is a Liquor store!"

Joe Gilchrist: I feel very privileged to have met a lot of United States Marines in my life, and Freddy carried that torch very well, and I'm very proud to see the Marines here. (cheers) One thing I was going to tell you is, I hang around a lot of the singer/songwriters, and most of them are pretty smart, but Freddy and Bo could stand some help! (laughs)

Bo Roberts: I got a mind like a steel trap.

Joe Gilchrist: Yeah, but the difference is, Bo can remember three or four songs, he writes one every year, but Freddy convinced me he was a lot smarter than he used to think he was when I got to know Catherine better. What a lucky guy, and what a lucky pair! I haven't had as much experience in marriage as Bo, I've only been married once…

Bo Roberts: Freddy had five kids, and I have five ex-wives. I was chasing the women and he… (laughs) He has five kids… (laughs)

Joe Gilchrist: I feel very fortunate that Fred and Catherine decided to come spend the last years of Freddy's life here, and I hope it was as enriching an experience for them as it's been for our little music community.

Bo Roberts: I got one more story… This is before Catherine settled him down, and Freddy loved women – hell, we all did – and I remember standing at this bar one night and this gal had been waiting on us for a couple of days, and she walked by and said to Freddy and I, "You guys alright?" And I said, "Yep," and Freddy looked at her and said, "You know, I had two wet dreams 'bout you," and she went, "Oh Freddy," and he told her, "Would have had another but I went to sleep!" (laughs)

Catherine Powers: Freddy was always a comedian! There were times where I'd just be setting there on the couch watching TV or whatever and he'd come out of the room and he'd walk into the room normally just like anyone else would, and out of nowhere, he'd get right in front of me and shake his body like a banshee! Then he'd just keep on walking, and do whatever he had to do in the house, then walk back into the living room like he wasn't even paying attention, get right in front of me, and randomly do the same thing all over again! (laughs) He'd never look me in the eyes, just keep right on walking…

Other times, I'd be looking outside, and seeing this guy standing there marching off in his own world, and I'd be sitting there looking at him going, "What are you doing?!!" But that was just Freddy – he didn't care if I knew for sure

I was watching, but just on the chance I'd be watching, and he'd just get up and do something crazy, all the time. I can tell all these stories because I was married to the man, and I mean, you learn to say the "F" word real quick when you start hanging out with a bunch of musicians – because its every other word!

Now, we'll hear a song from Christina Christian and Taylor Craven that they actually wrote about Freddy and I called "*The Book*."

Taylor Craven: I actually met Freddy Powers five or six years ago at the Frank Brown Songwriters Festival, and helped pick his wheelchair up with him in it to get him on the bus. Well, two years ago, we were up in the main room at the Flora-Bama and Chris Newbery was on stage, and he pointed to Freddy in his wheelchair with Catherine, and said, "That's the definition of love." I was staying at Mark Sherrill's condo by myself, so I went home that evening and started picking out this song on the guitar, and Christina Christian and I had a writing appointment the next day. Well, when she walked in, I hadn't been to sleep yet because I'd been up all night pickin' on this song and it was really about what Chris Newbery said, "Till death do us part," and Freddy and Catherine defined that. I had some situations in my family, Grandmothers and Aunts that had that same kind of commitment, and I always wanted to capture that.

Christina Christian: We finished the majority of the song in 2014, and we set it aside and let it marinate a little bit for about six months, and then finally the next year after we'd written the song all together, we were pretty excited about it because we did have Catherine listen to it on the same stage we're performing it on today, and she loved it and asked me to start playing that song for different Freddy events. I feel like it's a fitting tribute and Freddy heard the song before he passed, and we felt it was relevant to the two of them because when you were out at the Flora-Bama and you would see Catherine and Freddy together, or I would go over to their bus to visit, and she was just with him 24-7. Once I started seeing more of that, I was more connected to the song and it was a bit more emotional for me too, because there are just so many different lyrics in the song where you can really tell what they mean individually to Catherine and Freddy, and if you see how she took care of him while he was alive up through his passing, you just get every single line in this song about their love.

Catherine Powers: So this is what came out from hearing a story about Freddy and I…

The Book

(Written by Christina Christian, Taylor Craven,

and Megan McMillan)

Verse 1
They haven't given in or given out
'Cause giving up ain't what love's about
They've learned to lean on the vows they took
They keep turning pages
'Til it's time to close the book

Verse 2
She recalls every promise made that day
He can too, but he can't say
Until death will they be one
They keep turning pages
'Til the book is done

Chorus
There's laughter in the chapters of their past
With pages stained by tears that didn't last
There's no written rule how a happy ending looks
They keep turning pages, til it's time to close the book

Verse 3
From outside looking in no one can tell
How one look from him makes her heart swell
His hands are cool, but she melts at his touch
They keep turning pages, til it's time to close the book

Chorus
There's laughter in the chapters of their past

With pages stained by tears that didn't last
There's no written rule how a happy ending looks
They keep turning pages, til it's time to close the book

Turn Around
There's no written rule how a happy ending looks
They keep turning pages, til it's time to close the book

Tag
They haven't given in or given out
'Cause giving up ain't what loves about

Another touching tribute to Freddy came when our friend Ken Hart with Cary Stone wrote a salute to simply titled "THANK YOU FREDDY," that summed up perfectly why he'll be missed by so many.

Thank You Freddy

Once in a while someone comes along
Drives you wild with spcial little style of song
Makes you dance and makes you sing
Throws a little love in between
What a recipe he's famous for
He leaves his mark everywhere he goes
Plays his part but somehow steals the show
Puts a smile on your face
Boogies all your blues away

Guarantee, he'll always leave you wanting more

He gives you a taste but its never enough
Takes you away and always lifts you up
A natural high, you can't come down
It's the hottest thing in town
He's your friend in California that's for sure

So don't be late, tickets are going fast
Show starts at eight and its gonna be a blast
Just hold on
All night long
He never runs out of songs
One more stop on his never-ending tour

Just hold on
All night long
We know you never run out of songs
Thank You Freddy
Could you sing us just one more?

Catherine Powers: Finally, our dear friend Bo Porter, who started out playing with Freddy back on the Casino circuit in the 1970s, and has known us as a couple for over 30 years, wrote this beautiful poem about Freddy and my love story, and it was Freddy's wish that we close the show with it:

"The Powers In Love"
  Written by: Bo Roberts and Curly Corwin 2016

If someone should write a song about Freddy and Catherine
It would be so easy to write
Just picture all the love that they have for each other And write it down in every line
The powers in love
Is what keeps them together
Two hearts beating as one

If someone should write a song About Freddy and Catherine
It would be a sing-a-long love song
Oh they've tried to out love one another
A competition they'll have for life
Everyday there's something new
Every night there is two
Lovers on a natural high
Oh it ain't no big surprise Catherines had stars in her eyes
Since the night Freddy hung her the moon

And this song Ain't long enough to tell about all the love
Still going on between these two
Oh they've tried to out love one another
It's a competition that they'll have for life
Everyday there's something new
Every night there is two

Lovers on a natural high
Yes the powers in love
Is what keeps them together
Two lovers on a natural high

Discography

Freddy Powers co-produced, sang and played guitar on Willie Nelson's 'Somewhere Over The Rainbow' (Columbia Records, 1981).

Merle Haggard's recorded Freddy Powers' 'I Always Get Lucky With You' (co-written with Merle Haggard and Gary Church) and included the track on 'Big City' (Epic Records, 1981).

Merle Haggard recorded Freddy Powers' 'Lonely Night' and included the track on 'Going Home For Christmas' (Epic Records, 1982).

Merle Haggard and George Jones (Saturday 12 September 1931 - Friday 26 April 2013) recorded Freddy Powers' 'Silver Eagle' and included the track on 'A Taste Of Yesterday's Wine' (Epic Records, 1983); Freddy Powers also played guitar on the recording sessions for the album. George Jones (Saturday 12 September 1931 - Friday 26 April 2013) recorded Freddy Powers' 'I Always Get Lucky With You' (co-written with Merle Haggard) and included the track on 'Shine On' (Epic Records, 1983); the track was No.1 on the Billboard country music singles chart for one week in July/August 1983.

Merle Haggard and Leona Williams recorded Freddy

Powers' 'It's Cold In California Tonight' and included the track on 'Heart To Heart' (Mercury Records, 1983).
Ray Charles (Tuesday 23 September 1930 - Thursday 10 June 2004) recorded Freddy Powers' 'Little Hotel Room' and included the track on 'Friendship' (Columbia Records, 1984); the track was a duet with Merle Haggard.

Ray Charles' 'Friendship' (Columbia Records, 1984) was re-issued by Columbia/Legacy Records in 2005.
Merle Haggard recorded Freddy Powers' 'Let's Chase Each Other Around The Room' (co-written with Merle Haggard and Sherill Rodgers) and included the track on 'It's All In The Game' (Epic Records, 1984); the track was No.1 on the Billboard country music singles chart for one week in September 1984. Freddy Powers also played rhythm guitar on the album.

Merle Haggard recorded Freddy Powers' 'A Place To Fall Apart' (co-written with Merle Haggard and Willie Nelson) and included the track on 'It's All In The Game' (Epic Records, 1984); the track was No.1 on the Billboard country music singles chart for one week in February 1985. Janie Fricke provided harmony vocals on the track, while Freddy Powers played rhythm guitar on the album.

Merle Haggard recorded Freddy Powers' 'Natural High' and included the track on 'It's All In The Game' (Epic Records, 1984); the track was No.1 on the Billboard country music singles chart for one week in June 1985. The track, which was also included on 'Kern River' (Epic Records, 1984), featured Janie Fricke /index.php/janie-fricke.htmlon harmony vocals on the track, while Freddy Powers played rhythm guitar on both albums.

Merle Haggard recorded Freddy Powers' 'Little Hotel Room' and included the track on 'It's All In The Game' (Epic Records, 1984); Freddy Powers also played rhythm guitar on the album.

Merle Haggard recorded Freddy Powers' 'All I Want To Do Is Sing My Songs' and included the track on 'It's All In The Game' (Epic Records, 1984); Freddy Powers also played rhythm guitar on the album.

Merle Haggard recorded Freddy Powers' 'Ridin' High' and included the track on 'Kern River' (Epic Records, 1984); Janie Fricke provided harmony vocals on the track.
Merle Haggard recorded Freddy Powers' 'You Don't Love Me Anymore' and included the track on 'Kern River' (Epic Records, 1984).

Merle Haggard recorded Freddy Powers' 'Amber Waves Of Grain' and included the track on 'Amber Waves Of Grain' (Epic Records, 1985).

Merle Haggard recorded Freddy Powers' 'Friend In

California' and included the track on 'Friend In California' (Epic Records, 1986).

Merle Haggard recorded Freddy Powers' 'This Time I Really Do' and included the track on 'Friend In California' (Epic Records, 1986).

Merle Haggard recorded Freddy Powers' 'Texas' and included the track on 'Friend In California' (Epic Records, 1986).

Merle Haggard recorded Freddy Powers' 'Okie From Muskogee Is Comin' Home' and included the track on 'Friend In California' (Epic Records, 1986).

Merle Haggard recorded Freddy Powers' 'This Song Is For You' and included the track on 'Friend In California' (Epic Records, 1986).

Merle Haggard and Willie Nelson recorded Freddy Powers' 'Shotgun And A Pistol' and included the track on 'Seashores Of Old Mexico' (Columbia Records, 1987).

Merle Haggard recorded Freddy Powers' '1929' and included the track on 'Chill Factor' (Epic Records, 1987).

Merle Haggard recorded Freddy Powers' 'More Than This

Old Heart Can Take' and included the track on 'Chill Factor' (Epic Records, 1987).

Merle Haggard recorded Freddy Powers' 'Man From Another Time' and included the track on 'Chill Factor' (Epic Records, 1987).

Merle Haggard recorded Freddy Powers' 'Wouldn't That Be Something' and included the track on '5:01 Blues' (Epic Records, 1988).

Merle Haggard recorded Freddy Powers' 'Somewhere Down The Line' and included the track on '5:01 Blues' (Epic Records, 1988).

Merle Haggard recorded Freddy Powers' 'Blue Jungle' and included the track on 'Blue Jungle' (Curb Records, 1990).

Merle Haggard recorded Freddy Powers' 'Bar In Bakersfield' and included the track on 'Blue Jungle' (Curb Records, 1990).

Freddy Powers co-produced and played on Merle Haggard's pop standards album 'Unforgettable' (Capitol Records/Hag Records, 2004); Freddy also composed one of the featured tracks, 'Still Missing You'.

Merle Haggard recorded Freddy Powers' 'Wouldn't That Be Something' and included the track on 'The Bluegrass Sessions' (McCoury Music/Hag Records, 2007).

Merle Haggard recorded Freddy Powers' 'The Road To My Heart' and included the track on 'I Am What I Am' (Vanguard Records, 2010).

Bibliography of Freddy Powers Interview Sources

1. Source: Heritage of Texas / Enchanted Rock Magazine, Jan 1997

2./3./4./5. Source: Fretboard Journal, "On the Wagon: Following Paul Buskirk's Long, Dusty Trail," by Nathanial Riverhorse Nakadate

6. Source: Texas Music Magazine by Jason Hardison, June, 2006

7. Source: Heritage of Texas / Enchanted Rock Magazine, Jan 1997

8. Source: Austin Songwriter Magazine, May, 1997, by Sharon Jones-LeFlore

9. Source: Heritage of Texas / Enchanted Rock Magazine, Jan 1997

10. Source: Radio Host Randi O'Connor, Oct. 1987

11. Source: Heritage of Texas / Enchanted Rock Magazine, Jan 1997

12. Source: Texas Music Magazine by Jason Hardison, June, 2006

13. Source: "'Country Jazzman' Gets Lucky With 'New Country' Show", Robert K. Oermann

13a. Source: El Dorado Press Release

14./15 Source: Reno Gazette-Journal, After Dark, by Guy Richardson, June, 1992

16. Source: Stomp and Stammer Magazine, April, 2005, Dugan Trodglen

17./18./19. Source: to radio host Randi O'Connor, Oct. 1987

20. Source: Applause Magazine, December, 1996, by Kathleen Hudson

21. Source: Heritage of Texas / Enchanted Rock Magazine, Jan 1997

22. Source: Nevada Appeal, Star Talk, Thursday, Sept 21, 1989, by Pamela Bissell Crowell

23. Source: Heritage of Texas / Enchanted Rock Magazine, Jan 1997

24. Source: Conversation with radio host Johnny Johnson, KTRZ, Cortez, Colorado, Oct. 1987

25./26./27. Source: Conversation with radio host Johnny Johnson, KTRZ, Cortez, Colorado, Oct. 1987

28. Source: Radio Host Randi O'Connor, Oct. 1987

29. Source: Heritage of Texas / Enchanted Rock Magazine, Jan 1997

30. Source: Austin Songwriter Magazine, May, 1997, by Sharon Jones-LeFlore

31./32. Source: Conversation with radio host Randi O'Connor, Oct. 1987

33. Source: Fun and Gaming, June, 1992

34./35./36. Source: Motorcycles Magazine, July, 2007, Amy Edgerly

37. Source: Circus Circus Magazine, Inner View, by Kim Pryor

38./39. Source: Austin Songwriter Magazine, May, 1997, by Sharon Jones-LeFlore

40. Source: "Django Texas Style" by Sharon Jones

41. Source: San Antonio Express News, April, 2002, by John Goodspeed

42. Source: Austin Chronicle, August, 2008, by Doug Freeman

43./44. Source: Motorcycles Magazine, July, 2007, Amy Edgerly

45. Source: Austin Chronicle, August, 2008, by Doug Freeman

46. Source: Texas Music Magazine by Jason Hardison, June, 2006

47./48 Source: Motorcycles Magazine, July, 2007, Amy Edgerly

49./50. Source: Stomp and Stammer Magazine, April, 2005, by Dugan Trodglen

51. Source: Austin Chronicle, August, 2008, by Doug Freeman

52. Source: Motorcycles Magazine, July, 2007, Amy Edgerly

Author Bio

Award-winning Music biographer **Jake Brown** has written 43 published books since 2001, featuring many authorized collaborations with some of rock's biggest artists, including 2013 Rock & Roll Hall of Fame inductees **Heart** (with Ann and Nancy Wilson), living guitar legend **Joe Satriani**, country music legend **Merle Haggard**, heavy metal pioneers **Motorhead** (with **Lemmy Kilmister**), late hip hop icon **Tupac Shakur** (with the estate), celebrated Rock drummer **Kenny Aronoff**, late Funk pioneer **Rick James**, superstar country music anthology '*Nashville Songwriter*,' all-star Rock Drummers anthology '*Beyond the Beats*,' all-star rap producers HIP HOP HITS anthology, and the all-star rock producers anthology *Behind the Boards*, among many others.

Brown is a regular contributor to Tape Op has also appeared as the featured biographer of record on Fuse TV's *Live Through This* series and Bloomberg TV's *Game Changers* series, and received national press in Rolling Stone Magazine, CBS News, USA Today, MTV.com, The Hollywood Reporter, Parade Magazine, Billboard, etc. In 2012, Brown won the Association for Recorded Sound Collections Awards in the category of Excellence in Historical Recorded Sound Research.